Multilinear Analysis for

Students in Engineering and Science

Multilinear Analysis for

Students in Engineering and Science

G . A . H A W K I N S

Professor of Thermodynamics
and Dean of Engineering

Purdue University

John Wiley and Sons, Inc. / New York and London

Library of Congress Catalog Card Number: 63-17480
Printed in the United States of America

Preface

The objective of this book is to assist students interested in a self-study program of Multilinear Analysis or Tensor Analysis. It is not intended that this material be used as a text for a formal course nor as a treatise, but only as an aid in the pursuit of the subject on one's own.

The student who wishes to enhance his educational foundation must recognize that learning is a self discipline and, equally important, that it must be a lifelong process. Those who adopt this philosophy at the start of their learning career gain great satisfaction through self-study programs throughout their lives.

Thanks to my first mathematics instructor at the Colorado School of Mines, Professor Walter J. Risley, and later to my distinguished teacher, Andrey A. Potter, Emeritus Dean of Engineering at Purdue University, I early accepted these learning principles as a result of the scholarly lectures of these teachers and their informal talks with me. I absorbed their philosophy. They, along with other excellent teachers, showed me the way to lifelong learning.

The reader, no doubt, will wonder why I attempted to write this book after having completed others in different areas. This is my answer. In order to continue my study of how the Theory of the Continuum could be applied to special problems in thermodynamics and heat and mass transfer, it became evident that I must return to the role of the graduate student and reinforce my knowledge of vector and tensor analysis. After studying *Vector Analysis* by

J. G. Coffin many years ago, I critically reviewed a copy of *Vector and Tensor Analysis* by G. E. Hay. Later I had the privilege of informally studying the subject with Dr. Paul F. Chenea, Vice-President for Academic Affairs, Purdue University. At that time it was a Dean and an Associate Dean studying a subject of mutual interest. Then I attended the lectures of my colleague, Dr. A. Cemal Eringen, entitled "Theory of Continuous Media." During this course I noted how many students were struggling to acquire a knowledge of Multilinear Analysis. At this time I vowed to write a text for use as a self-study guide for students in this area. Later I had the pleasure of attending a course given by a colleague, Dr. Michael Golomb, which covered many advanced areas in modern mathematics. He encouraged me to complete this self study on Multilinear Analysis.

Before studying, it is imperative that the student review several concepts in mathematics which he may have forgotten during the course of his formal education. A restudy of these subjects is essential, and it may require considerable time. As an old student to a young one, I say "Do not take this statement lightly! If you do not have a full grasp of these parts, you will be lost and in hopeless confusion. Please take my advice and acquire the necessary information so that the details become as familiar to you as $2 + 2 = 4$." To those of you who do not take this advice seriously, I extend my sympathy. Unless you do, you cannot expect to use tensor analysis effectively in the solution of your problems. Multilinear analysis, tensor analysis, when thoroughly understood, is a very powerful tool and technique in the solution of problems in many areas of science and engineering.

The help given me during the past several years by my students and colleagues is greatly appreciated, and particularly that of Professor Marion B. Scott who has read much of the manuscript. It is sincerely hoped that this book will aid students in their quest for more knowledge.

Special thanks are due to my staff in the office of the Dean of Engineering and the Mathematical Sciences at Purdue University, particularly to Billie Bristow (Mrs. R.), Margaret Hill (Mrs. J. D.), and Doreen McClellan (Mrs. G. E.), for their untiring efforts in typing various aspects of the manuscript. Their task of keeping the superscripts and subscripts in their proper location is only appreciated by one familiar with the subject.

Limited space prevents the inclusion of a complete list of sources from which ideas and material have been taken; yet every effort has been made to give credit to those whose ideas have been consciously used. References for additional sources of study have been provided.

I am particularly indebted to my colleague, Mr. Richard M. McKinley, for his very careful and critical review of the text. The many suggestions made by him relative to the organization of the chapters and the methods of presentation of the material are deeply appreciated. He is, indeed, one who would be classed as a true scholar.

This book is dedicated to my understanding and lovely wife, Alma, who has suffered through many hours of loneliness during the preparation of my earlier books and now of this one.

G. A. HAWKINS

West Lafayette, Indiana
May, 1963

Contents

Review of Vector Analysis

1-1. Scalars and Vectors

Scalars are quantities which are designated by magnitude alone. Examples of scalars are mass, density, area, a quantity of heat, and energy per unit mass. A vector is a segment of a straight line which has a definite length and direction. Therefore a vector may be represented by an arrow. A vector **A** is shown in Fig. 1-1. The line of action is indicated by the broken line MM'. The origin of the vector is designated by the letter O. The end of the vector is called the terminus and is designated by the letter T. The magnitude (length) may be designated by $|\mathbf{A}|$ or A.

1-2. A Unit Vector

A unit vector is one having unit magnitude (length). Let **A** represent a vector having a magnitude A. The quantity $\mathbf{A}/A$ is a unit vector

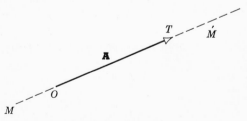

Fig. 1-1. Vector **A**.

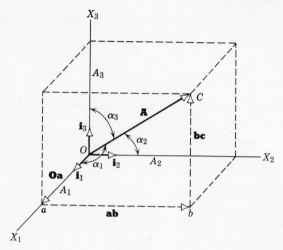

Fig. 1-2.

having the same direction as **A**. Any vector may be represented by the expression

$$\mathbf{A} = A\mathbf{a}$$

where **a** is a unit vector in the direction of **A**.

Consider the vector **A** in the rectangular Cartesian coordinate system shown in Fig. 1-2. The vectors $\mathbf{i}_j$ (that is, $\mathbf{i}_1$, $\mathbf{i}_2$, $\mathbf{i}_3$) are unit vectors having their lines of action along the coordinate axes.

The vector **A** is equal to the vector sum of the vectors **Oa**, **ab**, and **bc**. The magnitudes of these vectors are the distances measured along the coordinate axes, or A_1, A_2, and A_3. We may therefore write the vector identity:

$$\mathbf{A} = \mathbf{Oa} + \mathbf{ab} + \mathbf{bc} = A_1\mathbf{i}_1 + A_2\mathbf{i}_2 + A_3\mathbf{i}_3 \qquad (1\text{-}1)$$

The necessity for writing out the three components of the vector **A** may be eliminated by using a shorthand system. Thereby the three-term sum (1-1) will be represented by the single term $A_j\mathbf{i}_j$, where the subscripts j represent a summation over $j = 1, 2$, and 3 for a three-dimensional coordinate system. Hence the vector **A** may be expressed as

$$\mathbf{A} = A_j\mathbf{i}_j \qquad (1\text{-}2)$$

When a subscript is repeated as in equation (1-2), we shall infer that a summation is to be carried out, unless stated otherwise. The identical subscripts are called dummy indices.

If we should desire to add vectorially two vectors **A** and **B** represented as

$$\mathbf{A} = A_j \mathbf{i}_j \quad \text{and} \quad \mathbf{B} = B_k \mathbf{i}_k$$

we would obtain

$$\mathbf{A} + \mathbf{B} = A_j \mathbf{i}_j + B_k \mathbf{i}_k$$

Carrying out the summation gives

$$\mathbf{A} + \mathbf{B} = A_1 \mathbf{i}_1 + A_2 \mathbf{i}_2 + A_3 \mathbf{i}_3 + B_1 \mathbf{i}_1 + B_2 \mathbf{i}_2 + B_3 \mathbf{i}_3$$

Collecting terms yields

$$\mathbf{A} + \mathbf{B} = (A_1 + B_1)\mathbf{i}_1 + (A_2 + B_2)\mathbf{i}_2 + (A_3 + B_3)\mathbf{i}_3 = (A_j + B_j)\mathbf{i}_j$$

This is the familiar expression used in vector analysis.

The expression for the vector **A** in terms of its direction cosines is obtained by noting that

$$\frac{A_1}{|\mathbf{A}|} = \cos \alpha_1, \quad \frac{A_2}{|\mathbf{A}|} = \cos \alpha_2, \quad \frac{A_3}{|\mathbf{A}|} = \cos \alpha_3$$

Consequently the vector **A** may be expressed as

$$\mathbf{A} = |\mathbf{A}| (\cos \alpha_1 \, \mathbf{i}_1 + \cos \alpha_2 \, \mathbf{i}_2 + \cos \alpha_3 \, \mathbf{i}_3) = |\mathbf{A}| \cos \alpha_i \, \mathbf{i}_i \quad (1\text{-}3)$$

The magnitude of a vector may be found by use of the Pythagorean theorem; thus

$$A = |\mathbf{A}| = \sqrt{(A_1)^2 + (A_2)^2 + (A_3)^2}$$

Using the shorthand system allows us to write this expression as

$$A = |\mathbf{A}| = \sqrt{\sum (A_i)^2} = \sqrt{A_i A_i} \quad (1\text{-}4)$$

Here again the repeated indices i signify a summation.

1-3. The Scalar Product or Dot Product

The scalar or dot product of the two vectors **A** and **B** shown in Fig. 1-3 is defined by the relation

$$\mathbf{A} \cdot \mathbf{B} = |\mathbf{A}| \, |\mathbf{B}| \cos (\mathbf{A}, \mathbf{B}) = AB \cos \theta \quad (1\text{-}5)$$

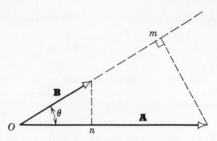

Fig. 1-3. Scalar product.

The expressions

$$On = |\mathbf{B}| \cos \theta \quad \text{and} \quad Om = |\mathbf{A}| \cos \theta$$

may be written. Substituting gives

$$\mathbf{A} \cdot \mathbf{B} = |\mathbf{A}| \, (On) = |\mathbf{B}| \, (Om)$$

If either $|\mathbf{A}|$ or $|\mathbf{B}|$ is zero, that is, a null vector, $\mathbf{A} \cdot \mathbf{B}$ is zero. If the vectors are at right angles, θ is $90°$ and $\mathbf{A} \cdot \mathbf{B}$ is zero. If θ is $0°$, the vectors are located on the same line of action, and $\mathbf{A} \cdot \mathbf{B}$ is equal to the product of the magnitudes of the vectors.

Consider the scalar products of the unit vectors in a Cartesian coordinate system.

$$\mathbf{i}_1 \cdot \mathbf{i}_1 = \mathbf{i}_2 \cdot \mathbf{i}_2 = \mathbf{i}_3 \cdot \mathbf{i}_3 = 1 \quad \text{since } \theta = 0°$$
$$\mathbf{i}_1 \cdot \mathbf{i}_2 = \mathbf{i}_2 \cdot \mathbf{i}_3 = \mathbf{i}_3 \cdot \mathbf{i}_1 = 0 \quad \text{since } \theta = 90°$$

These relations may be written in general form by introducing a symbol known as the Kronecker delta, δ_{jk}. This symbol is to equal zero unless j is the same as k, in which case it is to equal one. For example, $\delta_{11} = \delta_{22} = \delta_{33} = 1$ and all others are zero. The general expression for the scalar or the dot product of the unit vectors is then

$$\mathbf{i}_j \cdot \mathbf{i}_k = \delta_{jk} \tag{1-6}$$

Let A_j and B_k represent the rectangular Cartesian components of vectors $\mathbf{A}$ and $\mathbf{B}$. Then

$$\mathbf{A} \cdot \mathbf{B} = (A_j \mathbf{i}_j) \cdot (B_k \mathbf{i}_k) = A_j B_k (\mathbf{i}_j \cdot \mathbf{i}_k)$$

Substituting for $\mathbf{i}_j \cdot \mathbf{i}_k$ its equivalent δ_{jk} gives

$$\mathbf{A} \cdot \mathbf{B} = A_j B_k \, \delta_{jk}$$

When $j = k$, $\delta_{jk} = 1$; otherwise $\delta_{jk} = 0$. Hence the only terms remaining in the double summation above are those for which $j = k$:

$$\mathbf{A} \cdot \mathbf{B} = A_j B_j = A_1 B_1 + A_2 B_2 + A_3 B_3 \qquad (1\text{-}7)$$

Equation (1-7) is the familiar expression for the dot product of two vectors in terms of their Cartesian components A_i and B_i.

1-4. The Vector or Cross Product

The vector product is defined by the following equation, where $\mathbf{C}$ is a vector (see Fig. 1-4).

$$\mathbf{A} \times \mathbf{B} = \mathbf{C} = \mathbf{i}AB \sin (\mathbf{A}, \mathbf{B}) = \mathbf{i}AB \sin \alpha \qquad (1\text{-}8)$$

Here $\mathbf{i}$ is a unit vector normal to the plane of $\mathbf{A}$ and $\mathbf{B}$ and is so directed that, as the first-named vector $\mathbf{A}$ is turned (α is less than 180°) into the second vector $\mathbf{B}$, $\mathbf{i}$ points in the direction in which a right-handed screw would progress if turned in the same direction. The vector $\mathbf{C}$ is therefore normal to the plane containing $\mathbf{A}$ and $\mathbf{B}$ and in the direction of $\mathbf{i}$.

If either $\mathbf{A}$ or $\mathbf{B}$ is zero, that is, a null vector, then $\mathbf{A} \times \mathbf{B}$ is zero. If $\mathbf{A}$ and $\mathbf{B}$ are at right angles, then α is 90° and

$$\mathbf{A} \times \mathbf{B} = AB\mathbf{i}$$

If α is 0°, the vectors $\mathbf{A}$ and $\mathbf{B}$ are located on the same line of action and $\mathbf{A} \times \mathbf{B}$ is zero, since the sine of 0° is 0.

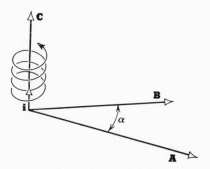

Fig. 1-4. Vector product.

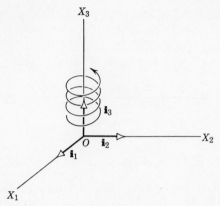

Fig. 1-5.

The vector product will now be applied to the unit vectors in a right-handed Cartesian coordinate system as shown in Fig. 1-5. The unit vectors are right-handed if and only if a right-handed screw advancing in the direction of i_3 rotates i_1 onto i_2. Applying the concept of the cross or vector product gives

$$i_1 \times i_1 = 0 \qquad i_1 \times i_2 = i_3 \qquad i_1 \times i_3 = -i_2$$
$$i_2 \times i_1 = -i_3 \qquad i_2 \times i_2 = 0 \qquad i_2 \times i_3 = i_1$$
$$i_3 \times i_1 = i_2 \qquad i_3 \times i_2 = -i_1 \qquad i_3 \times i_3 = 0$$

We now introduce a symbol e_{ijk} called a permutation symbol, the value of which may be 1, -1, or 0 according to the following schedule. If i, j, k are distinct and in cyclic order, the value is unity:

$$e_{123} = e_{312} = e_{231} = 1$$

If i, j, k are distinct but not in cyclic order, the value is -1:

$$e_{213} = e_{132} = e_{321} = -1$$

If any two indices are the same, the value is zero. For example,

$$e_{112} = e_{233} = 0$$

This symbol will be considered in greater detail later in the text.

We may now express in condensed form the relation for the cross products of the unit vectors.

$$i_j \times i_k = e_{ijk} i_i \qquad (1\text{-}9)$$

Let $j = 1$ and $k = 2$; then

$$\mathbf{i}_1 \times \mathbf{i}_2 = e_{i12}\mathbf{i}_i$$

Summing over i, since it is a dummy index, yields

$$\mathbf{i}_1 \times \mathbf{i}_2 = e_{112}\mathbf{i}_1 + e_{212}\mathbf{i}_2 + e_{312}\mathbf{i}_3 = 0 + 0 + \mathbf{i}_3$$

Hence

$$\mathbf{i}_1 \times \mathbf{i}_2 = \mathbf{i}_3$$

Let $j = 1$ and $k = 1$; then

$$\mathbf{i}_1 \times \mathbf{i}_1 = e_{i11}\mathbf{i}_i = 0$$

The general expression for $\mathbf{i}_j \times \mathbf{i}_k$ will now be used in the expression for $\mathbf{A} \times \mathbf{B}$:

$$\mathbf{A} \times \mathbf{B} = (A_j\mathbf{i}_j) \times (B_k\mathbf{i}_k) = A_jB_k\mathbf{i}_j \times \mathbf{i}_k$$

Substituting for $\mathbf{i}_j \times \mathbf{i}_k$ gives

$$\mathbf{A} \times \mathbf{B} = A_jB_ke_{ijk}\mathbf{i}_i \qquad (1\text{-}10)$$

Since a three-dimensional system is being considered, there are $(3)^3$ or 27 terms in the summation above. The only possible values which can be used for i, j, k are 1, 2, 3. Since all arrangements of i, j, k resulting in repeated indices gives a value of zero for e, only six or 3! terms are non-zero. They are

$$\mathbf{A} \times \mathbf{B} = A_2B_3e_{123}i_1 + A_3B_2e_{132}i_1 + A_1B_3e_{213}i_2$$
$$+ A_3B_1e_{231}i_2 + A_1B_2e_{312}i_3 + A_2B_1e_{321}i_3$$

Now

$$e_{123} = e_{231} = e_{312} = 1$$
$$e_{132} = e_{213} = e_{321} = -1$$

and therefore

$$\mathbf{A} \times \mathbf{B} = (A_2B_3 - A_3B_2)\mathbf{i}_1 + (A_3B_1 - A_1B_3)\mathbf{i}_2 + (A_1B_2 - A_2B_1)\mathbf{i}_3$$

This expression may also be represented by the determinant

$$\mathbf{A} \times \mathbf{B} = \begin{vmatrix} \mathbf{i}_1 & \mathbf{i}_2 & \mathbf{i}_3 \\ A_1 & A_2 & A_3 \\ B_1 & B_2 & B_3 \end{vmatrix} = A_jB_ke_{ijk}\mathbf{i}_i \qquad (1\text{-}11)$$

Expansion of the determinant gives the same result.

1-5. Base Vectors

A method for describing coordinate curves makes use of vector fields which are tangent to these curves. The describing vectors are often termed base vectors. To describe the three coordinate curves through point P in three-dimensional space it is necessary to define three base vectors.

The base vectors are used to define the coordinate curves describing the intersections of the coordinate surfaces* and are locally tangent to the coordinate curves. They may or may not be unit vectors. Consider the coordinate system shown by the X_i axes when $i = 1, 2,$ and 3 as illustrated in Fig. 1-6. The base vectors $\mathbf{e}_i$, that is, $\mathbf{e}_1$, $\mathbf{e}_2$, and $\mathbf{e}_3$, are tangent to the coordinate axes at the origin O. Consider a

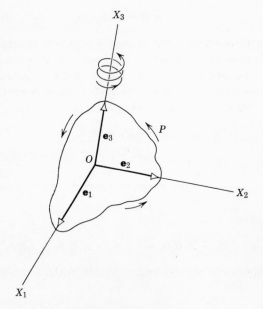

Fig. 1-6. Base vectors.

* A coordinate surface is a surface along which one of the three coordinates is constant. These surfaces are three mutually perpendicular planes in a Cartesian frame of reference.

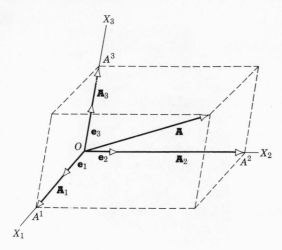

Fig. 1-7. Base vectors.

plane P passing through the terminal points of the three base vectors. On the side of the plane opposite the origin, draw arrows from the terminal points of the base vectors from e_1 to e_2, etc. These arrows are termed circulation arrows. If the circulation arrows are in a counterclockwise direction, the base vectors are called right-handed or dextral. If the arrows indicate a clockwise direction, the base vectors are called left-handed or sinistral. Note that e_1, e_2, e_3 are not necessarily orthogonal.

In another method of classifying the base vectors e_1 is rotated into e_2. If the axes of e_3 represent the direction in which a right-handed screw would rotate and advance, the system is right-handed; otherwise it is left-handed.

To obtain the components of a vector $\mathbf{A}$ along the base vectors (see Fig. 1-7), the vector $\mathbf{A}_1$ is constructed in the following manner: Through the terminus of vector $\mathbf{A}$ pass a plane parallel to the X_2X_3 plane and draw vector $\mathbf{A}_1$ from the origin O to the point where this plane intersects the X_1 axis. Obtain $\mathbf{A}_2$ in a similar manner but with a plane parallel to the X_1X_3 plane. For $\mathbf{A}_3$, use a plane parallel to the X_1X_2 plane.

Applying vector addition gives

$$\mathbf{A} = \mathbf{A}_1 + \mathbf{A}_2 + \mathbf{A}_3$$

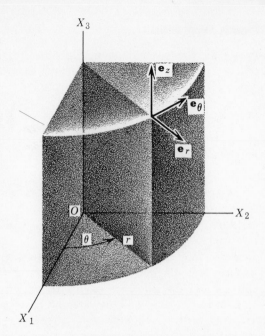

Fig. 1-8. Cylindrical coordinate system.

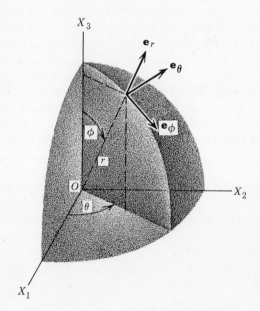

Fig. 1-9. Spherical coordinate system.

The vectors $\mathbf{e}_i$ are the base vectors, and for this case they will be considered unit base vectors. Hence the components of vector $\mathbf{A}$ may be expressed as

$$\mathbf{A}_1 = |\mathbf{A}_1|\,\mathbf{e}_1 = A^1\mathbf{e}_1$$
$$\mathbf{A}_2 = |\mathbf{A}_2|\,\mathbf{e}_2 = A^2\mathbf{e}_2$$
$$\mathbf{A}_3 = |\mathbf{A}_3|\,\mathbf{e}_3 = A^3\mathbf{e}_3$$

Substituting gives

$$\mathbf{A} = A^1\mathbf{e}_1 + A^2\mathbf{e}_2 + A^3\mathbf{e}_3 = A^i\mathbf{e}_i \tag{1-12}$$

The terms A^i are the lengths of the parallel projection of $\mathbf{A}$ onto the line of direction of the $\mathbf{e}_i$ vectors.*

The linearly independent base vectors $\mathbf{e}_1$, $\mathbf{e}_2$, $\mathbf{e}_3$ may be used to represent any arbitrary vector.

For Cartesian orthogonal coordinates the three families of co-ordinate surfaces are the planes $X = $ constant, $Y = $ constant, $Z = $ constant. In this case the base vectors are designated by the symbols $\mathbf{i}$, $\mathbf{j}$, $\mathbf{k}$, or $\mathbf{i}_1$, $\mathbf{i}_2$, and $\mathbf{i}_3$, and they are unit base vectors. The unit base vectors are oriented so that the rotation of $\mathbf{i}$ into $\mathbf{j}$ determines $\mathbf{k}$, and a rotation from $\mathbf{j}$ into $\mathbf{k}$ determines $\mathbf{i}$ according to the right-handed screw rule.

The base vectors for cylindrical coordinates are $\mathbf{e}_r$, $\mathbf{e}_\theta$, and $\mathbf{e}_z$ as shown in Fig. 1-8. These unit vectors are directed to indicate the direction of the increasing coordinate variable along the coordinate line. The ordered triad $\mathbf{e}_r$, $\mathbf{e}_\theta$, $\mathbf{e}_z$ form a right-handed system.

In spherical coordinates the unit base vectors are $\mathbf{e}_\theta$, $\mathbf{e}_r$, $\mathbf{e}_\phi$. The triad $\mathbf{e}_\theta$, $\mathbf{e}_r$, $\mathbf{e}_\phi$ forms a right-handed system as shown in Fig. 1-9.

Relations between the base vectors in cylindrical or spherical coordinate systems and the Cartesian orthogonal base vectors may be found by use of various trigonometric relations.

1-6. Reciprocal Base Vectors

Two sets of base vectors, $\mathbf{e}_1$, $\mathbf{e}_2$, $\mathbf{e}_3$ and $\mathbf{e}^1$, $\mathbf{e}^2$, $\mathbf{e}^3$, are called reciprocal if and only if the following relations are true.

$$\mathbf{e}_1 \cdot \mathbf{e}^1 = |\mathbf{e}_1|\,|\mathbf{e}^1|\cos(\mathbf{e}^1, \mathbf{e}_1) = 1; \quad \mathbf{e}_1 \cdot \mathbf{e}^2 = 0; \quad \mathbf{e}_1 \cdot \mathbf{e}^3 = 0$$
$$\mathbf{e}_2 \cdot \mathbf{e}^1 = 0; \qquad\qquad\qquad\qquad \mathbf{e}_2 \cdot \mathbf{e}^2 = 1; \quad \mathbf{e}_2 \cdot \mathbf{e}^3 = 0 \quad (1\text{-}13)$$
$$\mathbf{e}_3 \cdot \mathbf{e}^1 = 0; \qquad\qquad\qquad\qquad \mathbf{e}_3 \cdot \mathbf{e}^2 = 0; \quad \mathbf{e}_3 \cdot \mathbf{e}^3 = 1$$

* If the base vectors $\mathbf{e}_i$ are orthogonal, these parallel projections are also orthogonal projections.

By employing the Kronecker delta, these nine equations may be written in shorthand form:

$$\mathbf{e}_i \cdot \mathbf{e}^j = \delta_i{}^j \qquad (1\text{-}14)$$

Since the equations $\mathbf{e}_2 \cdot \mathbf{e}^1 = 0$ and $\mathbf{e}_3 \cdot \mathbf{e}^1 = 0$ express the fact that $\mathbf{e}^1$ is perpendicular to both $\mathbf{e}_2$ and $\mathbf{e}_3$, the following equation may be written:

$$\mathbf{e}^1 = C\mathbf{e}_2 \times \mathbf{e}_3$$

where C is a constant to be determined.

Taking the scalar product with $\mathbf{e}_1$ gives

$$\mathbf{e}_1 \cdot \mathbf{e}^1 = 1 = C\mathbf{e}_1 \cdot (\mathbf{e}_2 \times \mathbf{e}_3)$$

Let $\mathbf{e}_1 \cdot (\mathbf{e}_2 \times \mathbf{e}_3)$ be represented by the symbol E; then

$$C = (E)^{-1}$$

By using this expression, various relations may be established between the base vectors. For example,

$$\begin{aligned}
\mathbf{e}^1 &= (E)^{-1}\mathbf{e}_2 \times \mathbf{e}_3, \\
\mathbf{e}_1 &= E\mathbf{e}^2 \times \mathbf{e}^3.
\end{aligned} \qquad (1\text{-}15)$$

The symbol E is sometimes denoted by $[\mathbf{e}_1\mathbf{e}_2\mathbf{e}_3]$.

In shorthand form these equations may be represented as

$$\begin{aligned}
Ee_{ijk}\mathbf{e}^k &= \mathbf{e}_i \times \mathbf{e}_j \\
(E)^{-1}e^{ijk}\mathbf{e}_k &= \mathbf{e}^i \times \mathbf{e}^j
\end{aligned} \qquad (1\text{-}16)$$

In this expression e_{ijk} and e^{ijk} represent the permutation symbol and not a base vector.

A system of base vectors and their reciprocals are identical if

$$\mathbf{e}_i \cdot \mathbf{e}_j = \delta_{ij} \qquad (1\text{-}17)$$

This equation characterizes an orthonormal triple of unit vectors. Whenever triple orthonormal vectors are employed, there is no need to distinguish between their reciprocals. Thus there is no reason for using superscripts. The usual rectangular Cartesian system of base vectors is an example of this type.

In order to present a geometrical picture of base vectors and the equation $\mathbf{e}_i \cdot \mathbf{e}^j = \delta_i{}^j$ consider the two-dimensional vector space where $\mathbf{e}_1$ and $\mathbf{e}_2$ are two unit vectors on the X^1 and X^2 axes of Fig. 1-10.

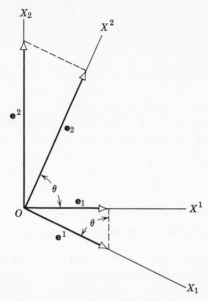

Fig. 1-10.

Construct a new set of axes (X_1, X_2) which are perpendicular to the (X^2, X^1) axes at the origin as shown in Fig. 1-10. Draw to the new axes lines from the ends of vectors $\mathbf{e}_1$ and $\mathbf{e}_2$ perpendicular to $\mathbf{e}_1$ and $\mathbf{e}_2$. Label the resulting vectors along the X_1 and X_2 axes $\mathbf{e}^1$ and $\mathbf{e}^2$, respectively. Now

$$OX_2 \text{ is perpendicular to } OX^1$$

and

$$OX_1 \text{ is perpendicular to } OX^2$$

Therefore

$$\mathbf{e}_1 \cdot \mathbf{e}^2 = |\mathbf{e}_1|\,|\mathbf{e}^2| \cos(90°) = 0$$

$$\mathbf{e}_2 \cdot \mathbf{e}^1 = 0$$

$$\mathbf{e}_1 \cdot \mathbf{e}^1 = |\mathbf{e}_1|\,|\mathbf{e}^1| \cos\left(\frac{\pi}{2} - \theta\right) = |\mathbf{e}_1||\mathbf{e}^1| \sin\theta$$

But

$$\sin\theta = \frac{|\mathbf{e}_1|}{|\mathbf{e}^1|}$$

Therefore

$$\mathbf{e}_1 \cdot \mathbf{e}^1 = |\mathbf{e}_1| \, |\mathbf{e}^1| \, \frac{|\mathbf{e}_1|}{|\mathbf{e}^1|} = |\mathbf{e}_1|^2 = |1|^2 = 1$$

Likewise $\mathbf{e}_2 \cdot \mathbf{e}^2 = 1$. Thus $\mathbf{e}^1$, $\mathbf{e}^2$ are the base vectors reciprocal to $\mathbf{e}_1$, $\mathbf{e}_2$.

Note that the scale of the magnitudes of $\mathbf{e}^i$ is different from those of $\mathbf{e}_j$. If $\mathbf{e}_j$ are unit vectors, $\mathbf{e}^j$ will have magnitudes larger than unity; that is,

$$|\mathbf{e}^1| = \frac{1}{\sin \theta} > 1$$

1-7. Covariant and Contravariant Components of a Vector

The parallel components of a vector with respect to base vectors $\mathbf{e}_i$ as described earlier are called contravariant components, and those obtained in a similar fashion along the base vectors $\mathbf{e}^j$ are called covariant components.

In order to study this statement from a geometrical standpoint, consider the vector $\mathbf{A}$ in two-dimensional space in which $\mathbf{e}_1$ and $\mathbf{e}_2$ are unit base vectors in the direction of X^1 and X^2 (see Fig. 1-11).

The components of vector $\mathbf{A}$ along the X^1 and X^2 axes are $\mathbf{A}^1$ and $\mathbf{A}^2$. The vector may therefore be expressed as

$$\mathbf{A} = \mathbf{A}^1 + \mathbf{A}^2 = A^1\mathbf{e}_1 + A^2\mathbf{e}_2 = A^i\mathbf{e}_i \tag{1-12}$$

These A^i are the contravariant components of the vector $\mathbf{A}$.

We now construct (see Fig. 1-12) the axes X_1 and X_2 such that X_1 is perpendicular to X^2 and X_2 is perpendicular to X^1.

The components of the vector $\mathbf{A}$ along the X_1 and X_2 axes are $\mathbf{A}_1$ and $\mathbf{A}_2$, respectively. The vector may be expressed as

$$\mathbf{A} = \mathbf{A}_1 + \mathbf{A}_2 = A_1\mathbf{e}^1 + A_2\mathbf{e}^2 = A_i\mathbf{e}^i \tag{1-18}$$

These A_i are the covariant components of the vector.

The same type of analysis may be expanded to include three-dimensional vector spaces. In general, therefore, the contravariant form of a vector may be written as

$$\mathbf{A} = A^i\mathbf{e}_i \tag{1-12}$$

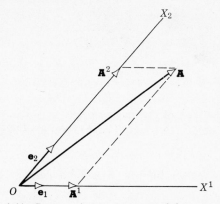

Fig. 1-11. Contravariant components of the vector **A**.

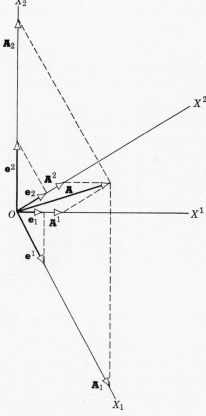

Fig. 1-12.

The scalar multiplication of this equation is performed with $\mathbf{e}^j$, or

$$\mathbf{A} \cdot \mathbf{e}^j = A^i \mathbf{e}_i \cdot \mathbf{e}^j$$

But

$$\mathbf{e}_i \cdot \mathbf{e}^j = \delta_i{}^j$$

Hence

$$\mathbf{A} \cdot \mathbf{e}^j = A^i \delta_i{}^j = A^j$$

The contravariant components of a vector are therefore expressed

$$A^i = \mathbf{A} \cdot \mathbf{e}^i \tag{1-19}$$

By a similar analysis the covariant components are

$$A_i = \mathbf{A} \cdot \mathbf{e}_i \tag{1-20}$$

1-8. Base Vectors and the Euclidean Metric and Conjugate Tensors

We introduce without definition for the present the Euclidean metric tensor g_{ij} and the conjugate tensor g^{ij}. The determinant of the metric tensor is

$$g = |g_{ij}| = \begin{vmatrix} g_{11} & g_{12} & g_{13} \\ g_{21} & g_{22} & g_{23} \\ g_{31} & g_{32} & g_{33} \end{vmatrix} = g_{i1} g_{j2} g_{k3} e^{ijk} \tag{1-21}$$

These tensors will be considered in detail in Chapters 7 and 8.

The components of the Euclidean metric and conjugate tensors in terms of the base vectors are obtained as follows.

Covariant components: $\mathbf{e}_i \cdot \mathbf{e}_j = g_{ij}$ $\qquad$ (1-22)

Contravariant components: $\mathbf{e}^i \cdot \mathbf{e}^j = g^{ij}$ $\qquad$ (1-23)

Mixed components: $\mathbf{e}_i \cdot \mathbf{e}^j = g_i{}^j = \delta_i{}^j$ $\qquad$ (1-24)

The components of the metric and conjugate tensors are symmetric; that is,

$$g_{ij} = g_{ji} \quad \text{and} \quad g^{ij} = g^{ji} \tag{1-25}$$

The scalar product of vectors $\mathbf{A}$ and $\mathbf{B}$ may be found in the following manner.

$$\mathbf{A} \cdot \mathbf{B} = (A^i \mathbf{e}_i) \cdot (B_j \mathbf{e}^j) = A^i B_j (\mathbf{e}_i \cdot \mathbf{e}^j)$$

But

$$\mathbf{e}_i \cdot \mathbf{e}^j = \delta_i{}^j$$

and hence

$$\mathbf{A} \cdot \mathbf{B} = A^i B_j \, \delta_i{}^j$$

In the summation on j the only non-zero term occurs when $j = i$; then $\delta_i{}^j = 1$, or

$$\mathbf{A} \cdot \mathbf{B} = A^i B_i = A_i B^i \tag{1-26}$$

An alternative expression for the scalar product is

$$\mathbf{A} \cdot \mathbf{B} = (A^i \mathbf{e}_i) \cdot (B^j \mathbf{e}_j) = A^i B^j (\mathbf{e}_i \cdot \mathbf{e}_j)$$

But

$$\mathbf{e}_i \cdot \mathbf{e}_j = g_{ij}$$

and hence

$$\mathbf{A} \cdot \mathbf{B} = A^i B^j g_{ij} = A_i B_j g^{ij} \tag{1-27}$$

The relationship between the covariant and contravariant components of $\mathbf{A}$ is now established:

$$A_j = \mathbf{A} \cdot \mathbf{e}_j = A^i \mathbf{e}_i \cdot \mathbf{e}_j = g_{ij} A^i \quad \text{and*} \quad A^i = g^{ij} A_j \tag{1-28}$$

The relationship between reciprocal base vectors may be obtained in a similar manner to the one used in establishing equations (1-28).

$$\mathbf{e}_i = g_{ij} \mathbf{e}^j \quad \text{and} \quad \mathbf{e}^i = g^{ij} \mathbf{e}_j \tag{1-29}$$

The contravariant and covariant components of the base vectors are related as follows:

$$\mathbf{e}_i \cdot \mathbf{e}^k = \delta_i{}^k \tag{1-24}$$

But $\mathbf{e}_i = g_{ij} \mathbf{e}^j$; hence

$$\delta_i{}^k = (g_{ij} \mathbf{e}^j) \cdot \mathbf{e}^k = g_{ij} (\mathbf{e}^j \cdot \mathbf{e}^k) = g_{ij} g^{jk} \tag{1-30}$$

By similar analysis,

$$\delta_i{}^j = g^{jk} g_{ki} \tag{1-31}$$

These equations are identical because g_{ij} and g^{ij} are symmetric.

Consider next the square of the magnitude of the length of a vector $\mathbf{A}$.

$$|\mathbf{A}|^2 = \mathbf{A} \cdot \mathbf{A} = A_i A^i = A^i A^j g_{ij} = A_i A_j g^{ij} \tag{1-32}$$

* By a similar procedure.

The cosine of the angle between two vectors $\mathbf{A}$ and $\mathbf{B}$ may be established as follows:

$$\cos(\mathbf{A}, \mathbf{B}) = \frac{\mathbf{A} \cdot \mathbf{B}}{|\mathbf{A}||\mathbf{B}|} = \frac{g_{ij}A^iB^j}{(g_{kl}A^kB^l)^{1/2}(g_{mn}B^mB^n)^{1/2}}$$

$$= \frac{g^{ij}A_iB_j}{(g^{kl}A_kA_l)^{1/2}(g^{mn}B_mB_n)^{1/2}} \quad (1\text{-}33)$$

The cross product of two base vectors may be written

$$\mathbf{e}^i \times \mathbf{e}^j = E^{-1}e^{ijk}\mathbf{e}_k \quad (1\text{-}16)$$

$\mathbf{A}$ and $\mathbf{B}$ may be expressed as

$$\mathbf{A} = A_i\mathbf{e}^i \quad \text{and} \quad \mathbf{B} = B_j\mathbf{e}^j$$

Forming the cross product,

$$\mathbf{A} \times \mathbf{B} = A_iB_j\mathbf{e}^i \times \mathbf{e}^j = E^{-1}e^{kij}\mathbf{e}_kA_iB_j$$
$$\mathbf{A} \times \mathbf{B} = E^{-1}e^{ijk}A_iB_j\mathbf{e}_k \quad (1\text{-}34)$$

Let $\mathbf{A} = \mathbf{e}_1$ and $\mathbf{B} = \mathbf{e}_2$; then

$$\mathbf{A} = A_i\mathbf{e}^i = \mathbf{e}_1 \qquad A_i = \mathbf{A} \cdot \mathbf{e}_i = \mathbf{e}_1 \cdot \mathbf{e}_i = g_{i1}$$
$$\mathbf{B} = B_j\mathbf{e}^j = \mathbf{e}_2 \qquad B_j = \mathbf{B} \cdot \mathbf{e}_j = \mathbf{e}_2 \cdot \mathbf{e}_j = g_{j2}$$

Substituting gives

$$\mathbf{e}_1 \times \mathbf{e}_2 = \frac{1}{E}e^{ijk}g_{i1}g_{j2}\mathbf{e}_k$$

Taking the scalar product with $\mathbf{e}_3$ yields

$$(\mathbf{e}_1 \times \mathbf{e}_2) \cdot \mathbf{e}_3 = \frac{1}{E}e^{ijk}g_{i1}g_{j2}(\mathbf{e}_k \cdot \mathbf{e}_3)$$

But $(\mathbf{e}_1 \times \mathbf{e}_2) \cdot \mathbf{e}_3$ equals E and $\mathbf{e}_k \cdot \mathbf{e}_3$ equals g_{k3}; hence

$$E = \frac{1}{E}e^{ijk}g_{i1}g_{j2}g_{k3}$$

According to equation 1-21 this becomes

$$E^2 = g = |g_{ij}|$$

Therefore

$$g = |g_{ij}| = \text{determinant}(\mathbf{e}_i \cdot \mathbf{e}_j) = [\mathbf{e}_1\mathbf{e}_2\mathbf{e}_3]^2 = E^2 \quad (1\text{-}35)$$

Similarly it can be shown that

$$\frac{1}{g} = |g^{ij}| = \text{determinant } (\mathbf{e}^i \cdot \mathbf{e}^j) = [\mathbf{e}^1\mathbf{e}^2\mathbf{e}^3]^2 = \frac{1}{E^2} \qquad (1\text{-}36)$$

Equation 1-16 may now be written as

$$\mathbf{e}^i \times \mathbf{e}^j = \frac{1}{\sqrt{g}} e^{ijk}\mathbf{e}_k$$

If $i = 1, j = 2$, and $k = 3$,

$$\mathbf{e}^1 \times \mathbf{e}^2 = \frac{1}{\sqrt{g}} e^{123}\mathbf{e}_3$$

But $e^{123} = 1$; hence

$$\mathbf{e}_3 = \sqrt{g}\,\mathbf{e}^1 \times \mathbf{e}^2$$

Two new symbols ϵ_{ijk} and ϵ^{ijk} are introduced at this point by the definitions

$$\epsilon_{ijk} = E e_{ijk} = \sqrt{g}\,e_{ijk} \qquad (1\text{-}37)$$

$$\epsilon^{ijk} = E^{-1}e^{ijk} = \frac{e^{ijk}}{\sqrt{g}} \qquad (1\text{-}38)$$

We shall see later that these definitions have certain transformation properties which are most convenient. Recasting equation (1-34) in terms of g rather than E gives

$$\mathbf{A} \times \mathbf{B} = \frac{e^{ijk}}{\sqrt{g}} A_i B_j \mathbf{e}_k$$

1-9. Problems

1-1. Using Cartesian coordinates, write in component form the expression for the vector which extends from: (a) $(1, 3, 0)$ to $(0, 4, 2)$; (b) $(-3, 2, 2)$ to $(0, 6, 1)$; and (c) the origin to $(0, 4, 7)$.

1-2. Determine the magnitude of the vectors: (a) $\mathbf{A} = 1\mathbf{i}_x + 2\mathbf{i}_y + \mathbf{i}_z$; (b) $\mathbf{A} = (1/\sqrt{2})\mathbf{i}_x + (1/\sqrt{2})\mathbf{i}_z$; and (c) $\mathbf{A} = \sin \alpha\mathbf{i}_x + \cos \alpha\mathbf{i}_y$.

1-3. Write the unit vectors in component form which lie in the direction defined by the vectors: (a) $\mathbf{A} = \mathbf{i}_x + 3\mathbf{i}_y + 2\mathbf{i}_z$; (b) $\mathbf{A} = 10\mathbf{i}_z$; and (c) $\mathbf{A} = 2\mathbf{i}_x + 7\mathbf{i}_z$.

1-4. Determine the scalar or dot product of the vectors $\mathbf{A}$ and $\mathbf{B}$ if: (a) $\mathbf{A} = 4\mathbf{i}_x + 4\mathbf{i}_y + 3\mathbf{i}_z, \mathbf{B} = 3\mathbf{i}_x + 2\mathbf{i}_y - 2\mathbf{i}_z$; (b) $\mathbf{A} = \mathbf{i}_x, \mathbf{B} = 2\mathbf{i}_y + 3\mathbf{i}_z$; (c) $\mathbf{A} = \mathbf{i}_x - 2\mathbf{i}_y - \mathbf{i}_z, \mathbf{B} = \mathbf{i}_x + 2\mathbf{i}_y - 3\mathbf{i}_z$.

1-5. Find the component of vector $C = -2i_x - 3i_y - 6i_z$ in the direction defined by the vector: (*a*) $2i_x + 4i_y$, and (*b*) $-3i_x - 4i_y - 9i_z$.

1-6. Show that the vectors $A = i_1 + 4i_2 + 3i_3$ and $B = 4i_1 + 2i_2 - 4i_3$ are perpendicular.

1-7. Find the projection of vector A on vector B if the vectors are represented by the equations $A = 2i_1 - 2i_2 + i_3$ and $B = 2i_1 - 4i_2 + 4i_3$.

1-8. Find the cross product of the vectors A and B for (*a*) $A = i_x - 2i_y + 3i_z$, $B = 2i_x - 4i_y + 5i_z$; (*b*) $A = 2i_y + 3i_z$, $B = i_x$; (*c*) $A = 4i_x + 3i_y + 2i_z$, $B = i_x - i_y + i_z$.

1-9. Two unit vectors e_A and e_B lying in the XY plane and passing through the origin make angles α_A and α_B with the X axis, respectively. Express each in Cartesian components. Take the scalar product and prove

$$\cos(\alpha_A - \alpha_B) = \cos \alpha_A \cos \alpha_B + \sin \alpha_A \sin \alpha_B$$

1-10. Prove that the vector fields $A = r \cos \phi r + r \sin \phi \phi + r k$ and $B = r \cos \phi r + r \sin \phi \phi - r k$ are perpendicular.

1-11. Prove that the vector fields

$$A = r \frac{\sin 2\theta}{r^2} + \frac{2\theta \sin \theta}{r^2} \quad \text{and} \quad B = r \cos \theta r + r \theta$$

are parallel.

1-12. Show that $(A - B) \times (A + B) = 2A \times B$.

1-13. Show that the scalar triple product of vectors A, B, and C is equal to any of the expressions

$$A \cdot (B \times C) = B \cdot (C \times A) = C \cdot (A \times B) = -C \cdot (B \times A)$$
$$= -A \cdot (C \times B) = -B \cdot (A \times C)$$

1-10. Suggested References

1-1. *Elementary Analysis*, H. C. Trimble and F. W. Lott, Jr., Prentice-Hall, Inc.

1-2. *Engineering Electromagnetics*, William H. Hayt, Jr., McGraw-Hill Book Company, Chapter 1.

1-3. *Engineering Mechanics, Statics*, Irving H. Shames, Prentice-Hall, Inc., Chapters 2 and 3.

1-4. *Vector Analysis*, Murray R. Spiegel, Schaum Publishing Company.

1-5. *Vector and Tensor Analysis*, G. E. Hay, Dover Publications, Inc.

1-6. *Vector and Tensor Analysis*, Nathaniel Coburn, The Macmillan Company.

1-7. *Vector Analysis*, Louis Brand, John Wiley and Sons, Inc.

1-8. *Vector Analysis with an Introduction to Tensor Analysis*, A. P. Wills, Dover Publications, Inc.

1-9. *Vector and Tensor Analysis*, Harry Lass, McGraw-Hill Book Company.

1-10. *Introduction to Vector Analysis*, Harry F. Davis, Allyn and Bacon, Inc.

1-11. *Vector Analysis*, J. Willard Gibbs, Dover Publications, Inc.

1-12. *Vector Analysis*, Manuel Schwartz, Simon Green, and W. A. Rutledge, Harper & Brothers.

1-13. *Vector Spaces and Matrices*, Robert M. Thrall, Leonard Tornheim, John Wiley and Sons, Inc.

1-14. *The Algebra of Vectors and Matrices*, Thomas L. Wade, Addison-Wesley Publishing Company.

1-15. *Elementary Vector Analysis*, C. E. Weatherburn, G. Bull and Sons, Ltd., London, 1948; Open Court Publishing Company, LaSalle, Ill.

1-16. *Introduction to Matrix Analysis*, Richard Bellman, McGraw-Hill Book Company.

1-17. *Advanced Calculus*, W. Kaplan, Addison-Wesley Publishing Co.

Review of Determinants

2-1. Introduction

In order to obviate the need for writing numerous terms in equations, and the elements of determinants, a shorthand system is introduced in this chapter. Later in the discussion the shorthand system will be expanded and considered in greater detail.

Consider first the following sum of four terms:

$$a_1 x_1 + a_2 x_2 + a_3 x_3 + a_4 x_4$$

This could be represented as a summation of the form

$$\sum_{i=1}^{4} a_i x_i = a_1 x_1 + a_2 x_2 + a_3 x_3 + a_4 x_4$$

In order to simplify the writing we use the expression $a_i x_i$ for the sum, keeping in mind that the i are summed from 1 to 4. The repeated index i is referred to as a dummy index, repeated index, or an umbral index. The value of the expression does not depend on the symbol used for the dummy index. On the other hand, an index which is not repeated is referred to as a free index, such as i in the expression $a_{ij} X^j$. Here j is the dummy index.

Using this form of notation we shall examine the expression $a_{ij} x_j$ where $i = 1, 2, 3$ and $j = 1, 2, 3, 4$. Here i is the identifying or free index and j is the summation or dummy index. The term

22

$a_{ij}x_j$ represents three different summations each containing 4 terms as follows:

when $i = 1$: $a_{1j}x_j = a_{11}x_1 + a_{12}x_2 + a_{13}x_3 + a_{14}x_4$

when $i = 2$: $a_{2j}x_j = a_{21}x_1 + a_{22}x_2 + a_{23}x_3 + a_{24}x_4$

when $i = 3$: $a_{3j}x_j = a_{31}x_1 + a_{32}x_2 + a_{33}x_3 + a_{34}x_4$

The coefficients a_{ij} may be real or complex.

We may agree that in general a summation will be represented by a single term such as $a_i x_i$ where the values of i range from 1 to n. Then

$$a_i x_i = a_1 x_1 + a_2 x_2 + \cdots + a_{(n)}x_{(n)}$$

Here $a_{(n)}x_{(n)}$ does not represent a summation; instead it is the nth term. In order to avoid confusion the parentheses will be employed when a summation is not intended.

An extension of this shorthand system to other relations will now be made. A quadratic of the form

$$\sum_{i=1}^{n} \sum_{j=1}^{n} a_{ij}x_i x_j$$

will now be expressed as

$$a_{ij}x_i x_j$$

This represents a bilinear form containing n^2 terms. If $n = 4$, writing out the detailed relations would be quite time-consuming. It is apparent that the shorthand system greatly simplifies the writing of such relations.

The system $a_{ij}a_{jk}$ represents n^2 sums of the form

$$a_{i1}a_{1k} + a_{i2}a_{2k} + \cdots + a_{i(n)}a_{(n)k} \qquad (i, k = 1, \ldots, n)$$

A linear combination of x^i with coefficients a_i may be written

$$a_i x^i$$

A bilinear combination of x_i and y_j with coefficients a^{ij} is expressed as

$$a^{ij}x_i y_j$$

In the analysis of problems in engineering and science it is often necessary to deal with rectangular arrays of numbers or functions. An array may be represented as follows.

$$\begin{pmatrix} a_{11} & a_{12} & \cdots & a_{1n} \\ a_{21} & a_{22} & \cdots & a_{2n} \\ \cdots\cdots\cdots\cdots\cdots\cdots \\ a_{m1} & a_{m2} & \cdots & a_{mn} \end{pmatrix}$$

The numbers or functions a_{ij} are called the elements of an array. A rectangular array of elements or functions is called a matrix. If the array has m rows and n columns, it is called an $m \times n$ (m by n) matrix and is represented as follows.

$$A = (a_{ij})_{(m,n)}$$

When the number of rows and the number of columns are the same ($m = n$), the matrix is called a square matrix or a matrix of order n, hence

$$A = (a_{ij})_{(n)}$$

Properties of matrices will be considered later.

We shall associate with each square matrix, $A = (a_{ij})_{(n)}$, $n \geqslant 1$, a uniquely defined scalar quantity called the determinant of A. The following symbols may be used for the scalar.

$$\det A = |a_{ij}| \quad \text{or} \quad |a^{ij}| \quad \text{or} \quad |a_j{}^i|$$

In these expressions the elements of the determinants are represented by the symbols a_{ij}, a^{ij}, or $a_j{}^i$. In the last representation, $a_j{}^i$, i identifies the row and j the column. That is,

$$\det A = \begin{vmatrix} a_1{}^1 & a_2{}^1 & \cdots & a_n{}^1 \\ a_1{}^2 & a_2{}^2 & \cdots & a_n{}^2 \\ \cdots\cdots\cdots\cdots\cdots\cdots \\ a_1{}^n & a_2{}^n & \cdots & a_n{}^n \end{vmatrix}$$

In determinants the principal or leading diagonal is the one from the upper left corner to the lower right corner. The diagonal from the lower left corner to the upper right corner is called the secondary diagonal. The principal diagonal of the preceding determinant is the one containing the elements $a_1{}^1, a_2{}^2, \ldots, a_n{}^n$. The secondary diagonal contains $a_n{}^1, \ldots, a_1{}^n$. The evaluation of a second- and a third-order determinant follows.

Second-order determinant:

$$|a_j{}^i| = \begin{vmatrix} a_1{}^1 & a_2{}^1 \\ a_1{}^2 & a_2{}^2 \end{vmatrix} = a_1{}^1 a_2{}^2 - a_1{}^2 a_2{}^1$$

Third-order determinant:

$$|a_j{}^i| = \begin{vmatrix} a_1{}^1 & a_2{}^1 & a_3{}^1 \\ a_1{}^2 & a_2{}^2 & a_3{}^2 \\ a_1{}^3 & a_2{}^3 & a_3{}^3 \end{vmatrix} = a_1{}^1 a_2{}^2 a_3{}^3 + a_3{}^1 a_1{}^2 a_2{}^3 + a_1{}^3 a_2{}^1 a_3{}^2$$

$$- a_3{}^1 a_2{}^2 a_1{}^3 - a_1{}^1 a_3{}^2 a_2{}^3 - a_3{}^3 a_2{}^1 a_1{}^2$$

$$= a_1{}^1 (a_2{}^2 a_3{}^3 - a_3{}^2 a_2{}^3) + a_2{}^1 (a_3{}^2 a_1{}^3 - a_3{}^3 a_1{}^2)$$

$$+ a_3{}^1 (a_1{}^2 a_2{}^3 - a_2{}^2 a_1{}^3)$$

The latter form provides a convenient calculational scheme.

Example 2-1

Find the value of the determinant

$$\begin{vmatrix} 1 & 0 & 3 \\ 2 & 8 & 4 \\ 2 & 1 & 2 \end{vmatrix} = 16 + 0 + 6 - 48 - 4 - 0 = -30$$

2-2. Some Properties of Determinants

1. If all elements in a row or column are zero, the determinant is zero.

$$\begin{vmatrix} a_1 & b_1 & c_1 \\ a_2 & b_2 & c_2 \\ 0 & 0 & 0 \end{vmatrix} = 0 \qquad \begin{vmatrix} 0 & b_1 & c_1 \\ 0 & b_2 & c_2 \\ 0 & b_3 & c_3 \end{vmatrix} = 0$$

2. The value of a determinant is not altered when the rows are changed to columns and the columns to rows, that is, when the rows and columns are interchanged.

3. The interchange of any two columns or any two rows of a determinant changes the sign of the determinant.

4. If two columns or two rows of a determinant are identical, the determinant is equal to zero.

5. If each element in any column or row of a determinant is expressed as the sum of two quantities, the determinant can be expressed as the sum of two determinants of the same order.

$$\begin{vmatrix} a_1 + d_1 & b_1 & c_1 \\ a_2 + d_2 & b_2 & c_2 \\ a_3 + d_3 & b_3 & c_3 \end{vmatrix} = \begin{vmatrix} a_1 & b_1 & c_1 \\ a_2 & b_2 & c_2 \\ a_3 & b_3 & c_3 \end{vmatrix} + \begin{vmatrix} d_1 & b_1 & c_1 \\ d_2 & b_2 & c_2 \\ d_3 & b_3 & c_3 \end{vmatrix}$$

6. Adding the same multiple of each element of one row to the corresponding element of another row does not change the value of the determinant. The same holds true for the columns.

$$\begin{vmatrix} a_1 & b_1 & c_1 \\ a_2 & b_2 & c_2 \\ a_3 & b_3 & c_3 \end{vmatrix} = \begin{vmatrix} (a_1 + nb_1) & b_1 & c_1 \\ (a_2 + nb_2) & b_2 & c_2 \\ (a_3 + nb_3) & b_3 & c_3 \end{vmatrix}$$

This result follows immediately from properties 4 and 5.

7. If all the elements in any column or row are multiplied by any factor, the determinant is multiplied by that factor.

$$\begin{vmatrix} ma_1 & b_1 & c_1 \\ ma_2 & b_2 & c_2 \\ ma_3 & b_3 & c_3 \end{vmatrix} = m \begin{vmatrix} a_1 & b_1 & c_1 \\ a_2 & b_2 & c_2 \\ a_3 & b_3 & c_3 \end{vmatrix}$$

$$\begin{vmatrix} \frac{1}{m} a_1 & b_1 & c_1 \\ \frac{1}{m} a_2 & b_2 & c_2 \\ \frac{1}{m} a_3 & b_3 & c_3 \end{vmatrix} = \frac{1}{m} \begin{vmatrix} a_1 & b_1 & c_1 \\ a_2 & b_2 & c_2 \\ a_3 & b_3 & c_3 \end{vmatrix}$$

8. The product of two determinants $A = |a_k{}^i|$ and $B = |b_j{}^k|$ is equal to a third determinant represented by $|a_k{}^i b_j{}^k| = |c_j{}^i|$.

The following examples illustrate the use of this rule. Let A and B represent the determinants

$$A = |a_k{}^i| = \begin{vmatrix} a_1{}^1 = 3 & a_2{}^1 = 2 & a_3{}^1 = -3 \\ a_1{}^2 = 1 & a_2{}^2 = 0 & a_3{}^2 = 2 \\ a_1{}^3 = 2 & a_2{}^3 = -1 & a_3{}^3 = -1 \end{vmatrix}$$

$$B = |b_j{}^k| = \begin{vmatrix} b_1{}^1 = 1 & b_2{}^1 = 2 & b_3{}^1 = 1 \\ b_1{}^2 = -1 & b_2{}^2 = 4 & b_3{}^2 = 5 \\ b_1{}^3 = 0 & b_2{}^3 = -4 & b_3{}^3 = 2 \end{vmatrix}$$

The product of A and B follows from the relation $c_j{}^i = a_k{}^i b_j{}^k$.

$$AB = \begin{vmatrix} \begin{pmatrix} a_1{}^1 b_1{}^1 + a_2{}^1 b_1{}^2 + a_3{}^1 b_1{}^3 \\ 3(1) + 2(-1) + (-3)0 \end{pmatrix} & \begin{pmatrix} a_1{}^1 b_2{}^1 + a_2{}^1 b_2{}^2 + a_3{}^1 b_2{}^3 \\ 3(2) + 2(4) - 3(-4) \end{pmatrix} & \begin{pmatrix} a_1{}^1 b_3{}^1 + a_2{}^1 b_3{}^2 + a_3{}^1 b_3{}^3 \\ 3(1) + 2(5) - 3(2) \end{pmatrix} \\ \begin{pmatrix} a_1{}^2 b_1{}^1 + a_2{}^2 b_1{}^2 + a_3{}^2 b_1{}^3 \\ 1(1) + 0(-1) + 2(0) \end{pmatrix} & \begin{pmatrix} a_1{}^2 b_2{}^1 + a_2{}^2 b_2{}^2 + a_3{}^2 b_2{}^3 \\ 1(2) + 0(4) + 2(-4) \end{pmatrix} & \begin{pmatrix} a_1{}^2 b_3{}^1 + a_2{}^2 b_3{}^2 + a_3{}^2 b_3{}^3 \\ 1(1) + 0(5) + 2(2) \end{pmatrix} \\ \begin{pmatrix} a_1{}^3 b_1{}^1 + a_2{}^3 b_1{}^2 + a_3{}^3 b_1{}^3 \\ 2(1) + -1(-1) - 1(0) \end{pmatrix} & \begin{pmatrix} a_1{}^3 b_2{}^1 + a_2{}^3 b_2{}^2 + a_3{}^3 b_2{}^3 \\ 2(2) - 1(4) - 1(-4) \end{pmatrix} & \begin{pmatrix} a_1{}^3 b_3{}^1 + a_2{}^3 b_3{}^2 + a_3{}^3 b_3{}^3 \\ 2(1) - 1(5) - 1(2) \end{pmatrix} \end{vmatrix}$$

$$= \begin{vmatrix} 1 & 26 & 7 \\ 1 & -6 & 5 \\ 3 & 4 & -5 \end{vmatrix} = 684$$

For the multiplication of more than two determinants, the product may be written in general form:

$$|d_j{}^i| = |a_k{}^i|\,|b_m{}^k|\,|c_j{}^m| = |a_k{}^i b_m{}^k c_j{}^m|$$

9. If the relation $a_{ij} = a_{ji}$ is valid, the element a_{ij} of the determinant is said to be symmetric.

10. If the relation $a_{ij} = -a_{ji}$ is valid, the element a_{ij} of the determinant is said to be skew-symmetric.

2-3. Minors

Consider a third-order determinant; for example,

$$a = |a_j{}^i| = \begin{vmatrix} a_1{}^1 & a_2{}^1 & a_3{}^1 \\ a_1{}^2 & a_2{}^2 & a_3{}^2 \\ a_1{}^3 & a_2{}^3 & a_3{}^3 \end{vmatrix}$$

If expanded, this determinant may be represented as

$$a = |a_j{}^i| = a_1{}^1 a_2{}^2 a_3{}^3 + a_2{}^1 a_3{}^2 a_1{}^3 + a_3{}^1 a_1{}^2 a_2{}^3$$
$$- a_3{}^1 a_2{}^2 a_1{}^3 - a_2{}^1 a_1{}^2 a_3{}^3 - a_1{}^1 a_3{}^2 a_2{}^3$$

Rearranging gives

$$a = a_1{}^1(a_2{}^2 a_3{}^3 - a_3{}^2 a_2{}^3) - a_1{}^2(a_2{}^1 a_3{}^3 - a_3{}^1 a_2{}^3)$$
$$+ a_1{}^3(a_2{}^1 a_3{}^2 - a_3{}^1 a_2{}^2)$$

The expressions in parentheses are recognized as second-order determinants; hence

$$a = |a_j{}^i| = a_1{}^1 \begin{vmatrix} a_2{}^2 & a_3{}^2 \\ a_2{}^3 & a_3{}^3 \end{vmatrix} - a_1{}^2 \begin{vmatrix} a_2{}^1 & a_3{}^1 \\ a_2{}^3 & a_3{}^3 \end{vmatrix} + a_1{}^3 \begin{vmatrix} a_2{}^1 & a_3{}^1 \\ a_2{}^2 & a_3{}^2 \end{vmatrix}$$

These second-order determinants are called the minors of the elements of the first column. A minor of an element is defined as the determinant of the next lower order which remains when the row and column in which the element stands are suppressed. Thus

$$\begin{vmatrix} a_2{}^2 & a_3{}^2 \\ a_2{}^3 & a_3{}^3 \end{vmatrix}$$

is the minor of $a_1{}^1$. The minor for elements in other locations of a determinant may be found in like manner.

Example 2-2

Establish the minors for the elements $a_2{}^1$, $a_2{}^2$, $a_2{}^3$, $a_1{}^1$, $a_2{}^1$, and $a_3{}^1$ in the determinant

$$a = |a_j{}^i| = \begin{vmatrix} a_1{}^1 & a_2{}^1 & a_3{}^1 \\ a_1{}^2 & a_2{}^2 & a_3{}^2 \\ a_1{}^3 & a_2{}^3 & a_3{}^3 \end{vmatrix}$$

$$\text{Minor of } a_2{}^1 = \begin{vmatrix} a_1{}^2 & a_3{}^2 \\ a_1{}^3 & a_3{}^3 \end{vmatrix} \qquad \text{Minor of } a_2{}^2 = \begin{vmatrix} a_1{}^1 & a_3{}^1 \\ a_1{}^3 & a_3{}^3 \end{vmatrix}$$

$$\text{Minor of } a_2{}^3 = \begin{vmatrix} a_1{}^1 & a_3{}^1 \\ a_1{}^2 & a_3{}^2 \end{vmatrix} \qquad \text{Minor of } a_1{}^1 = \begin{vmatrix} a_2{}^2 & a_3{}^2 \\ a_2{}^3 & a_3{}^3 \end{vmatrix}$$

$$\text{Minor of } a_2{}^1 = \begin{vmatrix} a_1{}^2 & a_3{}^2 \\ a_1{}^3 & a_3{}^3 \end{vmatrix} \qquad \text{Minor of } a_3{}^1 = \begin{vmatrix} a_1{}^2 & a_2{}^2 \\ a_1{}^3 & a_2{}^3 \end{vmatrix}$$

2-4. Cofactors

When a minor of an element is given the proper sign, the resulting term is called the cofactor of the element. If an element occurs in the pth row and in the mth column, the minor must be multiplied by the factor $(-1)^{m+p}$ to obtain the cofactor. If $m + p$ is odd, the sign is negative. If $m + p$ is even, the sign is positive. We may write the expression for the cofactor A and the minor M as follows:

$$A_{\text{cofactor}} = (-1)^{m+p} M_{\text{minor}}$$

Example 2-3

Determine the cofactor of the element $a_2{}^3$ in the determinant

$$a = |a_j{}^i| = \begin{vmatrix} a_1{}^1 & a_2{}^1 & a_3{}^1 \\ a_1{}^2 & a_2{}^2 & a_3{}^2 \\ a_1{}^3 & a_2{}^3 & a_3{}^3 \end{vmatrix}$$

The cofactor of $a_2{}^3$ equals

$$(-1)^{(3+2)} \begin{vmatrix} a_1{}^1 & a_3{}^1 \\ a_1{}^2 & a_3{}^2 \end{vmatrix} = - \begin{vmatrix} a_1{}^1 & a_3{}^1 \\ a_1{}^2 & a_3{}^2 \end{vmatrix}$$

Here $m = 2$ and $p = 3$ because the element occurs in the second column and third row.

2-5. Some Properties of Cofactors

The cofactor of an element $a_j{}^i$ in the determinant $|a_j{}^i|$ will be designated by the symbol $A_i{}^j$. The interchange of indices is arbitrary, and it is used to avoid confusion.

1. If all elements but one in a row or column are zero, the determinant is equal to the product of that element and its cofactor.

$$\begin{vmatrix} a_1{}^1 & a_2{}^1 & a_3{}^1 & 0 \\ a_1{}^2 & a_2{}^2 & a_3{}^2 & 0 \\ a_1{}^3 & a_2{}^3 & a_3{}^3 & a_4{}^3 \\ a_1{}^4 & a_2{}^4 & a_3{}^4 & 0 \end{vmatrix} = a_4{}^3(-1)^{(4+3)} \begin{vmatrix} a_1{}^1 & a_2{}^1 & a_3{}^1 \\ a_1{}^2 & a_2{}^2 & a_3{}^2 \\ a_1{}^4 & a_2{}^4 & a_3{}^4 \end{vmatrix} = a_4{}^3 A_3{}^4$$

2. If the elements of any column (or row) in a determinant are multiplied by the cofactors of the corresponding elements of any other column (or row), the sum of the products equals zero.

$$a = |a_j{}^i| = \begin{vmatrix} a_1{}^1 & a_2{}^1 & a_3{}^1 \\ a_1{}^2 & a_2{}^2 & a_3{}^2 \\ a_1{}^3 & a_2{}^3 & a_3{}^3 \end{vmatrix}$$

$$a_1{}^1 A_1{}^2 + a_1{}^2 A_2{}^2 + a_1{}^3 A_3{}^2 = 0 = a_j{}^i A_i{}^k \quad (j = 1, k = 2)$$

$$a_1{}^1 A_2{}^1 + a_2{}^1 A_2{}^2 + a_3{}^1 A_2{}^3 = 0 = a_i{}^j A_k{}^i \quad (j = 1, k = 2)$$

This may be expressed in general form as

$$a_j{}^i A_i{}^k = 0$$
$$\quad\quad\quad (k \neq j)$$
$$a_i{}^j A_k{}^i = 0$$

We now have use for the Kronecker delta, $\delta_j{}^i$, which was introduced in Chapter 1 and which has the special properties

$$\delta_j{}^i \text{ equals one if } i = j \quad \text{and zero if } i \neq j$$

That is,

$$\delta_j{}^i = \begin{cases} 1 & (i = j) \\ 0 & (i \neq j) \end{cases}$$

Example 2-4

If $i = 1, 2, 3$ and $j = 1, 2, 3$, determine the values for the 9 delta terms.

$$\delta_1{}^1 = \delta_2{}^2 = \delta_3{}^3 = 1$$
$$\delta_2{}^3 = \delta_3{}^1 = \delta_1{}^2 = \delta_3{}^2 = \delta_1{}^3 = \delta_2{}^1 = 0$$

3. The sum of the products of the elements of any row (or column) by the respective cofactors of any row (or column) of a determinant $|a_j{}^i|$ equals the product of the determinant and the Kronecker $\delta_k{}^i$. Hence

$$a_j{}^i A_k{}^j = a\delta_k{}^i \tag{2-1}$$

or

$$a_k{}^i A_j{}^k = a\delta_j{}^i \tag{2-2}$$

The proof of this may be demonstrated by expanding the left side. Thus

$$a_1{}^i A_k{}^1 + a_2{}^i A_k{}^2 + a_3{}^i A_k{}^3 + \cdots + a_{(n)}^i A_k^{(n)} = a\delta_k{}^i$$

$\delta_k{}^i$ can equal 1 only when $i = k$; therefore

$$a_1{}^i A_i{}^1 + a_2{}^i A_i{}^2 + a_3{}^i A_i{}^3 + \cdots + a_{(n)}^i A_i^{(n)} = a\delta_i{}^i = a$$

$$\text{(no summation on } i\text{)}$$

If the columns are used in place of the rows,

$$a_i{}^k A_k{}^j = a\delta_i{}^j$$

or

$$a_j{}^i A_i{}^k = a\delta_j{}^k$$

There are times when it is desirable to denote the elements of a determinant by the symbol a_{ij} and the cofactor by A_{ij} or A^{ij}; thus

$$a = |a_{ij}| = a_{(i)j} A_{(i)j} \quad \text{or} \quad a = |a_{ij}| = a_{(i)j} A^{(i)j}$$

Here the i's in parentheses do not represent a summation.

2-6. Evaluation of nth-Order Determinants

Equations (2-1) and (2-2) will be used to evaluate nth-order determinants. Consider equation (2-1). When $k = i$, then $\delta_k{}^i = 1$ and $a_j{}^i A_i{}^j = a$.

As an example consider the fourth-order determinant

$$\det a = |a_j{}^i| = \begin{vmatrix} a_1{}^1 & a_2{}^1 & a_3{}^1 & a_4{}^1 \\ a_1{}^2 & a_2{}^2 & a_3{}^2 & a_4{}^2 \\ a_1{}^3 & a_2{}^3 & a_3{}^3 & a_4{}^3 \\ a_1{}^4 & a_2{}^4 & a_3{}^4 & a_4{}^4 \end{vmatrix}$$

According to this relation, the determinant a then equals

$$\det a = |a_j{}^i| = a_1{}^1 \begin{vmatrix} a_2{}^2 & a_3{}^2 & a_4{}^2 \\ a_2{}^3 & a_3{}^3 & a_4{}^3 \\ a_2{}^4 & a_3{}^4 & a_4{}^4 \end{vmatrix} - a_1{}^2 \begin{vmatrix} a_2{}^1 & a_3{}^1 & a_4{}^1 \\ a_2{}^3 & a_3{}^3 & a_4{}^3 \\ a_2{}^4 & a_3{}^4 & a_4{}^4 \end{vmatrix}$$

$$+ a_1{}^3 \begin{vmatrix} a_2{}^1 & a_3{}^1 & a_4{}^1 \\ a_2{}^2 & a_3{}^2 & a_4{}^2 \\ a_2{}^4 & a_3{}^4 & a_4{}^4 \end{vmatrix} - a_1{}^4 \begin{vmatrix} a_2{}^1 & a_3{}^1 & a_4{}^1 \\ a_2{}^2 & a_3{}^2 & a_4{}^2 \\ a_2{}^3 & a_3{}^3 & a_4{}^3 \end{vmatrix}$$

2-7. Solution of Simultaneous Equations

Simultaneous equations may be solved by the use of determinants. The following procedure illustrates the method used to solve two simultaneous linear equations,

$$a_1 x + b_1 y = c_1$$
$$a_2 x + b_2 y = c_2$$

Multiply the first equation by b_2 and the second by $-b_1$.

$$a_1 b_2 x + b_1 b_2 y = c_1 b_2$$
$$-a_2 b_1 x - b_1 b_2 y = -c_2 b_1$$

Adding the equations gives

$$(a_1 b_2 - a_2 b_1)x = (b_2 c_1 - b_1 c_2)$$

Hence

$$x = \frac{b_2 c_1 - b_1 c_2}{a_1 b_2 - a_2 b_1}$$

This result is based on the premise that $a_1 b_2 - a_2 b_1$ is not equal to zero.

Now multiply the first and second equations by $-a_2$ and a_1, respectively, to obtain

$$-a_1 a_2 x - a_2 b_1 y = -a_2 c_1$$
$$a_1 a_2 x + a_1 b_2 y = a_1 c_2$$

Adding gives

$$(-a_2 b_1 + a_1 b_2)y = (-a_2 c_1 + a_1 c_2)$$

and solving for y gives

$$y = \frac{(a_1 c_2 - a_2 c_1)}{(a_1 b_2 - a_2 b_1)}$$

These relations may be written in determinant form:

$$x = \frac{\begin{vmatrix} c_1 & b_1 \\ c_2 & b_2 \end{vmatrix}}{\begin{vmatrix} a_1 & b_1 \\ a_2 & b_2 \end{vmatrix}}, \quad y = \frac{\begin{vmatrix} a_1 & c_1 \\ a_2 & c_2 \end{vmatrix}}{\begin{vmatrix} a_1 & b_1 \\ a_2 & b_2 \end{vmatrix}}$$

The determinants which constitute the denominators in the two preceding equations are equal, and they were formed from the coefficients of x and y in the original equations. The determinant in the numerator is found from the denominator by replacing the coefficients of the unknown sought (x or y) by the constant terms (c_1, c_2).

The discussion will be expanded to cover the problem of solving simultaneously n linear equations in n unknowns. Consider the system

$$a_{11}x_1 + a_{12}x_2 + \cdots + a_{1(n)}x_{(n)} = c_1$$

$$a_{21}x_1 + a_{22}x_2 + \cdots + a_{2(n)}x_{(n)} = c_2$$

$$\cdots \cdots \cdots \cdots \cdots \cdots \cdots \cdots \cdots \cdots \cdots \cdots \cdots$$

$$a_{n1}x_1 + a_{n2}x_2 + \cdots + a_{n(n)}x_{(n)} = c_n$$

The coefficients a_{ij} and the constants c_i are independent of $x_1, x_2, \ldots, x_n$ but are otherwise arbitrary. The coefficient matrix A will be defined as

$$A = (a_{ij})$$

A new matrix obtained by replacing the jth column of A by the column of c's is represented by A_j.

Cramer's rule states that, if the determinant of A is not equal to zero, the system of linear equations has only one solution given by the relation

$$x_j = \frac{\det A_j}{\det A}, \quad j = 1, 2, \ldots, n$$

Example 2-5

Solve the simultaneous equations

$$x + y + u = 1$$

$$-x + z + u = 0$$

$$y - z + u = 1$$

$$x - y + z = 0$$

The determinant A is expressed as

$$\begin{vmatrix} 1 & 1 & 0 & 1 \\ -1 & 0 & 1 & 1 \\ 0 & 1 & -1 & 1 \\ 1 & -1 & 1 & 0 \end{vmatrix} = (1) \begin{vmatrix} 0 & 1 & 1 \\ 1 & -1 & 1 \\ -1 & 1 & 0 \end{vmatrix}$$

$$- (1) \begin{vmatrix} -1 & 1 & 1 \\ 0 & -1 & 1 \\ 1 & 1 & 0 \end{vmatrix} + 0 \begin{vmatrix} -1 & 0 & 1 \\ 0 & 1 & 1 \\ 1 & -1 & 0 \end{vmatrix}$$

$$- (1) \begin{vmatrix} -1 & 0 & 1 \\ 0 & 1 & -1 \\ 1 & -1 & 1 \end{vmatrix} = -1 - 3 + 1 = -3$$

Now

$$x_1 = x = \frac{\det A_1}{\det A} = \frac{\begin{vmatrix} 1 & 1 & 0 & 1 \\ 0 & 0 & 1 & 1 \\ 1 & 1 & -1 & 1 \\ 0 & -1 & 1 & 0 \end{vmatrix}}{-3} =$$

$$\frac{1 \begin{vmatrix} 0 & 1 & 1 \\ 1 & -1 & 1 \\ -1 & 1 & 0 \end{vmatrix} - 1 \begin{vmatrix} 0 & 1 & 1 \\ 1 & -1 & 1 \\ 0 & 1 & 0 \end{vmatrix} + 0 \begin{vmatrix} 0 & 0 & 1 \\ 1 & 1 & 1 \\ 0 & -1 & 0 \end{vmatrix} - 1 \begin{vmatrix} 0 & 0 & 1 \\ 1 & 1 & -1 \\ 0 & -1 & 1 \end{vmatrix}}{-3} = \frac{1}{3}$$

$$x_2 = y = \frac{\det A_2}{\det A} = \frac{\begin{vmatrix} 1 & 1 & 0 & 1 \\ -1 & 0 & 1 & 1 \\ 0 & 1 & -1 & 1 \\ 1 & 0 & 1 & 0 \end{vmatrix}}{-3} =$$

$$\frac{1 \begin{vmatrix} 0 & 1 & 1 \\ 1 & -1 & 1 \\ 0 & 1 & 0 \end{vmatrix} - 1 \begin{vmatrix} -1 & 1 & 1 \\ 0 & -1 & 1 \\ 1 & 1 & 0 \end{vmatrix} + 0 \begin{vmatrix} -1 & 0 & 1 \\ 0 & 1 & 1 \\ 1 & 0 & 0 \end{vmatrix} - 1 \begin{vmatrix} -1 & 0 & 1 \\ 0 & 1 & -1 \\ 1 & 0 & 1 \end{vmatrix}}{-3}$$
$$= 0$$

$$x_3 = z = \frac{\det A_3}{\det A} = \frac{\begin{vmatrix} 1 & 1 & 1 & 1 \\ -1 & 0 & 0 & 1 \\ 0 & 1 & 1 & 1 \\ 1 & -1 & 0 & 0 \end{vmatrix}}{-3} =$$

$$\frac{\begin{vmatrix} 0 & 0 & 1 \\ 1 & 1 & 1 \\ -1 & 0 & 0 \end{vmatrix} - 1 \begin{vmatrix} -1 & 0 & 1 \\ 0 & 1 & 1 \\ 1 & 0 & 0 \end{vmatrix} + 1 \begin{vmatrix} -1 & 0 & 1 \\ 0 & 1 & 1 \\ 1 & -1 & 0 \end{vmatrix} - 1 \begin{vmatrix} -1 & 0 & 0 \\ 0 & 1 & 1 \\ 1 & -1 & 0 \end{vmatrix}}{-3}$$

$$= -\frac{1}{3}$$

$$x_4 = u = \frac{\det A_4}{\det A} = \frac{\begin{vmatrix} 1 & 1 & 0 & 1 \\ -1 & 0 & 1 & 0 \\ 0 & 1 & -1 & 1 \\ 1 & -1 & 1 & 0 \end{vmatrix}}{-3} =$$

$$\frac{\begin{vmatrix} 0 & 1 & 0 \\ 1 & -1 & 1 \\ -1 & 1 & 0 \end{vmatrix} - 1 \begin{vmatrix} -1 & 1 & 0 \\ 0 & -1 & 1 \\ 1 & 1 & 0 \end{vmatrix} + 0 \begin{vmatrix} -1 & 0 & 0 \\ 0 & 1 & 1 \\ 1 & -1 & 0 \end{vmatrix} - 1 \begin{vmatrix} -1 & 0 & 1 \\ 0 & 1 & -1 \\ 1 & -1 & 1 \end{vmatrix}}{-3}$$

$$= \frac{2}{3}$$

2-8. Differentiation of a Determinant

Consider a determinant $|a_s{}^r| = a$ whose elements are functions of the independent variables $x^1, x^2, x^3, \ldots, x^n$. We wish to determine the derivative $\partial a / \partial x^t$, where $t = 1, 2, 3, \ldots, n$. Now

$$a_s{}^r = a_s{}^r(x^1, x^2, x^3, \ldots, x^n)$$

and

$$a = a(a_s{}^r)$$

By the chain rule

$$\frac{\partial a}{\partial x^t} = \frac{\partial a}{\partial a_s{}^r} \frac{\partial a_s{}^r}{\partial x^t} \tag{2-3}$$

In terms of the cofactors the determinant $a = |a_s{}^r|$ may be expressed as

$$a = a_k{}^1 A_1{}^k = a_1{}^1 A_1{}^1 + a_2{}^1 A_1{}^2 + \cdots + a_n{}^1 A_1{}^n$$

In this expression the $a_k{}^1$ are explicit and do not occur in the $A_1{}^k$ terms. Thus we may write

$$\frac{\partial a}{\partial a_1{}^1} = A_1{}^1, \quad \frac{\partial a}{\partial a_2{}^1} = A_1{}^2, \quad \text{etc.}$$

Hence

$$\frac{\partial a}{\partial a_k{}^1} = A_1{}^k$$

In general,

$$\frac{\partial a}{\partial a_s{}^r} = A_r{}^s$$

Substituting gives

$$\frac{\partial a}{\partial x^t} = \frac{\partial a}{\partial a_s{}^r}\frac{\partial a_s{}^r}{\partial x^t} = A_r{}^s \frac{\partial a_s{}^r}{\partial x^t} \tag{2-4}$$

which is a sum of n determinants, each one differing from the original determinant, a, only in that one row (or column) has been differentiated with respect to x^t starting with the first row (or column) and progressing to the nth row (or column). For example, if

$$a = \begin{vmatrix} a_1{}^1 & a_2{}^1 \\ a_1{}^2 & a_2{}^2 \end{vmatrix}$$

then

$$\frac{\partial a}{\partial x^t} = \begin{vmatrix} \dfrac{\partial a_1{}^1}{\partial x^t} & \dfrac{\partial a_2{}^1}{\partial x^t} \\ a_1{}^2 & a_2{}^2 \end{vmatrix} + \begin{vmatrix} a_1{}^1 & a_2{}^1 \\ \dfrac{\partial a_1{}^2}{\partial x^t} & \dfrac{\partial a_2{}^2}{\partial x^t} \end{vmatrix}$$

2-9. Problems

2-1. Evaluate $a = |a_j{}^i|$ if

$$(a_j{}^i) = \begin{pmatrix} 1 & 4 & 3 \\ 1 & 2 & 5 \\ 3 & 0 & 1 \end{pmatrix}$$

2-2. Solve for x and y:
$$3x + 2y = 23$$
$$5x - 2y = 29$$

2-3. Solve for x and y:
$$8x + 7y = 14$$
$$5x - 18y = -12$$

2-4. Solve for x and y:
$$\frac{x}{3} + \frac{y}{7} = 9$$
$$\frac{x}{5} + \frac{y}{5} = 3$$

2-5. Solve for x and y:
$$\frac{x + y}{5} + \frac{y - x}{7} = 8$$
$$\frac{x}{7} + \frac{x + y}{4} = 7$$

2-6. Find the nine cofactors for the following set of $a_j{}^i$'s:
$$(a_j{}^i) = \begin{pmatrix} 1 & 4 & 3 \\ 1 & 2 & 5 \\ 3 & 0 & 1 \end{pmatrix}$$

2-7. Evaluate $a = |a_j{}^i|$ when the $a_j{}^i$ are those found in Problem 2-6.

2-8. If (a) is any scalar, show that
$$|a\,\delta_j{}^i| = a^3 \qquad (i, j = 1, 2, 3)$$

2-9. Given that α is a scalar and
$$(a_{ij}) = \begin{pmatrix} 1 & \alpha & \alpha \\ \alpha & 1 & \alpha \\ \alpha & \alpha & 1 \end{pmatrix}$$

find the values for $a = |a_{ij}|$, A^{ij}, and $A = |A^{ij}|$.

2-10. If a_{ij} is symmetric, that is, $a_{ij} = a_{ji}$, prove that A^{ji} is symmetric.

2-11. If a_{ij} is antisymmetric that is $a_{ij} = -a_{ji}$, is A^{ji} antisymmetric?

2-12. Prove that $a_k{}^i A_i{}^k = 3a$ $(i, k = 1, 2, 3)$.

2-13. If $a_k{}^i A_j{}^k = a\delta_j{}^i$, show that $A = |A_j{}^i| = a^{n-1}$.

2-14. Given $S = a_{ij} X^i X^j = 0$. If the a_{ij}'s do not vanish, show that they are antisymmetric.

2-15. Show that
$$\mathbf{A} \cdot (\mathbf{B} \times \mathbf{C}) = \begin{vmatrix} A_1 & A_2 & A_3 \\ B_1 & B_2 & B_3 \\ C_1 & C_2 & C_3 \end{vmatrix}$$

2-16. Show that

$$[A \cdot (B \times C)](f \times g) = \begin{vmatrix} A & B & C \\ f \cdot A & f \cdot B & f \cdot C \\ g \cdot A & g \cdot B & g \cdot C \end{vmatrix}$$

2-17. Show that

$$[A \cdot (B \times C)][a \cdot (b \times c)] = \begin{vmatrix} A \cdot a & A \cdot b & A \cdot c \\ B \cdot a & B \cdot b & B \cdot c \\ C \cdot a & C \cdot b & C \cdot c \end{vmatrix}$$

Here **a**, **b**, and **c** are unit vectors whose lines of action are the same as those for the vectors **A**, **B**, and **C**.

2-10. Suggested References

2-1. *Elementary Analysis*, H. C. Trimble and Fred W. Lott, Jr., Prentice-Hall, Inc.

2-2. *Elementary Matrix Algebra*, Franz E. Hohn, The Macmillan Company.

2-3. *Mathematics of Physics and Modern Engineering*, I. S. Sokolnikoff and R. M. Redheffer, McGraw-Hill Book Company.

2-4. *Introduction to Matrices and Linear Transformations*, Daniel T. Finkbeiner II, W. H. Freeman and Company.

2-5. *Application of the Theory of Matrices*, F. R. Gantmacher, Interscience Publishers, Inc.

2-6. *Introduction to Matrix Analysis*, Richard Bellman, McGraw-Hill Book Company.

2-7. *Theory of Matrices*, S. Perlis, Addison-Wesley Publishing Company.

3

Matrices

3-1. Introduction

Matrix algebra is useful in performing the various operations involved in the application of tensor analysis to the solution of engineering problems. The solution of sets of simultaneous equations and the transformation of variables may be conveniently carried out with this technique. As only a brief introduction to matrix algebra is presented here, the reader should consult textbooks on the subject for a more thorough coverage. (See references at end of this chapter.)

An ordered set of mn numbers called elements arranged in a rectangular array of m rows and n columns is called a matrix with m rows and n columns. If $a_j{}^i$ represents the element in the ith row and jth column, the matrix may be expressed by any of the pictorial forms

$$A = (a_j{}^i) \quad \text{or} \quad \begin{pmatrix} a_1{}^1 & a_2{}^1 & \cdots & a_n{}^1 \\ a_1{}^2 & a_2{}^2 & \cdots & a_n{}^2 \\ \hdotsfor{4} \\ \hdotsfor{4} \\ a_1{}^m & a_2{}^m & \cdots & a_n{}^m \end{pmatrix}$$

or $\qquad\qquad\qquad\qquad\qquad\qquad\qquad\qquad\qquad\qquad$ (3-1)

$$\begin{Vmatrix} a_1{}^1 & a_2{}^1 & \cdots & a_n{}^1 \\ a_1{}^2 & a_2{}^2 & \cdots & a_n{}^2 \\ \hdotsfor{4} \\ \hdotsfor{4} \\ a_1{}^m & a_2{}^m & \cdots & a_n{}^m \end{Vmatrix}$$

A matrix having m rows and n columns is called a matrix of order (m, n) or an $m \times n$ matrix. When $m = n$, the matrix is called a square matrix of order n. A matrix having more than one row and more than one column is referred to as a 2-way matrix. A matrix having one row and more than one column or vice versa is referred to as a 1-way matrix. These are often referred to as row or column matrices, which are illustrated below.

Row matrix:

$$(a_1{}^1 \quad a_2{}^1 \quad \cdots \quad a_n{}^1) \quad \text{or} \quad \|a_1{}^1 \quad a_2{}^1 \quad \cdots \quad a_n{}^1\| \qquad (3\text{-}2)$$

Column matrix:

$$\begin{pmatrix} a_1{}^1 \\ a_1{}^2 \\ \cdot \\ \cdot \\ \cdot \\ a_1{}^m \end{pmatrix} \quad \text{or} \quad \begin{Vmatrix} a_1{}^1 \\ a_1{}^2 \\ \cdot \\ \cdot \\ \cdot \\ a_1{}^m \end{Vmatrix} \qquad (3\text{-}3)$$

A 3-way matrix may be visualized as three matrices forming the faces of a cube.

Two $m \times n$ matrices $A = (a_j{}^i)$ and $B = (b_j{}^i)$ are equal if and only if $a_j{}^i$ and $b_j{}^i$ are equal for each value of i and j. In other words, elements in like positions of the two matrices must be equal. In equation form, this means that $a_j{}^i = b_j{}^i$ for each i and j.

A symmetric matrix is one which is symmetrical about the main diagonal.

$$A = \begin{pmatrix} a & d & e \\ d & b & f \\ e & f & c \end{pmatrix}$$

A skew-symmetric matrix has equal elements about the main diagonal, but the elements are of opposite sign.

$$A = \begin{pmatrix} a & d & e \\ -d & b & f \\ -e & -f & c \end{pmatrix}$$

By definition a zero or null matrix 0 is a square matrix wherein all the elements are zero; that is,

$$(0) = \begin{pmatrix} 0 & 0 & \cdots & 0 \\ 0 & 0 & \cdots & 0 \\ \cdots\cdots\cdots\cdots \\ 0 & 0 & \cdots & 0 \end{pmatrix} \tag{3-4}$$

The square unit matrix is one in which all the elements on the principal diagonal are unity and all others are zero:

$$I = \begin{pmatrix} 1 & 0 & 0 & 0 \\ 0 & 1 & 0 & 0 \\ 0 & 0 & 1 & 0 \\ 0 & 0 & 0 & 1 \end{pmatrix} \tag{3-5}$$

It is immediately apparent that the Kronecker delta $\delta_j{}^i$ satisfies this condition, since it is unity only when $i = j$. We may, therefore, express the unit matrix in terms of $\delta_j{}^i$ as

$$I = (\delta_j{}^i) \tag{3-6}$$

If I represents the unity matrix,

$$IA = AI = A$$

A square matrix whose determinant is zero is called a singular matrix.

A square diagonal matrix is one where all elements except those on the principal diagonal are zero. Hence

$$A = (a_j{}^i) = \begin{pmatrix} a_1{}^1 & 0 & 0 \\ 0 & a_2{}^2 & 0 \\ 0 & 0 & a_3{}^3 \end{pmatrix}, \quad a_j{}^i = 0 \quad \text{for} \quad i \neq j$$

A square scalar matrix is one in which all elements along the principal diagonal are equal and all others are zero.

3-2. Addition of Matrices

The sum of two matrices which have the same number of rows and the same number of columns may be expressed as follows:

$$A + B = C = (c_j{}^i) \qquad (3\text{-}7)$$

where $(c_j{}^i) = (a_j{}^i + b_j{}^i)$.

In order to calculate the sum of two matrices of the same type, we compute the matrix whose elements are the numerical sum of the corresponding elements of the given matrices.

Example 3-1

Determine the sum of the two matrices

$$A = (a_j{}^i) = \begin{array}{c} l \\ m \\ n \end{array}\!\!\begin{pmatrix} 1 & 2 & 3 \\ 3 & 1 & 4 \\ 5 & 2 & 2 \end{pmatrix}, \quad B = (b_j{}^i) = \begin{array}{c} l \\ m \\ n \end{array}\!\!\begin{pmatrix} 2 & 1 & 3 \\ 2 & 2 & 1 \\ 5 & 1 & 6 \end{pmatrix}$$

with identification indices l, m, n across the columns.

$$A + B = (a_j{}^i) + (b_j{}^i) = \begin{pmatrix} 1 & 2 & 3 \\ 3 & 1 & 4 \\ 5 & 2 & 2 \end{pmatrix} + \begin{pmatrix} 2 & 1 & 3 \\ 2 & 2 & 1 \\ 5 & 1 & 6 \end{pmatrix}$$

$$= \begin{pmatrix} 1+2 & 2+1 & 3+3 \\ 3+2 & 1+2 & 4+1 \\ 5+5 & 2+1 & 2+6 \end{pmatrix} = \begin{pmatrix} 3 & 3 & 6 \\ 5 & 3 & 5 \\ 10 & 3 & 8 \end{pmatrix}$$

In this example the letters *l*, *m*, and *n* are used to identify the rows and columns of the matrix. For convenience we shall call these letters identification indices.

There are times when two or more matrices with different identification indices need to be added to form a single matrix. To perform the addition it is assumed that each matrix contains all the identification indices; however, the elements of the non-existing identification indices in each matrix are taken to be zero. An example will illustrate the procedure for adding two such matrices.

Example 3-2

Determine the sum of the two matrices

$$A = (a_j{}^i) = \begin{array}{c} \\ l \\ m \end{array}\overset{\begin{array}{cc} l & m \end{array}}{\begin{pmatrix} 1 & 2 \\ 3 & 1 \end{pmatrix}}, \quad B = (b_j{}^i) = \begin{array}{c} \\ m \\ n \end{array}\overset{\begin{array}{cc} m & n \end{array}}{\begin{pmatrix} 2 & 1 \\ 1 & 6 \end{pmatrix}}$$

Now

$$A + B = (a_j{}^i) + (b_j{}^i) = \begin{array}{c} \\ l \\ m \\ n \end{array}\overset{\begin{array}{ccc} l & m & n \end{array}}{\begin{pmatrix} 1 & 2 & 0 \\ 3 & 1 & 0 \\ 0 & 0 & 0 \end{pmatrix}} + \begin{array}{c} \\ l \\ m \\ n \end{array}\overset{\begin{array}{ccc} l & m & n \end{array}}{\begin{pmatrix} 0 & 0 & 0 \\ 0 & 2 & 1 \\ 0 & 1 & 6 \end{pmatrix}} = \begin{pmatrix} 1 & 2 & 0 \\ 3 & 3 & 1 \\ 0 & 1 & 6 \end{pmatrix}$$

This procedure is extensively used in electrical engineering for adding the impedances of one network to those of another to obtain the over-all impedance.

In matrix addition the commutative law holds; thus, if A and B are two matrices of the same type,

$$A + B = B + A$$

and, if A, B, and C are three matrices of the same type, the associative law also holds for matrix addition; thus

$$(A + B) + C = A + (B + C)$$

If 0 is the zero matrix,

$$0 + A = A$$

3-3. Subtraction of Matrices

If A and B are two matrices of the same order, the difference between the two may be expressed as

$$A - B = C = (c_j{}^i) \tag{3-8}$$

where $(c_j{}^i) = (a_j{}^i - b_j{}^i)$.

In order to calculate the difference of two like matrices, compute a matrix whose elements are the numerical difference between the corresponding elements of the given matrices.

44   *Multilinear Analysis*

Example 3-3

Find the difference of the following matrices.

$$A = (a_j{}^i) = \begin{pmatrix} 5 & 3 & 1 \\ 4 & 7 & 6 \\ 1 & 2 & 4 \end{pmatrix}, \quad B = (b_j{}^i) = \begin{pmatrix} 4 & 2 & 4 \\ 3 & 1 & 7 \\ 8 & 4 & 6 \end{pmatrix}$$

$$A - B = (a_j{}^i) - (b_j{}^i) = \begin{pmatrix} 5 & 3 & 1 \\ 4 & 7 & 6 \\ 1 & 2 & 4 \end{pmatrix} - \begin{pmatrix} 4 & 2 & 4 \\ 3 & 1 & 7 \\ 8 & 4 & 6 \end{pmatrix}$$

$$= \begin{pmatrix} 5-4 & 3-2 & 1-4 \\ 4-3 & 7-1 & 6-7 \\ 1-8 & 2-4 & 4-6 \end{pmatrix} = \begin{pmatrix} 1 & 1 & -3 \\ 1 & 6 & -1 \\ -7 & -2 & -2 \end{pmatrix}$$

3-4. Multiplication of Matrices

The product of a matrix A and a constant α is a matrix wherein every element is multiplied by the constant. Hence we may write

$$A = (\alpha a_j{}^i) = \begin{pmatrix} \alpha a_1{}^1 & \alpha a_2{}^1 & \alpha a_3{}^1 \\ \alpha a_1{}^2 & \alpha a_2{}^2 & \alpha a_3{}^2 \\ \alpha a_1{}^3 & \alpha a_2{}^3 & \alpha a_3{}^3 \end{pmatrix} \tag{3-9}$$

Multiplication of two 1-way matrices is analogous to carrying out the scalar or dot product in vector analysis.

$$e_k i^k = \mathbf{e} \cdot \mathbf{i} = (e_1 e_2 e_3)(i^1 i^2 i^3) = e_1 i^1 + e_2 i^2 + e_3 i^3$$

The product of two matrices of the same type results in a matrix C which is defined as

$$C = (c_j{}^i)$$
where
$$c_j{}^i = a_k{}^i b_j{}^k \tag{3-10}$$

Determine the product of the following matrices.

$$A = \begin{pmatrix} a_1{}^1 & a_2{}^1 & a_3{}^1 \\ a_1{}^2 & a_2{}^2 & a_3{}^2 \\ a_1{}^3 & a_2{}^3 & a_3{}^3 \end{pmatrix}, \quad B = \begin{pmatrix} b_1{}^1 & b_2{}^1 & b_3{}^1 \\ b_1{}^2 & b_2{}^2 & b_3{}^2 \\ b_1{}^3 & b_2{}^3 & b_3{}^3 \end{pmatrix}$$
$$c_j{}^i = a_1{}^i b_j{}^1 + a_2{}^i b_j{}^2 + a_3{}^i b_j{}^3$$

$$AB = \begin{pmatrix} \left\{ \begin{array}{c} i=1, \ j=1 \\ c_1{}^1 = a_1{}^1 b_1{}^1 + a_2{}^1 b_1{}^2 + a_3{}^1 b_1{}^3 \end{array} \right\} & \left\{ \begin{array}{c} i=1, \ j=2 \\ c_2{}^1 = a_1{}^1 b_2{}^1 + a_2{}^1 b_2{}^2 + a_3{}^1 b_2{}^3 \end{array} \right\} \\ \left\{ \begin{array}{c} i=2, \ j=1 \\ c_1{}^2 = a_1{}^2 b_1{}^1 + a_2{}^2 b_1{}^2 + a_3{}^2 b_1{}^3 \end{array} \right\} & \left\{ \begin{array}{c} i=2, \ j=2 \\ c_2{}^2 = a_1{}^2 b_2{}^1 + a_2{}^2 b_2{}^2 + a_3{}^2 b_2{}^3 \end{array} \right\} \\ \left\{ \begin{array}{c} i=3, \ j=1 \\ c_1{}^3 = a_1{}^3 b_1{}^1 + a_2{}^3 b_1{}^2 + a_3{}^3 b_1{}^3 \end{array} \right\} & \left\{ \begin{array}{c} i=3, \ j=2 \\ c_2{}^3 = a_1{}^3 b_2{}^1 + a_2{}^3 b_2{}^2 + a_3{}^3 b_2{}^3 \end{array} \right\} \end{pmatrix}$$

$$\begin{pmatrix} \left\{ \begin{array}{c} i=1, \ j=3 \\ c_3{}^1 = a_1{}^1 b_3{}^1 + a_2{}^1 b_3{}^2 + a_3{}^1 b_3{}^3 \end{array} \right\} \\ \left\{ \begin{array}{c} i=2, \ j=3 \\ c_3{}^2 = a_1{}^2 b_3{}^1 + a_2{}^2 b_3{}^2 + a_3{}^2 b_3{}^3 \end{array} \right\} \\ \left\{ \begin{array}{c} i=3, \ j=3 \\ c_3{}^3 = a_1{}^3 b_3{}^1 + a_2{}^3 b_3{}^2 + a_3{}^3 b_3{}^3 \end{array} \right\} \end{pmatrix}$$

That is, the elements of the rows of the first matrix A are multiplied by the correspondingly located elements in the columns of the second matrix B, so that the ijth element in $C = AB$ is obtained by multiplying the elements in the ith row of A by the corresponding elements in the jth column of B.

Example 3-4

Determine the product of the following matrices.

$$A = \begin{pmatrix} a_1{}^1 & a_2{}^1 & a_3{}^1 \\ a_1{}^2 & a_2{}^2 & a_3{}^2 \\ a_1{}^3 & a_2{}^3 & a_3{}^3 \end{pmatrix}, \quad B = \begin{pmatrix} b_1{}^1 \\ b_1{}^2 \\ b_1{}^3 \end{pmatrix}.$$

Since terms $b_2{}^1$, $b_2{}^2$, $b_2{}^3$, $b_3{}^1$, $b_3{}^2$, and $b_3{}^3$ do not exist, the product AB is a matrix represented by

$$AB = \begin{pmatrix} c_1{}^1 \\ c_1{}^2 \\ c_1{}^3 \end{pmatrix}$$

where the $c_1{}^1$, $c_1{}^2$, and $c_1{}^3$ elements are the same as in the previous example.

In general, the matrix product AB is defined for all matrices A, B for which the number of columns of A is equal to the number of rows of B.

Example 3-5

Determine the product of the matrices Z_{jk} and i^k.

$$Z_{jk} = \begin{matrix} & a & b & c \\ a & \\ b & \\ c & \end{matrix} \begin{pmatrix} Z_{11} & Z_{12} & Z_{13} \\ Z_{21} & Z_{22} & Z_{23} \\ Z_{31} & Z_{32} & Z_{33} \end{pmatrix}, \quad i^k = \begin{matrix} & a \\ a & \\ b & \\ c & \end{matrix} \begin{pmatrix} i^{11} \\ i^{21} \\ i^{31} \end{pmatrix}$$

The product is a column matrix.

$$Z_{jk}i^k = \begin{pmatrix} Z_{11} & Z_{12} & Z_{13} \\ Z_{21} & Z_{22} & Z_{23} \\ Z_{31} & Z_{32} & Z_{33} \end{pmatrix} \begin{pmatrix} i^{11} \\ i^{21} \\ i^{31} \end{pmatrix} = \begin{pmatrix} (Z_{11}i^{11} + Z_{12}i^{21} + Z_{13}i^{31}) & 0 & 0 \\ (Z_{21}i^{11} + Z_{22}i^{21} + Z_{23}i^{31}) & 0 & 0 \\ (Z_{31}i^{11} + Z_{32}i^{21} + Z_{33}i^{31}) & 0 & 0 \end{pmatrix}$$

The product of two diagonal matrices where all elements except those in the main diagonals are zero is commutative; that is, $AB = BA$. This may be shown as follows:

$$\begin{pmatrix} a_1{}^1 & 0 & 0 \\ 0 & a_2{}^2 & 0 \\ 0 & 0 & a_3{}^3 \end{pmatrix} \begin{pmatrix} b_1{}^1 & 0 & 0 \\ 0 & b_2{}^2 & 0 \\ 0 & 0 & b_3{}^3 \end{pmatrix} = \begin{pmatrix} a_1{}^1 b_1{}^1 & 0 & 0 \\ 0 & a_2{}^2 b_2{}^2 & 0 \\ 0 & 0 & a_3{}^3 b_3{}^3 \end{pmatrix}$$

In general, however, $AB \neq BA$ for arbitrary matrices A and B; hence ordering of factors in a matrix product is quite important. For example, if

$$A = \begin{pmatrix} 1 & 1 & 0 \\ 0 & 0 & 0 \\ 0 & 1 & 0 \end{pmatrix}, \quad B = \begin{pmatrix} 0 & 0 & 0 \\ 0 & 0 & 0 \\ 1 & 0 & 0 \end{pmatrix}$$

Then $AB = 0$, but

$$BA = \begin{pmatrix} 0 & 0 & 0 \\ 0 & 0 & 0 \\ 1 & 1 & 0 \end{pmatrix} \neq 0$$

The product of three matrices A, B, and C may be expressed in one of the following forms (associative law for multiplication):

$$(AB)C = A(BC)$$

The product of a matrix C and the sum of matrices A and B is (distributive law for multiplication)

$$C(A + B) = CA + CB$$

or

$$(A + B)C = AC + BC$$

The product of two matrices may be a zero matrix even in the event that neither of the matrices is a zero matrix.

Example 3-6

Determine the product of the matrices A and B.

$$A = \begin{pmatrix} 1 & 1 & 0 \\ 0 & 0 & 0 \\ 0 & 1 & 0 \end{pmatrix}, \quad B = \begin{pmatrix} 0 & 0 & 0 \\ 0 & 0 & 0 \\ 1 & 0 & 0 \end{pmatrix}$$

The product AB is zero although $A \neq 0$, $B \neq 0$:

$$AB = \begin{pmatrix} 0 & 0 & 0 \\ 0 & 0 & 0 \\ 0 & 0 & 0 \end{pmatrix}$$

The following equations exemplify some properties which combine addition and multiplication of matrices.

$$A(B + C) = AB + AC$$

$$(A + B)C = AC + BC$$

$$A(B - C) = AB - AC$$

$$(A + B)(C + D) = AC + BC + AD + BD$$

$$(A + B)^2 = A^2 + BA + AB + B^2$$

$$(A - B)^2 = A^2 - BA - AB + B^2$$

$$(A + B)(A - B) = A^2 + BA - AB - B^2$$

$$A(B + C + D) = AB + AC + AD$$

$$-(A + B + C) = (-A) + (-B) + (-C)$$

$$-A = (-I)A$$

3-5. Transpose of a Matrix

The transpose of a matrix is obtained by interchanging the rows and columns. This is equivalent to rotating the elements of the matrix about the principal diagonal.

Example 3-7

Determine the transpose of the matrix A.

$$A = \begin{pmatrix} a & b & c \\ d & m & n \\ f & g & p \end{pmatrix}$$

The transpose is

$$A_t = \begin{pmatrix} a & d & f \\ b & m & g \\ c & n & p \end{pmatrix}$$

The transpose of a product of two matrices is equal to the product of the transposes of the two matrices with the order of multiplication reversed.

$$(AB)_t = B_t A_t \tag{3-11}$$

Example 3-8

$$A = \begin{pmatrix} a & b \\ c & d \end{pmatrix}, \quad B = \begin{pmatrix} l & m \\ n & p \end{pmatrix}$$

Now

$$A_t = \begin{pmatrix} a & c \\ b & d \end{pmatrix}, \quad B_t = \begin{pmatrix} l & n \\ m & p \end{pmatrix}$$

$$(AB) = \begin{pmatrix} a & b \\ c & d \end{pmatrix}\begin{pmatrix} l & m \\ n & p \end{pmatrix} = \begin{pmatrix} al + bn & am + bp \\ cl + dn & cm + dp \end{pmatrix}$$

$$(AB)_t = \begin{pmatrix} al + bn & cl + dn \\ am + bp & cm + dp \end{pmatrix}$$

$$B_t A_t = \begin{pmatrix} l & n \\ m & p \end{pmatrix}\begin{pmatrix} a & c \\ b & d \end{pmatrix} = \begin{pmatrix} al + bn & cl + dn \\ am + bp & cm + dp \end{pmatrix}$$

Therefore

$$(AB)_t = B_t A_t$$

3-6. Inverse of a Matrix

The reciprocal or inverse of a real number a is defined as $1/a$ or a^{-1} if $a \neq 0$. An analogous operation exists for square matrices. Let A represent a square matrix of order n. If the determinant $|a_j{}^i| \neq 0$, there exists a matrix A^{-1} in analogy to the inverse of a real number, which has the following important properties:

$$AA^{-1} = I = A^{-1}A$$

Here I is the unit matrix. The matrix A^{-1} is called the inverse matrix of A.

In general the method of obtaining the inverse of a 2-way matrix is analogous to division. The steps in finding the inverse are:

Procedure A	Procedure B
1. Interchange the rows and columns of the matrix, thus producing the transpose of the matrix.	1. Compute the cofactors of the original matrix. Using the cofactors as elements, establish a new matrix.
2. Compute the cofactors of the transpose of the matrix. Using the cofactors as elements, establish a new matrix.	2. Form the transpose of this matrix.
3. Divide each element of the new matrix by the value of the determinant of the original matrix. The result is the inverse of the original matrix.	3. Divide each element by the value of the determinant of the original matrix. The result is the inverse of the original matrix.

Example 3-9

Determine the inverse of the matrix shown by means of the two procedures.

$$A = \begin{pmatrix} 3 & 2 & 1 \\ 4 & 6 & 5 \\ 3 & 8 & 4 \end{pmatrix}$$

The determinant is equal to

$$\begin{vmatrix} 3 & 2 & 1 \\ 4 & 6 & 5 \\ 3 & 8 & 4 \end{vmatrix} = 72 + 30 + 32 - 18 - 120 - 32 = -36$$

<table>
<tr><td>

Method 1

1. Interchange the rows and columns, obtaining the transpose

$$A_t = \begin{pmatrix} 3 & 4 & 3 \\ 2 & 6 & 8 \\ 1 & 5 & 4 \end{pmatrix}$$

2. Compute the cofactors of the transpose of the matrix. Consider each of the elements by starting with the first column and proceeding downward; then proceed downward in the second column, etc.

</td><td>

Method 2

1. Compute the cofactors of the original matrix. Consider each of the elements by starting with the first column and proceeding downward; then proceed downward in the second column, etc.

</td></tr>
</table>

Element	Cofactor		Element	Cofactor
(3)	$(-1)^2 \begin{vmatrix} 6 & 8 \\ 5 & 4 \end{vmatrix} = 24 - 40 = -16$		(3)	$(-1)^2 \begin{vmatrix} 6 & 5 \\ 8 & 4 \end{vmatrix} = 24 - 40 = -16$
(2)	$(-1)^3 \begin{vmatrix} 4 & 3 \\ 5 & 4 \end{vmatrix} = -16 + 15 = -1$		(4)	$(-1)^3 \begin{vmatrix} 2 & 1 \\ 8 & 4 \end{vmatrix} = -8 + 8 = 0$
(1)	$(-1)^4 \begin{vmatrix} 4 & 3 \\ 6 & 8 \end{vmatrix} = 32 - 18 = 14$		(3)	$(-1)^4 \begin{vmatrix} 2 & 1 \\ 6 & 5 \end{vmatrix} = 10 - 6 = 4$
(4)	$(-1)^3 \begin{vmatrix} 2 & 8 \\ 1 & 4 \end{vmatrix} = -8 + 8 = 0$		(2)	$(-1)^3 \begin{vmatrix} 4 & 5 \\ 3 & 4 \end{vmatrix} = -16 + 15 = -1$
(6)	$(-1)^4 \begin{vmatrix} 3 & 3 \\ 1 & 4 \end{vmatrix} = 12 - 3 = 9$		(6)	$(-1)^4 \begin{vmatrix} 3 & 1 \\ 3 & 4 \end{vmatrix} = 12 - 3 = 9$
(5)	$(-1)^5 \begin{vmatrix} 3 & 3 \\ 2 & 8 \end{vmatrix} = -24 + 6 = -18$		(8)	$(-1)^5 \begin{vmatrix} 3 & 1 \\ 4 & 5 \end{vmatrix} = -15 + 4 = -11$
(3)	$(-1)^4 \begin{vmatrix} 2 & 6 \\ 1 & 5 \end{vmatrix} = 10 - 6 = 4$		(1)	$(-1)^4 \begin{vmatrix} 4 & 6 \\ 3 & 8 \end{vmatrix} = 32 - 18 = 14$
(8)	$(-1)^5 \begin{vmatrix} 3 & 4 \\ 1 & 5 \end{vmatrix} = -15 + 4 = -11$		(5)	$(-1)^5 \begin{vmatrix} 3 & 2 \\ 3 & 8 \end{vmatrix} = -24 + 6 = -18$
(4)	$(-1)^6 \begin{vmatrix} 3 & 4 \\ 2 & 6 \end{vmatrix} = 18 - 8 = 10$		(4)	$(-1)^6 \begin{vmatrix} 3 & 2 \\ 4 & 6 \end{vmatrix} = 18 - 8 = 10$

<table>
<tr><td>

The new matrix involving the cofactor is

$$A_c = \begin{pmatrix} -16 & 0 & 4 \\ -1 & 9 & -11 \\ 14 & -18 & 10 \end{pmatrix}$$

</td><td>

The new matrix involving the cofactor is

$$A_c = \begin{pmatrix} -16 & -1 & 14 \\ 0 & 9 & -18 \\ 4 & -11 & 10 \end{pmatrix}$$

</td></tr>
</table>

2. The transpose of this matrix is

$$A = \begin{pmatrix} -16 & 0 & 4 \\ -1 & 9 & -11 \\ 14 & -18 & 10 \end{pmatrix}$$

3. Dividing each element of this matrix by the value of the determinant of the original matrix gives the inverse of the original matrix. Hence

$$A^{-1} = \begin{pmatrix} \dfrac{-16}{-36} & \dfrac{0}{-36} & \dfrac{4}{-36} \\ \dfrac{-1}{-36} & \dfrac{9}{-36} & \dfrac{-11}{-36} \\ \dfrac{14}{-36} & \dfrac{-18}{-36} & \dfrac{10}{-36} \end{pmatrix}$$

or

$$A^{-1} = \begin{pmatrix} \frac{4}{9} & 0 & -\frac{1}{9} \\ \frac{1}{36} & -\frac{1}{4} & \frac{11}{36} \\ -\frac{7}{18} & \frac{1}{2} & -\frac{5}{18} \end{pmatrix}$$

3. Dividing each element of this matrix by the value of the determinant of the original matrix gives the inverse of the original matrix. Hence

$$A^{-1} = \begin{pmatrix} \dfrac{-16}{-36} & \dfrac{0}{-36} & \dfrac{4}{-36} \\ \dfrac{-1}{-36} & \dfrac{9}{-36} & \dfrac{-11}{-36} \\ \dfrac{14}{-36} & \dfrac{-18}{-36} & \dfrac{10}{-36} \end{pmatrix}$$

or

$$A^{-1} = \begin{pmatrix} \frac{4}{9} & 0 & -\frac{1}{9} \\ \frac{1}{36} & -\frac{1}{4} & \frac{11}{36} \\ -\frac{7}{18} & \frac{1}{2} & -\frac{5}{18} \end{pmatrix}$$

By matrix multiplication we see that

$$AA^{-1} = A^{-1}A = \begin{pmatrix} 1 & 0 & 0 \\ 0 & 1 & 0 \\ 0 & 0 & 1 \end{pmatrix}$$

For a square matrix of two rows and two columns, the determinant of which is not zero, the inverse may be established by the following very simple procedure. Interchange the position of the diagonal elements a_{11} and a_{22}, reverse the sign of the non-diagonal elements, and divide all four elements by the determinant.

Example 3-10

Determine the inverse of matrix A.

$$A = \begin{pmatrix} a & b \\ c & d \end{pmatrix} \qquad \text{Determinant} = \begin{vmatrix} a & b \\ c & d \end{vmatrix} = D$$

$$A^{-1} = \begin{pmatrix} \dfrac{d}{D} & \dfrac{-b}{D} \\ \dfrac{-c}{D} & \dfrac{a}{D} \end{pmatrix}$$

The inverse of a product of two matrices is equal to the product of the inverses of the two matrices but in reverse order, that is,

$$(AB)^{-1} = B^{-1}A^{-1} \tag{3-12}$$

3-7. Differentiation of a Matrix

The derivative of a matrix with respect to a parameter is obtained by differentiating each element in the matrix with respect to the parameter.

Example 3-11

Determine the derivative of matrix A_{ij} with respect to θ.

$$(A_{ij}) = \begin{pmatrix} 1 & 0 & 0 \\ 0 & \cos\theta & -\sin\theta \\ 0 & \sin\theta & \cos\theta \end{pmatrix}$$

$$\frac{\partial(A_{ij})}{\partial\theta} = \frac{\partial}{\partial\theta}\begin{pmatrix} 1 & 0 & 0 \\ 0 & \cos\theta & -\sin\theta \\ 0 & \sin\theta & \cos\theta \end{pmatrix} = \begin{pmatrix} 0 & 0 & 0 \\ 0 & \dfrac{\partial\cos\theta}{\partial\theta} & -\dfrac{\partial\sin\theta}{\partial\theta} \\ 0 & \dfrac{\partial\sin\theta}{\partial\theta} & \dfrac{\partial\cos\theta}{\partial\theta} \end{pmatrix}$$

$$= \begin{pmatrix} 0 & 0 & 0 \\ 0 & -\sin\theta & -\cos\theta \\ 0 & \cos\theta & -\sin\theta \end{pmatrix}$$

3-8. Partitioning of Matrices

In dealing with simple problems involving only a few variables, the corresponding matrices have few elements and can be handled in the usual manner. However, in complicated systems involving many variables the matrices are of large dimensions, and the tasks of multiplication, taking inverses, and other operations becomes extremely difficult. In order to overcome this situation, large matrices may be partitioned or subdivided into smaller ones which are more easily handled. This procedure has already been used in evaluating determinants having more than three columns and three rows by the use of cofactors.

Consider the various possible ways of partitioning the following matrix.

$$A = \begin{pmatrix} 2 & 0 \\ -1 & 4 \\ 3 & 1 \end{pmatrix}$$

First possibility:

$$A = B_1 + B_2 = \begin{pmatrix} 2 & 0 \\ -1 & 0 \\ 3 & 0 \end{pmatrix} + \begin{pmatrix} 0 & 0 \\ 0 & 4 \\ 0 & 1 \end{pmatrix}$$

Second possibility:

$$A = \begin{pmatrix} C_1 \\ C_2 \\ C_3 \end{pmatrix} \quad \text{where } C_1 = (2, 0), \quad C_2 = (-1, 4), \quad C_3 = (3, 1)$$

Third possibility:

$$A = \begin{pmatrix} D_1 \\ D_2 \end{pmatrix} \quad \text{where } D_1 = \begin{pmatrix} 2 & 0 \\ -1 & 4 \end{pmatrix} \quad \text{and} \quad D_2 = (3 \quad 1)$$

Dashed lines are often used to indicate the manner in which a matrix is to be partitioned into submatrices.

$$\begin{pmatrix} 6 & 1 & 4 \\ -2 & 3 & 7 \\ 4 & 5 & 9 \end{pmatrix} = \begin{pmatrix} 6 & 1 & | & 4 \\ -2 & 3 & | & 7 \\ \hline 4 & 5 & | & 9 \end{pmatrix} = \begin{pmatrix} A & B \\ C & D \end{pmatrix}$$

Here A, B, C, and D are the submatrices.

When the submatrices are used in computations, all the laws of matrix algebra apply. Consider the addition of two matrices having the submatrices indicated.

$$\begin{pmatrix} A_1 & B_1 \\ C_1 & D_1 \end{pmatrix} + \begin{pmatrix} A_2 & B_2 \\ C_2 & D_2 \end{pmatrix} = \begin{pmatrix} A_1 + A_2 & B_1 + B_2 \\ C_1 + C_2 & D_1 + D_2 \end{pmatrix}$$

This relation is valid if A_1 and A_2 are of the same order, and similarly for B_1 and B_2, C_1 and C_2, D_1 and D_2.

Two matrices A and B are identically partitioned if the resulting matrices of submatrices contain the same number of rows and the same number of columns, and corresponding blocks have the same order. The following matrices are identically partitioned.

$$\begin{pmatrix} 6 & -1 & \vdots & 4 \\ 5 & 2 & \vdots & 9 \\ \cdots & \cdots & & \cdots \\ 1 & 8 & \vdots & 7 \end{pmatrix} \quad \text{and} \quad \begin{pmatrix} a & b & \vdots & c \\ d & e & \vdots & f \\ \cdots & \cdots & & \cdots \\ g & h & \vdots & k \end{pmatrix}$$

Thus we may say that identically partitioned matrices are equal if and only if the corresponding submatrices are equal throughout the matrices.

Submatrices are often used in the multiplication of complicated matrices. Suppose the two matrices A and B having the submatrices shown are to be multiplied.

$$A = \begin{pmatrix} L & \vdots & M \\ \cdots & & \cdots \\ N & \vdots & O \end{pmatrix}, \quad B = \begin{pmatrix} P & \vdots & Q \\ \cdots & & \cdots \\ R & \vdots & S \end{pmatrix}$$

The multiplication involving the submatrices follows.

$$AB = \begin{pmatrix} L & M \\ N & O \end{pmatrix}\begin{pmatrix} P & Q \\ R & S \end{pmatrix} = \begin{pmatrix} LP + MR & \vdots & LQ + MS \\ \cdots & & \cdots \\ NP + OR & \vdots & NQ + OS \end{pmatrix}$$

if the partition is such that the matrix products are defined.

Example 3-12

Determine the product of matrices A and B partitioned as shown.

$$A = \begin{pmatrix} 1 & 3 & \vdots & 1 \\ 2 & 1 & \vdots & -1 \end{pmatrix}, \quad B = \begin{pmatrix} 1 & 2 \\ 3 & 0 \\ \cdots & \cdots \\ 2 & -1 \end{pmatrix}$$

$$AB = \left(\begin{bmatrix} 1 & 3 \\ 2 & 1 \end{bmatrix}\begin{bmatrix} 1 \\ -1 \end{bmatrix} \right) \begin{pmatrix} \begin{bmatrix} 1 & 2 \\ 3 & 0 \end{bmatrix} \\ [2 \quad -1] \end{pmatrix}$$

$$= \left(\begin{bmatrix} 1 & 3 \\ 2 & 1 \end{bmatrix}\begin{bmatrix} 1 & 2 \\ 3 & 0 \end{bmatrix} + \begin{bmatrix} 1 \\ -1 \end{bmatrix}[2 \quad -1] \right)$$

$$AB = \left(\begin{bmatrix} 1+9 & 2+0 \\ 2+3 & 4+0 \end{bmatrix} + \begin{bmatrix} 2 & -1 \\ -2 & 1 \end{bmatrix} \right)$$

$$= \left(\begin{bmatrix} 10+2 \\ 5+4 \end{bmatrix} + \begin{bmatrix} 2 & -1 \\ -2 & 1 \end{bmatrix} \right) = \begin{pmatrix} 12 & 1 \\ 3 & 5 \end{pmatrix}$$

Example 3-13

Determine the product of matrices A and B.

$$A = \left(\begin{matrix} 1 & 0 & 0 & \vdots & 1 & 0 \\ 0 & 1 & 0 & \vdots & 0 & 1 \\ 0 & 0 & 1 & \vdots & -1 & 1 \end{matrix} \right), \quad B = \left(\begin{matrix} 5 & 2 & 1 \\ 2 & 3 & 1 \\ 5 & 4 & 4 \\ \hline 7 & 3 & 0 \\ 3 & 7 & 7 \end{matrix} \right)$$

$$AB = \left(\begin{bmatrix} 1 & 0 & 0 \\ 0 & 1 & 0 \\ 0 & 0 & 1 \end{bmatrix} \begin{bmatrix} 1 & 0 \\ 0 & 1 \\ -1 & 1 \end{bmatrix} \right) \left(\begin{bmatrix} 5 & 2 & 1 \\ 2 & 3 & 1 \\ 5 & 4 & 4 \end{bmatrix} \\ \begin{bmatrix} 7 & 3 & 0 \\ 3 & 7 & 7 \end{bmatrix} \right)$$

$$= \left(\begin{bmatrix} 1 & 0 & 0 \\ 0 & 1 & 0 \\ 0 & 0 & 1 \end{bmatrix} \begin{bmatrix} 5 & 2 & 1 \\ 2 & 3 & 1 \\ 5 & 4 & 4 \end{bmatrix} + \begin{bmatrix} 1 & 0 \\ 0 & 1 \\ -1 & 1 \end{bmatrix} \begin{bmatrix} 7 & 3 & 0 \\ 3 & 7 & 7 \end{bmatrix} \right)$$

$$= \left(\begin{bmatrix} 5+0+0 & 2+0+0 & 1+0+0 \\ 0+2+0 & 0+3+0 & 0+1+0 \\ 0+0+5 & 0+0+4 & 0+0+4 \end{bmatrix} \right.$$

$$+ \left. \begin{bmatrix} 7+0 & 3+0 & 0+0 \\ 0+3 & 0+7 & 0+7 \\ -7+3 & -3+7 & 0+7 \end{bmatrix} \right) = \begin{pmatrix} 12+5+1 \\ 5+10+8 \\ 1+8+11 \end{pmatrix}$$

Example 3-14

Determine the product of matrices A and B.

$$A = \left(\begin{array}{cc:ccc}
1 & 2 & 3 & -1 & 0 \\
2 & -1 & 0 & 0 & 0 \\
\hdashline
1 & 0 & 1 & 0 & 0 \\
3 & 2 & 0 & 1 & 0 \\
2 & 1 & 0 & 0 & 1
\end{array}\right), \quad
B = \left(\begin{array}{cc:ccc}
1 & 0 & 1 & 3 & 1 \\
0 & 1 & 0 & 1 & 3 \\
\hdashline
0 & 0 & 1 & 1 & 1 \\
0 & 1 & 0 & 2 & 1 \\
1 & 0 & 0 & 0 & 0
\end{array}\right)$$

$$AB = \begin{pmatrix}
\begin{bmatrix}1 & 2\\2 & -1\end{bmatrix} & \begin{bmatrix}3 & -1\\0 & 0\end{bmatrix} & \begin{bmatrix}0\\1\end{bmatrix} & \begin{bmatrix}1 & 3\\0 & 1\end{bmatrix} & \begin{bmatrix}1\\3\end{bmatrix} \\[12pt]
\begin{bmatrix}1\\2\end{bmatrix} & \begin{bmatrix}0 & 1\\2 & 0\end{bmatrix} & \begin{bmatrix}0\\1\end{bmatrix} & \begin{bmatrix}1 & 1\\2 & 1\end{bmatrix} & \begin{bmatrix}0\\0\end{bmatrix}
\end{pmatrix}$$

$$\begin{bmatrix} 1 & 2 \\ 2 & -1 \end{bmatrix} \begin{bmatrix} 1 & 3 & 1 \\ 0 & 1 & 3 \end{bmatrix} + \begin{bmatrix} 3 & -1 \\ 0 & 0 \end{bmatrix} \begin{bmatrix} 1 & 1 & 1 \\ 0 & 2 & 1 \\ 0 & 0 & 0 \end{bmatrix}$$

$$\begin{bmatrix} 1 & 0 \\ 0 & 1 \end{bmatrix} \begin{bmatrix} 1 & 2 \\ 2 & -1 \end{bmatrix} + \begin{bmatrix} 3 & -1 \\ 0 & 0 \end{bmatrix} \begin{bmatrix} 0 & 0 \\ 0 & 1 \\ 1 & 0 \end{bmatrix}$$

$$=$$

$$\begin{bmatrix} 1 & 0 \\ 2 & 0 \end{bmatrix} \begin{bmatrix} 3 & 1 \\ 2 & 3 \end{bmatrix} + \begin{bmatrix} 1 & 3 & 1 \\ 0 & 1 & 3 \end{bmatrix} \begin{bmatrix} 1 & 1 & 1 \\ 0 & 2 & 1 \\ 0 & 0 & 0 \end{bmatrix}$$

$$\begin{bmatrix} 1 & 0 \\ 2 & 0 \end{bmatrix} + \begin{bmatrix} 0 & 1 \\ 0 & 1 \end{bmatrix} \begin{bmatrix} 0 & 0 \\ 0 & 1 \\ 1 & 0 \end{bmatrix}$$

$$=$$

$$\begin{bmatrix} 1+0 & 0+2 \\ 2+0 & 0-1 \end{bmatrix} \begin{bmatrix} 1+0 & 3+2 & 1+6 \\ 2+0 & 6-1 & 2-3 \end{bmatrix} \begin{bmatrix} 3-0 & 3-2+0 & 3-1+0 \\ 0+0+0 & 0+0+0 & 0+0+0 \end{bmatrix}$$

$$\begin{bmatrix} 1+2 & 0-1+0 \\ 2+0 & 0-1 \end{bmatrix} + \begin{bmatrix} 0+0+0 & 0-1+0 \\ 0+0+0 & 0+0+0 \end{bmatrix}$$

$$\begin{bmatrix} 1+0 & 0+0 \\ 3+0 & 0+2 \\ 2+0 & 0+1 \end{bmatrix} \begin{bmatrix} 1+0 & 3+0 & 1+0 \\ 3+0 & 9+2 & 3+6 \\ 2+0 & 6+1 & 2+3 \end{bmatrix} \begin{bmatrix} 1+0+0 & 1+0+0 & 1+0+0 \\ 0+0+0 & 0+2+0 & 0+1+0 \\ 0+0+0 & 0+0+0 & 0+0+0 \end{bmatrix}$$

$$\begin{bmatrix} 0+0+0 & 0+0+0 \\ 0+0+0 & 0+0+0 \\ 0+0+1 & 0+0+0 \end{bmatrix}$$

$$=$$

$$\begin{bmatrix} 1 & 2 \\ 2 & -1 \end{bmatrix} \begin{bmatrix} 3 & 1 \\ 2 & 3 \end{bmatrix} + \begin{bmatrix} 3 & 1 \\ 0 & 0 \end{bmatrix} \begin{bmatrix} 1 & 1 & 1 \\ 0 & 2 & 1 \\ 0 & 0 & 0 \end{bmatrix}$$

$$\begin{bmatrix} 1 & 2 \\ 2 & -1 \end{bmatrix} \begin{bmatrix} 0 & -1 \\ 0 & 0 \end{bmatrix} + \begin{bmatrix} 0 & 0 \\ 0 & 1 \\ 1 & 0 \end{bmatrix}$$

$$\begin{bmatrix} 1 & 3 & 1 \\ 2 & 5 & 7 \\ 2 & 5 & -1 \end{bmatrix} \begin{bmatrix} 1 & 3 & 1 \\ 3 & 11 & 9 \\ 2 & 7 & 5 \end{bmatrix}$$

$$=$$

$$\begin{bmatrix} 1 & 1 & 1 & 2 & 1 & 9 \\ 2 & -1 & 1 & 0 & 2 & 4 & 6 & -1 \\ 1 & 3 & 3 & 1 & 13 & 10 \\ 3 & 1 & 2 & 7 & 5 \end{bmatrix}$$

3-9. The Determinant of a Product of Two Square Matrices

The theorem that the determinant of the product of two square matrices of order n is equal to the product of their determinants will be found very useful in the section dealing with relative tensors.

According to the rules governing matrix multiplication the following equality exists.

$$\begin{pmatrix} 3 & -1 \\ 4 & 2 \end{pmatrix}\begin{pmatrix} w & x \\ y & z \end{pmatrix} = \begin{pmatrix} 3w - y & 3x - z \\ 4w + 2y & 4x + 2z \end{pmatrix}$$

Taking the determinants of these matrices gives

$$(6 + 4)(wz - yx) = (3w - y)(4x + 2z) - (3x - z)(4w + 2y)$$

$$10wz - 10yx = 12wx - 4xy + 6wz - 2yz - 12xw$$
$$+ 4zw - 6xy + 2yz = 10wz - 10yx$$

Consider the following matrix transformation relation for a primed coordinate system and an unprimed one.

$$A'^{rs} = \frac{\partial x'^r}{\partial x^i} A^{ij} \frac{\partial x'^s}{\partial x^j}$$

Taking the determinants of these matrices gives

$$|A'^{rs}| = \left| \frac{\partial x'^r}{\partial x^i} \right| |A^{ij}| \left| \frac{\partial x'^s}{\partial x^j} \right|$$

$$\left| \frac{\partial x^i}{\partial x'^r} \right| \quad \text{and} \quad \left| \frac{\partial x^j}{\partial x'^s} \right|$$

are transformation Jacobians, J; hence the expression may be written

$$|A'^{rs}| = J^{-2} |A^{ij}|$$

3-10. Problems

3-1. If

$$(a_j{}^i) = \begin{pmatrix} 1 & 0 & 4 \\ 3 & 2 & 1 \\ 2 & 1 & 4 \end{pmatrix} \quad \text{and} \quad (b_j{}^i) = \begin{pmatrix} 4 & 3 & 2 \\ 1 & 0 & 4 \\ 3 & 2 & 1 \end{pmatrix}$$

determine (*a*) the nine quantities $p_j{}^i = a_k{}^i b_j{}^k$ and (*b*) the nine quantities $q_j{}^i = a_j{}^k b_k{}^i$.

3-2. If $p_j{}^i$ and $q_j{}^i$ are defined as in Problem 3-1, show that

$$p = |p_j{}^i| = q = |q_j{}^i| = 15$$

by direct expansion.

3-3. Given the three matrices

$$A = \begin{pmatrix} 1 & 2 & 1 & -4 \\ -1 & 2 & -1 & 3 \\ 0 & 4 & 4 & -1 \\ 1 & 1 & 0 & -1 \end{pmatrix}, \quad B = \begin{pmatrix} 1 & 2 & 4 & -1 \\ -1 & 3 & -1 & 3 \\ 1 & 2 & 2 & -1 \\ 0 & 3 & -1 & 4 \end{pmatrix},$$

$$C = \begin{pmatrix} 4 & 0 & -1 & 3 \\ 4 & 4 & -1 & 2 \\ 3 & -1 & 2 & 5 \\ 1 & 2 & 4 & 0 \end{pmatrix}$$

determine (*a*) $A + B$; (*b*) $A + C$; (*c*) $B + C$; (*d*) $A + B + C$.

3-4. By the rules governing the addition of matrices, prove that the multiplication of a matrix by a scalar is the same as multiplying each of the elements by the scalar.

3-5. Using the matrices in Problem 3-3, solve for (*a*) $A - B$; (*b*) $B - A$; (*c*) $A - C$; (*d*) $C - A$; (*e*) $B - C$; (*f*) $C - B$; (*g*) $A - B - C$; (*h*) $C - B - A$.

3-6. Given the matrices

$$A = \begin{pmatrix} 0 & 2 & 1 \\ 1 & 3 & 2 \\ -1 & 2 & 1 \end{pmatrix}, \quad B = \begin{pmatrix} 3 & 2 & 1 \\ -1 & 1 & 0 \\ 2 & 3 & 2 \end{pmatrix}, \quad C = \begin{pmatrix} 3 & 1 & 4 \\ 3 & 2 & 3 \\ -4 & 1 & 2 \end{pmatrix}$$

determine (*a*) AB; (*b*) AC; (*c*) BC; (*d*) ABC.

3-7. Prove the following matrix relations.

$$(A + B)(C + D) = AC + BC + AD + BD$$
$$(A + B)^2 = A^2 + BA + AB + B^2$$
$$(A - B)^2 = A^2 - BA - AB + B^2$$
$$(A + B)(A - B) = A^2 + BA - AB - B^2$$

3-8. Given the matrices

$$A = \begin{pmatrix} 1 & 2 & 3 \\ 4 & 5 & 6 \\ 7 & 8 & 9 \end{pmatrix}, \quad B = \begin{pmatrix} 1 & 2 & 4 \\ 5 & 2 & 7 \\ 3 & 2 & 1 \end{pmatrix}, \quad C = \begin{pmatrix} 1 & 2 & 1 \\ 3 & 4 & 0 \\ 0 & 5 & 2 \end{pmatrix}$$

determine (a) A_t; (b) B_t; (c) C_t; (d) $A_t B_t$; (e) $A_t C_t$; (f) $C_t B_t$; (g) $A_t B_t C_t$.

3-9. Given the three matrices

$$
A = \begin{array}{c} a \\ b \\ c \end{array}\begin{pmatrix} 3 \\ 2 \\ -1 \end{pmatrix}\begin{array}{c} a \end{array}, \quad
B = \begin{array}{c} a \\ b \\ c \end{array}\begin{pmatrix} 2 & 4 & 1 \\ -1 & 2 & 3 \\ 1 & 3 & 0 \end{pmatrix}, \quad
C = \begin{array}{c} a \\ c \end{array}\begin{pmatrix} 1 & 2 \\ 3 & 4 \end{pmatrix}
$$

determine (a) BA; (b) CA; (c) $B + C$; (d) $(B + C)A$; (e) $BA + CA$; (f) B^{-1}; (g) C^{-1}; (h) $(B + C)^{-1}$; (i) BB^{-1}; (j) CC^{-1}; (k) $(B + C)(B + C)^{-1}$; (l) $B^{-1}(BA)$; (m) $C^{-1}(CA)$; (n) $(B + C)^{-1}(BA + CA)$; (o) $(BA)A$; (p) $(CA)A$; (q) $(BA + CA)A$.

What conclusions can you draw from your results?

3-10. Show that the inverse of the transpose is equal to the transpose of the inverse of a matrix.

3-11. Show that the following relation is true.

$$(AB)^{-1} = B^{-1}A^{-1}$$

3-12. Compute the product of matrices A and B, using the indicated partitioning.

$$
A = \left(\begin{array}{ccc|c}
2 & 1 & 4 & 3 \\
1 & 2 & 0 & -1 \\ \hline
-2 & 3 & 2 & 2 \\
1 & 1 & 3 & 4
\end{array} \right), \quad
B = \left(\begin{array}{cc|cc}
1 & 3 & 1 & 2 \\
2 & 0 & 2 & 4 \\
2 & 2 & -3 & 1 \\ \hline
-1 & 2 & 0 & 2
\end{array} \right)
$$

3-11. Suggested References

3-1. *Elementary Matrix Algebra*, F. E. Hohn, The Macmillan Company.
3-2. *Elementary Analysis*, H. C. Trimble and F. W. Lott, Jr., Prentice-Hall, Inc.
3-3. *Introduction to Matrices and Linear Transformations*, D. T. Finkbeiner II, W. H. Freeman and Company.
3-4. *Applications of the Theory of Matrices*, F. R. Gantmacher, Interscience Publishers, Inc.
3-5. *Tensor Analysis of Electric Circuits and Machines*, L. V. Bewley, The Ronald Press Company.
3-6. *Matrix and Tensor Calculus*, A. D. Michal, John Wiley and Sons.
3-7. *Introduction to Matrix Analysis*, Richard Bellman, McGraw-Hill Book Company.
3-8. *Theory of Matrices*, S. Perlis, Addison-Wesley Publishing Company.

4

Summation Convention

4-1. Introduction

Of the various notations devised for the tensor calculus the index notation offers many advantages; hence it will be used throughout the text. Latin letters, i, j, k, etc., and Greek letters, $\alpha, \beta, \gamma, \ldots$, etc., will be used for indices, both as subscripts (a_i) and as superscripts (a^i). Hence the three quantities a^1, a^2, and a^3 will be denoted by the symbol a^i. Symbolically this may be written

$$a^i = (a^1, a^2, a^3)$$

It must be remembered that a in this relation is simply a set of three quantities. No operation such as multiplication or division is implied. For i and j ranging from 1 to 3 independently the symbols $a_j{}^i$, a_{ij}, and a^{ij} represent nine quantities.

According to the summation convention a summation is implied when an index is repeated. For example,

$$b_i c_j{}^i = b_1 c_j{}^1 + b_2 c_j{}^2 + b_3 c_j{}^3 \qquad (j = 1, 2, 3)$$

A repeated index is called a dummy index, a repeated index, or an umbral index, because the value of the term does not depend on the symbol used.

An index which is not repeated is called a free index.

The subjects of range and the summation convention will now be discussed in detail for purposes of review.

When a suffix occurs unrepeated in a term, it will be understood that it takes the values from the set $(1, 2, 3, \ldots, n)$, where n is a

specified integer called the range. Evaluating $a_i = b_i$ for the range
(1, 2, 3) gives

$$a_1 = b_1, \quad a_2 = b_2, \quad a_3 = b_3$$

Throughout the study of engineering problems one is often confronted with sums of the type

$$S = a_1 x_1 + a_2 x_2 + \cdots + a_{(n)} x_{(n)}$$

As stated in an earlier section, this may be shortened as follows

$$S = \sum_{i=1}^{n} a_i x_i$$

It is often much more convenient to replace the subscript of the quantities $x_1, x_2, \ldots, x_n$ by superscripts $x^1, x^2, \ldots, x^n$. The sum can now be expressed as

$$S = \sum_{i=1}^{n} a_i x^i$$

We can now eliminate the Σ sign, if we remember that two repeated indices represent a summation from 1 to n. This notation was introduced by Einstein.

The index of summation is a dummy index since the final result is independent of the letter used. For example,

$$S = a_i x^i = a_j x^j = a_\alpha x^\alpha = a_B x^B$$

Examples are presented here to demonstrate the summation procedure once more.

Example 4-1

(a) Expand $a_i a^i$ for $(i = 1, 2, 3, \ldots, n)$.

$$a_i a^i = a_1 a^1 + a_2 a^2 + a_3 a^3 + \cdots + a_{(n)} a^{(n)}$$

(b) Expand $a_{ij} b^j$ for $(j = 1, 2, 3)$.

$$a_{ij} b^j = a_{i1} b^1 + a_{i2} b^2 + a_{i3} b^3$$

(c) Expand $a_j{}^i a_i{}^k$ for $(i = 1, 2, 3, \ldots, n)$.

$$a_j{}^i a_i{}^k = a_j{}^1 a_1{}^k + a_j{}^2 a_2{}^k + a_j{}^3 a_3{}^k + \cdots + a_j{}^{(n)} a_{(n)}{}^k$$

(d) Write out the expression $a_{ijk} X^k$ for $k = 1, 2, 3, \ldots, n$.

$$a_{ijk} X^k = a_{ij1} X^1 + a_{ij2} X^2 + a_{ij3} X^3 + \cdots + a_{ij(n)} X^{(n)}$$

Any change in a free index must be made in every term of an equation, but a dummy index may be changed in the individual terms of the equation.

Example 4-2

(a) Expand the following relation for $i = 1, 2, 3$ and $j = 1, 2, 3, 4$.

$$a_{ij}x_j$$

This expression represents three linear relations having the following form, since j is summed from 1 to 4.

$$a_{1j}x_j = a_{11}x_1 + a_{12}x_2 + a_{13}x_3 + a_{14}x_4$$
$$a_{2j}x_j = a_{21}x_1 + a_{22}x_2 + a_{23}x_3 + a_{24}x_4$$
$$a_{3j}x_j = a_{31}x_1 + a_{32}x_2 + a_{33}x_3 + a_{34}x_4$$

(b) Write out in full the expression for $\mathbf{a} = a^i\mathbf{e}_i$ for $i = 1, 2, 3$.

$$\mathbf{a} = a^1\mathbf{e}_1 + a^2\mathbf{e}_2 + a^3\mathbf{e}_3$$

(c) Write in full $a_\alpha{}^i x^\alpha = b^i$ for $i, \alpha = 1, 2, 3$.
Consider the α summation first.

$$a_\alpha{}^i x^\alpha, \qquad a_1{}^i x^1 + a_2{}^i x^2 + a_3{}^i x^3 = b^i$$

Consider the i range next.

$$a_\alpha{}^1 x^\alpha, \qquad a_1{}^1 x^1 + a_2{}^1 x^2 + a_3{}^1 x^3 = b^1$$
$$a_\alpha{}^2 x^\alpha, \qquad a_1{}^2 x^1 + a_2{}^2 x^2 + a_3{}^2 x^3 = b^2$$
$$a_\alpha{}^3 x^\alpha, \qquad a_1{}^3 x^1 + a_2{}^3 x^2 + a_3{}^3 x^3 = b^3$$

(d) Expand $a_{ij}x_i x_j$ for $i = 1, 2, 3$ and $j = 1, 2, 3$.

$$a_{ij}x_i x_j = a_{11}x_1 x_1 + a_{12}x_1 x_2 + a_{13}x_1 x_3$$
$$+ a_{21}x_2 x_1 + a_{22}x_2 x_2 + a_{23}x_2 x_3$$
$$+ a_{31}x_3 x_1 + a_{32}x_3 x_2 + a_{33}x_3 x_3$$

Example 4-3

Evaluate $S = g_{\alpha\beta}x^\alpha x^\beta$.
Since there are two repeated indices, there are two summations. This is the same as Example 4-2d except for the position of the indices.
Assume first that α is summed from 1 to 3. Hence

$$S = g_{1\beta}x^1 x^\beta + g_{2\beta}x^2 x^\beta + g_{3\beta}x^3 x^\beta$$

Now sum β from 1 to 3, as an example.

$$S = g_{11}x^1 x^1 + g_{21}x^2 x^1 + g_{31}x^3 x^1$$
$$+ g_{12}x^1 x^2 + g_{22}x^2 x^2 + g_{32}x^3 x^2$$
$$+ g_{13}x^1 x^3 + g_{23}x^2 x^3 + g_{33}x^3 x^3$$

Hence $S = g_{\alpha\beta}x^\alpha x^\beta$ represents the double summation

$$S = \sum_{\beta=1}^{3}\sum_{\alpha=1}^{3}g_{\alpha\beta}x^\alpha x^\beta$$

Note also that $g_{\alpha\beta}$ may be represented as the elements of a square matrix, such as

$$\begin{pmatrix} g_{11} & g_{12} & g_{13} \\ g_{21} & g_{22} & g_{23} \\ g_{31} & g_{32} & g_{33} \end{pmatrix}$$

Example 4-4

If $y^i = a_\alpha{}^i x^\alpha$ and $z^i = b_\alpha{}^i y^\alpha$, show that

$$z^i = b_\alpha{}^i a_\beta{}^\alpha x^\beta$$

Let the summation on α be from 1 to 3.

$$y^i = a_1{}^i x^1 + a_2{}^i x^2 + a_3{}^i x^3$$
$$z^i = b_1{}^i y^1 + b_2{}^i y^2 + b_3{}^i y^3$$

where, when $i = 1$,

$$y^1 = a_1{}^1 x^1 + a_2{}^1 x^2 + a_3{}^1 x^3$$

when $i = 2$,

$$y^2 = a_1{}^2 x^1 + a_2{}^2 x^2 + a_3{}^2 x^3$$

and, when $i = 3$,

$$y^3 = a_1{}^3 x^1 + a_2{}^3 x^2 + a_3{}^3 x^3$$

Substituting these expressions for y^i in the z^i equation gives

$$\begin{aligned} z^i = \; & b_1{}^i(a_1{}^1 x^1 + a_2{}^1 x^2 + a_3{}^1 x^3) \\ & + b_2{}^i(a_1{}^2 x^1 + a_2{}^2 x^2 + a_3{}^2 x^3) \\ & + b_3{}^i(a_1{}^3 x^1 + a_2{}^3 x^2 + a_3{}^3 x^3) \end{aligned}$$

This may be written in abbreviated form:

$$z^i = b_\alpha{}^i a_\beta{}^\alpha x^\beta$$

Example 4-5

Write out the following expressions for a range n.

(a)
$$\frac{\partial f_i}{\partial x_j}\,dx_j$$

This is a summation on j.

$$\frac{\partial f_i}{\partial x_j}\,dx_j = \frac{\partial f_i}{\partial x_1}\,dx_1 + \frac{\partial f_i}{\partial x_2}\,dx_2 + \cdots + \frac{\partial f_i}{\partial x_{(n)}}\,dx_{(n)} = df_i$$

(b)
$$a^i = \frac{\partial x^i}{\partial y^j}\,b^j$$

This is a summation in j.

$$a^i = \frac{\partial x^i}{\partial y^j} b^j = \frac{\partial x^i}{\partial y^1} b^1 + \frac{\partial x^i}{\partial y^2} b^2 + \cdots + \frac{\partial x^i}{\partial y^{(n)}} b^{(n)}$$

(c)
$$g_{ij} = \frac{\partial y^k}{\partial x^i} \frac{\partial y^k}{\partial x^j}$$

This is a summation in k.

$$g_{ij} = \frac{\partial y^1}{\partial x^i} \frac{\partial y^1}{\partial x^j} + \frac{\partial y^2}{\partial x^i} \frac{\partial y^2}{\partial x^j} + \cdots + \frac{\partial y^{(n)}}{\partial x^i} \frac{\partial y^{(n)}}{\partial x^j}$$

Example 4-6

Express in summation notation the value of df/dt for the equation
$$f = f(x^1, x^2, \ldots, x^n).$$

According to the calculus we may write.

$$df = \frac{\partial f}{\partial x^1} dx^1 + \frac{\partial f}{\partial x^2} dx^2 + \cdots + \frac{\partial f}{\partial x^{(n)}} dx^{(n)}$$

$$= \sum_{i=1}^{n} \frac{\partial f}{\partial x^i} dx^i$$

Changing the dummy index and eliminating the Σ sign gives

$$df = \frac{\partial f}{\partial x^\alpha} dx^\alpha$$

Now

$$\frac{df}{dt} = \frac{\partial f}{\partial x^\alpha} \frac{dx^\alpha}{dt}$$

4-2. The Kronecker Deltas

If $x^1, x^2, \ldots, x^n$ are n independent variables, $\partial x^i/\partial x^j = \delta_j{}^i$. Here $\delta_j{}^i$ is known as the Kronecker delta.

If $i = j$, $\partial x^i/\partial x^j = 1$.

If $i \neq j$, there is no change in the variable x^i if we change x^j, since they are independent variables, hence $\partial x^i/\partial x^j = 0$.

The Kronecker deltas, δ_{ij}, $\delta_i{}^j$, δ^{ij}, are symbols carrying two indices, and they are defined such that $\delta_i{}^j = 1$ when $i = j$ and $\delta_i{}^j = 0$ when $i \neq j$.

When $j = i$, the term $\delta_i{}^j$ becomes $\delta_{(i)}^{(i)}$. Here we have a repeated index which does not represent a summation as we previously defined it.

Suppose $j = i$ and values for i range from 1 to n; then

$$\delta_i{}^j = \delta_1{}^1 = \delta_2{}^2 = \delta_3{}^3 = \cdots = \delta_{(n)}^{(n)} = 1$$

If $j = 1$ and i ranges from 2 to n,

$$\delta_i{}^j = \delta_2{}^1 = \delta_3{}^1 = \delta_4{}^1 = \cdots = \delta_n{}^1 = 0$$

Let $j = i$ and i range from 1 to 4; then

$$\delta_j{}^i = \delta_1{}^1 = \delta_2{}^2 = \delta_3{}^3 = \delta_4{}^4 = 1$$

The sum of the four deltas would be 4; therefore, we may write in general terms the relation

$$\delta_i{}^i = \delta_1{}^1 + \cdots + \delta_{(n)}^{(n)} = \underbrace{1 + \cdots + 1}_{n \text{ times}} = n$$

Example 4-7

Write out the following expression in full.

$$\delta_{ij}a_j$$

This represents a summation in j:

$$\delta_{ij}a_j = \delta_{i1}a_1 + \delta_{i2}a_2 + \delta_{i3}a_3 + \delta_{i4}a_4 + \cdots + \delta_{i(n)}a_{(n)}$$

If $i = 1$, the only non-zero term is $\delta_{11}a_1$; hence

$$\delta_{ij}a_j = \delta_{11}a_1 = a_1$$

If $i = 2$,

$$\delta_{ij}a_j = \delta_{22}a_2 = a_2$$

In general terms the expression is

$$\delta_{ij}a_j = a_i \qquad (i = 1, \ldots, n)$$

Example 4-8

Evaluate

(*a*)
$$\frac{\partial a_i}{\partial a^j} = \delta_i{}^j$$

If $i = j$,

$$\frac{\partial a^i}{\partial a^j} = \delta_{(i)}^{(i)} = 1$$

If $i \neq j$, there is no change in the variable a^i if we change a^j, since the variables are independent; hence $\partial a^i / \partial a^j = 0$.

(*b*)
$$a_i{}^j \delta_j{}^i$$

This is a double summation in i and j. $\delta_j{}^i$ is zero for all cases, except when $i = j$; therefore

$$a_i{}^j \delta_j{}^i = a_i{}^i = a_j{}^j = a_1{}^1 + a_2{}^2 + \cdots + a_{(n)}^{(n)}$$

Example 4-9

If $S = a_\alpha x^\alpha$ and the a_α are constants, show that $\partial(a_\alpha x^\alpha)/\partial x^u = a_u$.

$$\frac{\partial S}{\partial x^u} = a_\alpha \frac{\partial x^\alpha}{\partial x^u} = a_\alpha \delta_u{}^\alpha$$

$$\delta_u{}^\alpha = 0 \quad \text{except when} \quad \alpha = u$$

Hence

$$\frac{\partial(a_\alpha x^\alpha)}{\partial x^u} = a_\alpha \delta_u{}^\alpha = a_u$$

Example 4-10

$S = a_{\alpha\beta} x^\alpha x^\beta = 0$ for all values of the variables $x^1, x^2, x^3, \ldots, x^n$. Show that $a_{ji} + a_{ij} = 0$.

First differentiate S with respect to x^i.

$$\frac{\partial S}{\partial x^i} = a_{\alpha\beta} x^\alpha \frac{\partial x^\beta}{\partial x^i} + a_{\alpha\beta} x^\beta \frac{\partial x^\alpha}{\partial x^i} = 0$$

$$= a_{\alpha\beta} x^\alpha \delta_i{}^\beta + a_{\alpha\beta} x^\beta \delta_i{}^\alpha = 0$$

$$= a_{\alpha i} x^\alpha + a_{i\beta} x^\beta = 0$$

Now differentiate with respect to x^j.

$$\frac{\partial^2 S}{\partial x^j\,\partial x^i} = a_{\alpha i} \frac{\partial x^\alpha}{\partial x^j} + a_{i\beta} \frac{\partial x^\beta}{\partial x^j} = 0$$

$$= a_{\alpha i} \delta_j{}^\alpha + a_{i\beta} \delta_j{}^\beta = 0$$

$$= a_{ji} + a_{ij} = 0$$

Example 4-11

If $a_{\alpha\beta\gamma} x^\alpha x^\beta x^\gamma = 0$ for all values of x^i, show that $a_{kji} + a_{jki} + a_{ikj} + a_{ijk} + a_{kij} + a_{jik} = 0$.

First differentiate with respect to x^i.

$$a_{\alpha\beta\gamma} x^\alpha x^\beta \frac{\partial x^\gamma}{\partial x^i} + a_{\alpha\beta\gamma} x^\beta x^\gamma \frac{\partial x^\alpha}{\partial x^i} + a_{\alpha\beta\gamma} x^\alpha x^\gamma \frac{\partial x^\beta}{\partial x^i} = 0$$

$$a_{\alpha\beta\gamma} x^\alpha x^\beta \delta_i{}^\gamma + a_{\alpha\beta\gamma} x^\beta x^\gamma \delta_i{}^\alpha + a_{\alpha\beta\gamma} x^\alpha x^\gamma \delta_i{}^\beta = 0$$

$$a_{\alpha\beta i} x^\alpha x^\beta + a_{i\beta\gamma} x^\beta x^\gamma + a_{\alpha i\gamma} x^\alpha x^\gamma = 0$$

Now differentiate with respect to x^j.

$$a_{\alpha\beta i} x^\alpha \frac{\partial x^\beta}{\partial x^j} + a_{\alpha\beta i} x^\beta \frac{\partial x^\alpha}{\partial x^j} + a_{i\beta\gamma} x^\beta \frac{\partial x^\gamma}{\partial x^j} + a_{i\beta\gamma} x^\gamma \frac{\partial x^\beta}{\partial x^j}$$

$$+ a_{\alpha i\gamma} x^\alpha \frac{\partial x^\gamma}{\partial x^j} + a_{\alpha i\gamma} x^\gamma \frac{\partial x^\alpha}{\partial x^j} = 0$$

$$a_{\alpha j i} x^\alpha + a_{j\beta i} x^\beta + a_{i\beta j} x^\beta + a_{ij\gamma} x^\gamma + a_{\alpha i j} x^\alpha + a_{ji\gamma} x^\gamma = 0$$

Differentiate with respect to x^k.

$$a_{\alpha ji}\frac{\partial x^\alpha}{\partial x^k} + a_{j\beta i}\frac{\partial x^\beta}{\partial x^k} + a_{i\beta j}\frac{\partial x^\beta}{\partial x^k} + a_{ij\gamma}\frac{\partial x^\gamma}{\partial x^k} + a_{\alpha ij}\frac{\partial x^\alpha}{\partial x^k} + a_{ji\gamma}\frac{\partial x^\gamma}{\partial x^k} = 0$$

Hence

$$a_{kji} + a_{jki} + a_{ikj} + a_{ijk} + a_{kij} + a_{jik} = 0$$

4-3. The Number of Equations and Quantities in an Indexed Equation

Consider a three-dimensional space, that is, $n = 3$. How many different expressions are represented by the following term?

$$A_n{}^m B_{pq}{}^n C_s{}^{qr}$$

When one of the expressions is expanded, how many terms will it contain?

The number of expressions is determined by the number of free indices according to the equation

$$\text{Number of expressions} = n^f$$

Here n is the number of dimensions of the space and f represents the number of free indices.

In the original expression there are four free indices; therefore the number of expressions is

$$n^f = 3^4 = 81$$

This means that the original group of symbols represents 81 different expressions.

Since repeated indices indicate a summation, the number of terms in any one expression is n^r, where r represents the number of repeated indices.

In the original group of symbols there are two repeated indices; therefore the number of terms in each expression is

$$n^r = 3^2 = 9$$

The total number of terms represented is 9×81 or 729.

4-4. Problems

4-1. Expand the expression $a^i a_i$ for $i = 1, 2, 3, \ldots, n$.

4-2. Expand the expressions $a_j{}^i a_i{}^k$ and $a_{ij} x^i x^j$. Assume that $n = 3$.

4-3. Show that

(a)
$$a_i \delta_j{}^i = a_j$$

(b)
$$a^i \delta_i{}^j = a^j$$

(c)
$$a_i{}^j \delta_j{}^i = a_i{}^i$$

4-4. If $S = a_i x^i$ show that

$$\frac{\partial S}{\partial a_j} = x^j \quad \text{and} \quad \frac{\partial S}{\partial x^j} = a_j$$

4-5. If $S = a_{ij} x^i x^j$, show that

(a)
$$\frac{\partial S}{\partial x^k} = (a_{ik} + a_{ki})x^i$$

(b)
$$\frac{\partial^2 S}{\partial x^k \partial x^l} = a_{lk} + a_{kl}$$

(c)
$$\frac{\partial S}{\partial a_{ij}} = x^i x^j$$

4-6. If $x^i = x^i(\mathbf{x}^1, \mathbf{x}^2, \mathbf{x}^3)$ and $\mathbf{x}^i = \mathbf{x}^i(x^1, x^2, x^3)$ show that

$$\frac{\partial x^p}{\partial \mathbf{x}^q} \frac{\partial \mathbf{x}^q}{\partial x^r} = \delta_r{}^p$$

4-7. Expand the following.

(a)
$$\delta_j{}^i a^j$$

(b)
$$\delta_{ij} x^i x^j$$

(c)
$$\delta_{ij} a_j$$

4-8. If a_i are three independent quantities, show that

$$\frac{\partial a_i}{\partial a_j} = \delta_i{}^j$$

4-9. Show that

(a)
$$\delta_j{}^i \delta_k{}^j = \delta_k{}^i$$

(b)
$$\delta_i{}^i = 3 \text{ for } n = 3$$

(c)
$$\delta_j{}^i \delta_i{}^j = 3 \text{ for } n = 3$$

(d)
$$a^j a_i \delta_j{}^i = a^i a_i \text{ or } a^j a_j$$

4-5. Suggested References

4-1. *Tensor Analysis: Theory and Applications,* I. S. Sokolnikoff, John Wiley and Sons, Inc.
4-2. *Vector and Tensor Analysis,* Harry Lass, McGraw-Hill Book Company.

Transformations

5-1. The Direction Cosines of Vectors

Consider the vector $\mathbf{P}$ as shown in Fig. 5-1. The angles $(\mathbf{P}, \mathbf{i}_1)$, $(\mathbf{P}, \mathbf{i}_2)$, and $(\mathbf{P}, \mathbf{i}_3)$ are called the direction angles of the vector $\mathbf{P}$.

In solid analytic geometry, the direction of a vector is conveniently given by the cosines of the direction angles, which are called the direction cosines of the vector.

Consider the two vectors $\mathbf{A}_1$ and $\mathbf{A}_2$ acting in the directions shown in Fig. 5-2. Since $\mathbf{A}_1$ and $\mathbf{A}_2$ do not pass through the origin, construct two unit vectors $\mathbf{a}_1$ and $\mathbf{a}_2$ radiating from the origin and parallel to $\mathbf{A}_1$ and $\mathbf{A}_2$. The direction cosines for these unit vectors are:

for $\mathbf{a}_1$, $\qquad \cos(\mathbf{a}_1, \mathbf{i}_1), \cos(\mathbf{a}_1, \mathbf{i}_2), \cos(\mathbf{a}_1, \mathbf{i}_3)$

for $\mathbf{a}_2$, $\qquad \cos(\mathbf{a}_2, \mathbf{i}_1), \cos(\mathbf{a}_2, \mathbf{i}_2), \cos(\mathbf{a}_2, \mathbf{i}_3)$

The projection of vectors $\mathbf{a}_1$ and $\mathbf{a}_2$ on the X^1, X^2, and X^3 axes are found by use of the scalar product. The scalar coefficients of the vector components of $\mathbf{a}_1$ and $\mathbf{a}_2$ are

$$\mathbf{a}_1 \cdot \mathbf{i}_1 = |\mathbf{a}_1| \, |\mathbf{i}_1| \cos(\mathbf{a}_1, \mathbf{i}_1) = 1(1) \cos(\mathbf{a}_1, \mathbf{i}_1) = \cos(\mathbf{a}_1, \mathbf{i}_1)$$
$$\mathbf{a}_1 \cdot \mathbf{i}_2 = \cos(\mathbf{a}_1, \mathbf{i}_2)$$
$$\mathbf{a}_1 \cdot \mathbf{i}_3 = \cos(\mathbf{a}_1, \mathbf{i}_3)$$

and

$$\mathbf{a}_2 \cdot \mathbf{i}_1 = |\mathbf{a}_2| \, |\mathbf{i}_1| \cos(\mathbf{a}_2, \mathbf{i}_1) = 1(1) \cos(\mathbf{a}_2, \mathbf{i}_1) = \cos(\mathbf{a}_2, \mathbf{i}_1)$$
$$\mathbf{a}_2 \cdot \mathbf{i}_2 = \cos(\mathbf{a}_2, \mathbf{i}_2)$$
$$\mathbf{a}_2 \cdot \mathbf{i}_3 = \cos(\mathbf{a}_2, \mathbf{i}_3)$$

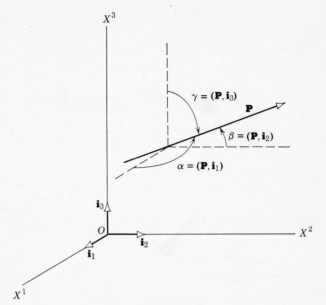

Fig. 5-1.

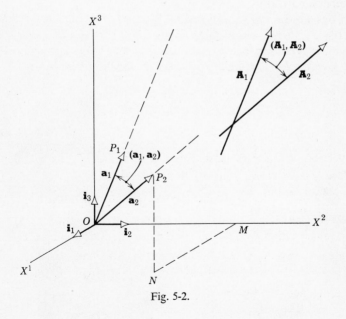

Fig. 5-2.

The vector components of $\mathbf{a}_1$ and $\mathbf{a}_2$ along the X^1, X^2, and X^3 axes may be formed by multiplying the scalar coefficients by the respective unit vectors; hence the vector components are:

for $\mathbf{a}_2$: $\cos(\mathbf{a}_2, \mathbf{i}_1)\mathbf{i}_1$, $\cos(\mathbf{a}_2, \mathbf{i}_2)\mathbf{i}_2$, $\cos(\mathbf{a}_2, \mathbf{i}_3)\mathbf{i}_3$

for $\mathbf{a}_1$: $\cos(\mathbf{a}_1, \mathbf{i}_1)\mathbf{i}_1$, $\cos(\mathbf{a}_1, \mathbf{i}_2)\mathbf{i}_2$, $\cos(\mathbf{a}_1, \mathbf{i}_3)\mathbf{i}_3$

The projection of vector $\mathbf{a}_2$ on $\mathbf{a}_1$ may be found by projecting the vector components of $\mathbf{a}_2$ along the X^1, X^2, and X^3 axes on $\mathbf{a}_1$ and

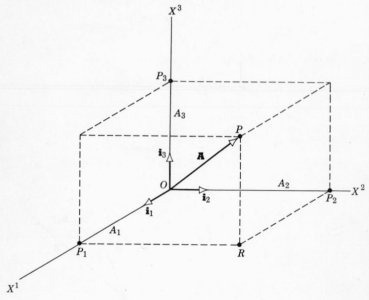

Fig. 5-3.

summing, or taking the scalar product of $\mathbf{a}_2$ and $\mathbf{a}_1$ directly. Hence the projection of $\mathbf{a}_2$ on $\mathbf{a}_1$ may be expressed as

$$\mathbf{a}_2 \cdot \mathbf{a}_1 = \cos(\mathbf{a}_2, \mathbf{i}_1)\mathbf{i}_1 \cdot \mathbf{a}_1 + \cos(\mathbf{a}_2, \mathbf{i}_2)\mathbf{i}_2 \cdot \mathbf{a}_1 + \cos(\mathbf{a}_2, \mathbf{i}_3)\mathbf{i}_3 \cdot \mathbf{a}_1$$

According to the commutative law for dot products, $\mathbf{i}_1 \cdot \mathbf{a}_1 = \mathbf{a}_1 \cdot \mathbf{i}_1$, etc. Substituting the previous results for the dot product gives

$$\mathbf{a}_2 \cdot \mathbf{a}_1 = \cos(\mathbf{a}_2, \mathbf{i}_1)\cos(\mathbf{a}_1, \mathbf{i}_1) + \cos(\mathbf{a}_2, \mathbf{i}_2)\cos(\mathbf{a}_1, \mathbf{i}_2)$$
$$+ \cos(\mathbf{a}_2, \mathbf{i}_3)\cos(\mathbf{a}_1, \mathbf{i}_3)$$

By the direct scalar product one obtains

$$\mathbf{a}_2 \cdot \mathbf{a}_1 = (1)(1)\cos(\mathbf{a}_2, \mathbf{a}_1) = \cos(\mathbf{a}_2, \mathbf{a}_1)$$

Consider the vector **A** having the components A_1, A_2, and A_3 as shown in Fig. 5-3. The magnitude of the vector **A** will be designated by $|A|$. The Cartesian rectangular components may be expressed as follows in terms of the direction cosines.

$$\cos (\mathbf{i}_1, \mathbf{A}) = \frac{A_1}{|A|} \quad \text{or} \quad A_1 = |A| \cos (\mathbf{i}_1, \mathbf{A})$$

$$\cos (\mathbf{i}_2, \mathbf{A}) = \frac{A_2}{|A|} \quad \text{or} \quad A_2 = |A| \cos (\mathbf{i}_2, \mathbf{A})$$

$$\cos (\mathbf{i}_3, \mathbf{A}) = \frac{A_3}{|A|} \quad \text{or} \quad A_3 = |A| \cos (\mathbf{i}_3, \mathbf{A})$$

According to the Pythagorean theorem,

$$(OP)^2 = |A|^2 = (OP_1)^2 + (OP_2)^2 + (OP_3)^2$$

or

$$|A|^2 = (A_1)^2 + (A_2)^2 + (A_3)^2$$

Substituting for A_1, A_2, and A_3 gives

$$|A|^2 = |A|^2 \cos^2 (\mathbf{i}_1, \mathbf{A}) + |A|^2 \cos^2 (\mathbf{i}_2, \mathbf{A}) + |A|^2 \cos^2 (\mathbf{i}_3, \mathbf{A})$$

Dividing through by $|A|^2$ gives

$$\cos^2 (\mathbf{i}_1, \mathbf{A}) + \cos^2 (\mathbf{i}_2, \mathbf{A}) + \cos^2 (\mathbf{i}_3, \mathbf{A}) = 1$$

which is the so-called normalization equation for direction cosines.

5-2. Transformations of Coordinates by Use of Direction Cosines

Now we consider the transformation of the coordinates of a point P from one Cartesian coordinate system to another.

$\dot{X}^1$, $\dot{X}^2$, $\dot{X}^3$ are new axes which are obtained by rotating the old axes X^1, X^2, X^3 as shown in Fig. 5-4.

The point P has coordinates of x^1, x^2, x^3 with respect to the X^1, X^2, and X^3 axes, and coordinates of $\dot{x}^1$, $\dot{x}^2$, and $\dot{x}^3$ along the $\dot{X}^1$, $\dot{X}^2$, and $\dot{X}^3$ axes.

The position vector **A** may be expressed by the relations

$$\mathbf{A} = x^1 \mathbf{i}_1 + x^2 \mathbf{i}_2 + x^3 \mathbf{i}_3 = \dot{x}^1 \dot{\mathbf{i}}_1 + \dot{x}^2 \dot{\mathbf{i}}_2 + \dot{x}^3 \dot{\mathbf{i}}_3$$

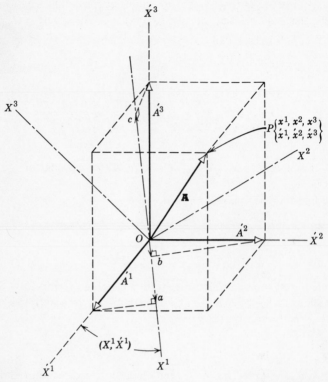

Fig. 5-4. Oa = component of $\overset{'}{A}{}^1$ or $\overset{'}{x}{}^1$ along the X^1 axis; Ob = component of $\overset{'}{A}{}^2$ or $\overset{'}{x}{}^2$ along the X^1 axis; Oc = component of $\overset{'}{A}{}^3$ or $\overset{'}{x}{}^3$ along the X^1 axis.

The component along X^1 of the position vector $\mathbf{A}$ in terms of the components in the $\overset{'}{X}{}^1$, $\overset{'}{X}{}^2$, and $\overset{'}{X}{}^3$ frame is

$$\mathbf{A} \cdot \mathbf{i}_1 = x^1 = \overset{'}{x}{}^1 \overset{'}{\mathbf{i}}_1 \cdot \mathbf{i}_1 + \overset{'}{x}{}^2 \overset{'}{\mathbf{i}}_2 \cdot \mathbf{i}_1 + \overset{'}{x}{}^3 \overset{'}{\mathbf{i}}_3 \cdot \mathbf{i}_1$$

However,

$$\overset{'}{\mathbf{i}}_1 \cdot \mathbf{i}_1 = (1)\,(1) \cos (\overset{'}{\mathbf{i}}_1, \mathbf{i}_1) = (1)\,(1) \cos (\mathbf{i}_1, \overset{'}{\mathbf{i}}_1),\ \text{etc.}$$

Hence

$$x^1 = \overset{'}{x}{}^1 \cos (\mathbf{i}_1, \overset{'}{\mathbf{i}}_1) + \overset{'}{x}{}^2 \cos (\mathbf{i}_1, \overset{'}{\mathbf{i}}_2) + \overset{'}{x}{}^3 \cos (\mathbf{i}_1 \cdot \overset{'}{\mathbf{i}}_3)$$

In a similar manner the x^2 and x^3 components may be established:

$$x^2 = \overset{'}{x}{}^1 \cos (\mathbf{i}_2, \overset{'}{\mathbf{i}}_1) + \overset{'}{x}{}^2 \cos (\mathbf{i}_2, \overset{'}{\mathbf{i}}_2) + \overset{'}{x}{}^3 \cos (\mathbf{i}_2, \overset{'}{\mathbf{i}}_3)$$

$$x^3 = \overset{'}{x}{}^1 \cos (\mathbf{i}_3, \overset{'}{\mathbf{i}}_1) + \overset{'}{x}{}^2 \cos (\mathbf{i}_3, \overset{'}{\mathbf{i}}_2) + \overset{'}{x}{}^3 \cos (\mathbf{i}_3, \overset{'}{\mathbf{i}}_3)$$

These three equations represent the transformation equations between the two Cartesian coordinate systems. The cosines in these equations form the elements of a three-by-three coefficient matrix as shown below.

$$
\begin{array}{cccc}
 & \overset{'}{x}^1 & \overset{'}{x}^2 & \overset{'}{x}^3 \\
x^1 & \begin{pmatrix} \cos(\mathbf{i}_1, \overset{'}{\mathbf{i}}_1) & \cos(\mathbf{i}_1, \overset{'}{\mathbf{i}}_2) & \cos(\mathbf{i}_1, \overset{'}{\mathbf{i}}_3) \\ \end{pmatrix} \\
x^2 & \begin{pmatrix} \cos(\mathbf{i}_2, \overset{'}{\mathbf{i}}_1) & \cos(\mathbf{i}_2, \overset{'}{\mathbf{i}}_2) & \cos(\mathbf{i}_2, \overset{'}{\mathbf{i}}_3) \end{pmatrix} \\
x^3 & \begin{pmatrix} \cos(\mathbf{i}_3, \overset{'}{\mathbf{i}}_1) & \cos(\mathbf{i}_3, \overset{'}{\mathbf{i}}_2) & \cos(\mathbf{i}_3, \overset{'}{\mathbf{i}}_3) \end{pmatrix}
\end{array}
$$

Let a_{11} represent $\cos(\mathbf{i}_1, \overset{'}{\mathbf{i}}_1)$, etc. The matrix above becomes

$$
\begin{array}{cccc}
 & \overset{'}{x}^1 & \overset{'}{x}^2 & \overset{'}{x}^3 \\
x^1 & \begin{pmatrix} a_{11} & a_{12} & a_{13} \\ \end{pmatrix} \\
x^2 & \begin{pmatrix} a_{21} & a_{22} & a_{23} \end{pmatrix} \\
x^3 & \begin{pmatrix} a_{31} & a_{32} & a_{33} \end{pmatrix}
\end{array}
$$

Utilizing the summation convention and letting a_{ij} represent the direction cosines, the preceding equations for x^1, x^2, and x^3 may all be expressed by the equation

$$ x^i = a_{ij} \overset{'}{x}^j $$

Let $i = 1$; then

$$ x^1 = a_{1j} \overset{'}{x}^j = a_{11} \overset{'}{x}^1 + a_{12} \overset{'}{x}^2 + a_{13} \overset{'}{x}^3 $$

which is the first transformation equation. We found earlier that

$$ \cos^2(\mathbf{i}_1, \mathbf{a}) + \cos^2(\mathbf{i}_2, \mathbf{a}) + \cos^2(\mathbf{i}_3, \mathbf{a}) = 1 $$

for any vector $\mathbf{a}$. In particular, the relation holds for the three vectors whose lengths are x^1, x^2, and x^3, respectively, and also for the three vectors whose lengths are $\overset{'}{x}^1$, $\overset{'}{x}^2$, $\overset{'}{x}^3$. Therefore

$$
\begin{array}{ll}
a_{11}{}^2 + a_{12}{}^2 + a_{13}{}^2 = 1 & a_{11}{}^2 + a_{21}{}^2 + a_{31}{}^2 = 1 \\
a_{21}{}^2 + a_{22}{}^2 + a_{23}{}^2 = 1 & a_{12}{}^2 + a_{22}{}^2 + a_{32}{}^2 = 1 \qquad (5\text{-}1) \\
a_{31}{}^2 + a_{32}{}^2 + a_{33}{}^2 = 1 & a_{13}{}^2 + a_{23}{}^2 + a_{33}{}^2 = 1
\end{array}
$$

These relations will also be established in another manner.

The origin remains fixed and the terminal point of the vector $\mathbf{A}$ is unaltered by the axes selected. For one set of coordinate axes the coordinates for point P are x^1, x^2, and x^3; for the other, $\overset{'}{x}^1$, $\overset{'}{x}^2$, $\overset{'}{x}^3$.

The length of the vector **A** remains the same for the two sets of coordinate axes; hence

$$|\mathbf{x}|^2 = x^i x^i$$

$$|\mathbf{x'}|^2 = x'^i x'^i$$

However, $|\mathbf{x}| = |\mathbf{x'}|$; therefore

$$x^i x^i = x'^i x'^i \tag{5-2}$$

The transformation relation between x^i and x'^i was given earlier as follows:

$$x^i = a_{ij} x'^j \quad \text{with the restriction that} \quad |a_{ij}| \neq 0 \tag{5-3}$$

Inserting in equation (5-2) values from equation (5-3) and changing one set of dummy indices gives

$$(a_{ij} x'^j)(a_{ik} x'^k) = x'^i x'^i \qquad (i, j, k = 1, 2, 3)$$

or

$$a_{ij} a_{ik} x'^j x'^k = x'^i x'^i$$

Another relation may be found by interchanging the dummy indices j and k; thus

$$a_{ik} a_{ij} x'^k x'^j = x'^i x'^i$$

Equating shows that

$$a_{ij} a_{ik} = a_{ik} a_{ij}$$

The relation is symmetric in j and k since the order is immaterial to the result.

We may also write the equation

$$\delta_{jk} x'^j x'^k = x'^i x'^i$$

Comparing this expression with the one above for $x'^i x'^i$, we see that

$$a_{ij} a_{ik} x'^j x'^k = \delta_{jk} x'^j x'^k$$

or

$$(a_{ij} a_{ik} - \delta_{jk}) x'^j x'^k = 0$$

Since x'^i is an arbitrary vector, the last expression can be true if and only if the coefficient of the term $x'^j x'^k$ plus the coefficient of the term $x'^k x'^j$ add to zero; that is,

$$(a_{ij} a_{ik} + a_{ik} a_{ij}) - (\delta_{jk} + \delta_{kj}) = 0$$

Since symmetry in j and k exists, the last result may be written

$$2 a_{ij} a_{ik} = 2 \delta_{jk} \quad \text{or} \quad a_{ij} a_{ik} = \delta_{jk} \tag{5-4}$$

This is based on the fact that the length of a vector remains the same in the given transformation from one set of axes to another.

Only if $j = k$ will $\delta_{jk} = 1$; therefore, for $j = 1$ and $i = 1, 2, 3$, we obtain

$$a_{11}^2 + a_{21}^2 + a_{31}^2 = 1$$

for $j = 2$ and $i = 1, 2, 3$,

$$a_{12}^2 + a_{22}^2 + a_{32}^2 = 1$$

for $j = 3$ and $i = 1, 2, 3$,

$$a_{13}^2 + a_{23}^2 + a_{33}^2 = 1$$

If we repeat the previous derivation using the inverse transformation

$$x^{'i} = a_{ji}x^j$$

we obtain

$$a_{ij}a_{kj} = \delta_{ik}$$

The last result gives: for $i = 1$ and $j = 1, 2, 3$,

$$a_{11}^2 + a_{12}^2 + a_{13}^2 = 1$$

for $i = 2$ and $j = 1, 2, 3$,

$$a_{21}^2 + a_{22}^2 + a_{23}^2 = 1$$

for $i = 3$ and $j = 1, 2, 3$,

$$a_{31}^2 + a_{32}^2 + a_{33}^2 = 1$$

This shows that the sum of the squares of each of the elements in a row or column of the (a_{ij}) array is equal to unity.

If $j \neq k$, then $\delta_{jk} = 0$, and

$$a_{ij}a_{ik} = 0$$

For $j = 1$ and $k = 2$,

$$a_{i1}a_{i2} = a_{11}a_{12} + a_{21}a_{22} + a_{31}a_{32} = 0$$

For $j = 1$ and $k = 3$,

$$a_{i1}a_{i3} = a_{11}a_{13} + a_{21}a_{23} + a_{31}a_{33} = 0$$

For $j = 2$ and $k = 1$,

$$a_{i2}a_{i1} = a_{12}a_{11} + a_{22}a_{21} + a_{32}a_{31} = 0$$

For $j = 2$ and $k = 3$,

$$a_{i2}a_{i3} = a_{12}a_{13} + a_{22}a_{23} + a_{32}a_{33} = 0$$

(5-5)

In summary,

$$
\left.
\begin{aligned}
{a_{11}}^2 + {a_{21}}^2 + {a_{31}}^2 &= 1 \\
{a_{12}}^2 + {a_{22}}^2 + {a_{32}}^2 &= 1 \\
{a_{13}}^2 + {a_{23}}^2 + {a_{33}}^2 &= 1
\end{aligned}
\right\}
\qquad (5\text{-}1)
$$

$$
\left.
\begin{aligned}
a_{12}a_{13} + a_{22}a_{23} + a_{32}a_{33} &= 0 \\
a_{13}a_{11} + a_{23}a_{21} + a_{33}a_{31} &= 0 \\
a_{11}a_{12} + a_{21}a_{22} + a_{31}a_{32} &= 0
\end{aligned}
\right\}
\qquad (5\text{-}5)
$$

5-3. Transformations by Use of the Scalar Product

The transformation of the components of a vector from Cartesian coordinates into the components in cylindrical coordinates will be considered to illustrate what is meant by a transformation of a vector from one coordinate system to another.

Consider the position vector $\mathbf{A}$ shown in Fig. 5-5 which in Cartesian coordinates may be expressed as

$$\mathbf{A} = A_x \mathbf{i}_x + A_y \mathbf{i}_y + A_z \mathbf{i}_z$$

Here A_x, A_y, and A_z are the components of $\mathbf{A}$ along the X, Y, and Z axes.

The same vector referred to a cylindrical coordinate system will have the form

$$\mathbf{A} = A_r \mathbf{e}_r + A_\theta \mathbf{e}_\theta + A_z \mathbf{e}_z$$

The following relationships are evident from Fig. 5-5.

$$x = r \cos \theta, \quad y = r \sin \theta$$
$$z = z$$

There is no change in the variable z and the unit vectors $\mathbf{i}_z$ and $\mathbf{e}_z$ are the same for both coordinate systems.

The components A_r, A_θ, A_z may be obtained by taking the dot product of the vector and a unit vector in the direction desired, as this gives the component in that direction. Hence

$$
\begin{aligned}
A_r = \mathbf{A} \cdot \mathbf{e}_r &= (A_x \mathbf{i}_x + A_y \mathbf{i}_y + A_z \mathbf{i}_z) \cdot \mathbf{e}_r \\
&= A_x \mathbf{i}_x \cdot \mathbf{e}_r + A_y \mathbf{i}_y \cdot \mathbf{e}_r + A_z \mathbf{i}_z \cdot \mathbf{e}_r \\
A_\theta = \mathbf{A} \cdot \mathbf{e}_\theta &= A_x \mathbf{i}_x \cdot \mathbf{e}_\theta + A_y \mathbf{i}_y \cdot \mathbf{e}_\theta + A_z \mathbf{i}_z \cdot \mathbf{e}_\theta
\end{aligned}
$$

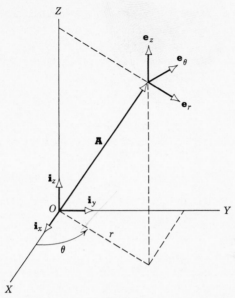

Fig. 5-5.

Since we are dealing with unit vectors, the scalar product may be expressed as

$$\mathbf{i}_x \cdot \mathbf{e}_r = |1|\,|1| \cos \alpha_{(x,r)}$$

Values for the scalar products are

$$\mathbf{i}_x \cdot \mathbf{e}_r = \cos \theta$$
$$\mathbf{i}_y \cdot \mathbf{e}_r = \sin \theta$$
$$\mathbf{i}_z \cdot \mathbf{e}_r = \cos 90^\circ = 0$$
$$\mathbf{i}_x \cdot \mathbf{e}_\theta = -\sin \theta$$
$$\mathbf{i}_y \cdot \mathbf{e}_\theta = \cos \theta$$
$$\mathbf{i}_z \cdot \mathbf{e}_\theta = \cos 90^\circ = 0$$

Substituting gives the expressions for A_r and A_θ.

$$A_r = A_x \cos \theta + A_y \sin \theta + A_z 0$$
$$A_\theta = -A_x \sin \theta + A_y \cos \theta + A_z 0$$

The final expression for the vector $\mathbf{A}$ in cylindrical coordinates is

$$\mathbf{A} = (A_x \cos \theta + A_y \sin \theta)\mathbf{e}_r + (-A_x \sin \theta + A_y \cos \theta)\mathbf{e}_\theta + A_z\mathbf{e}_z$$

In a similar manner expressions can be developed for transforming from Cartesian coordinates to spherical coordinates or vice versa. Relations pertaining to a change of variable and a change of components for Cartesian and cylindrical coordinates are presented in Table 5-1. Similar information regarding Cartesian and spherical coordinates is included in Table 5-2. An example will show the use of these tables.

TABLE 5-1

Relations between the Variables and Vector components of the Cartesian and Cylindrical Coordinate Systems

Change of Variable		Change of Component	
Cartesian to Cylindrical	Cylindrical to Cartesian	Cartesian to Cylindrical	Cylindrical to Cartesian
$x = r \cos \theta$	$r = \sqrt{x^2 + y^2}$	$A_r = A_x \cos \theta + A_y \sin \theta$	$A_x = A_r \dfrac{x}{\sqrt{x^2 + y^2}} - A_\theta \dfrac{y}{\sqrt{x^2 + y^2}}$
$y = r \sin \theta$	$\theta = \tan^{-1} \dfrac{y}{x}$	$A_\theta = -A_x \sin \theta + A_y \cos \theta$	$A_y = A_r \dfrac{y}{\sqrt{x^2 + y^2}} + A_\theta \dfrac{x}{\sqrt{x^2 + y^2}}$
$z = z$	$z = z$	$A_z = A_z$	$A_z = A_z$

Example 5-1

Transform the following vector from cylindrical coordinates to Cartesian coordinates.

$$\mathbf{A} = r \cos \theta \mathbf{e}_r - r \sin \theta \mathbf{e}_\theta = A_r \mathbf{e}_r - A_\theta \mathbf{e}_\theta$$

Values for the coordinates r and θ in terms of x, y, and z may be found by referring to Table 5-1. Thus

$$A_r = r \cos \theta = \sqrt{x^2 + y^2} \frac{x}{\sqrt{x^2 + y^2}} = x$$

$$-A_\theta = -r \sin \theta = \sqrt{x^2 + y^2} \frac{-y}{\sqrt{x^2 + y^2}} = -y$$

The general form of the vector in Cartesian coordinates is

$$\mathbf{A} = A_x \mathbf{i}_x + A_y \mathbf{i}_y$$

TABLE 5-2

Equations between the Variables and Vector Components of the Cartesian and Spherical Coordinate Systems

	Change of Variable		Change of Component	
Cartesian to Spherical		Spherical to Cartesian	Cartesian to Spherical	Spherical to Cartesian
$x = r \sin\phi \cos\theta$		$r = \sqrt{x^2 + y^2 + z^2}$	$A_r = A_x \sin\phi\cos\theta + A_y \sin\phi \sin\theta + A_z \cos\phi$	$A_x = \dfrac{A_r x}{\sqrt{x^2 + y^2 + z^2}} + \dfrac{A_\phi xz}{\sqrt{(x^2 + y^2)(x^2 + y^2 + z^2)}} - \dfrac{A_\theta y}{\sqrt{x^2 + y^2}}$
$y = r \sin\phi \sin\theta$		$\phi = \cos^{-1}\dfrac{z}{\sqrt{x^2 + y^2 + z^2}}$	$A_\phi = A_x \cos\phi\cos\theta + A_y \cos\phi \sin\theta - A_z \sin\phi$	$A_y = \dfrac{A_r y}{\sqrt{x^2 + y^2 + z^2}} + \dfrac{A_\phi yz}{\sqrt{(x^2 + y^2)(x^2 + y^2 + z^2)}} + \dfrac{A_\theta x}{\sqrt{x^2 + y^2}}$
$z = r \cos\phi$		$\theta = \tan^{-1}\dfrac{y}{x}$	$A_\theta = -A_x \sin\theta + A_y \cos\theta$	$A_z = \dfrac{A_r z}{\sqrt{x^2 + y^2 + z^2}} - \dfrac{A_\phi \sqrt{x^2 + y^2}}{\sqrt{x^2 + y^2 + z^2}}$

Values for A_x and A_y are given in the same table. Substituting give

$$\mathbf{A} = \left(A_r \frac{x}{\sqrt{x^2+y^2}} - A_\theta \frac{y}{\sqrt{x^2+y^2}}\right)\mathbf{i}_x$$
$$+ \left(A_r \frac{y}{\sqrt{x^2+y^2}} + A_\theta \frac{x}{\sqrt{x^2+y^2}}\right)\mathbf{i}_y$$

Substituting for A_r and A_θ gives

$$\mathbf{A} = \left(\frac{x^2}{\sqrt{x^2+y^2}} + \frac{y^2}{\sqrt{x^2+y^2}}\right)\mathbf{i}_x + \left(\frac{xy}{\sqrt{x^2+y^2}} - \frac{yx}{\sqrt{x^2+y^2}}\right)\mathbf{i}_y$$
$$\mathbf{A} = \sqrt{x^2+y^2}\,\mathbf{i}_x$$

5-4. Linear Transformations and Matrices

Consider a set of equations such as

$$y_1 = a_{11}x_1 + a_{12}x_2 + \cdots + a_{1(n)}x_{(n)}$$
$$y_2 = a_{21}x_1 + a_{22}x_2 + \cdots + a_{2(n)}x_{(n)}$$
$$\cdots \cdots \cdots \cdots \cdots \cdots \cdots$$
$$\cdots \cdots \cdots \cdots \cdots \cdots \cdots$$
$$y_n = a_{n1}x_1 + a_{n2}x_2 + \cdots + a_{n(n)}x_{(n)}$$

By means of these relations n numbers $(x_1, x_2, \ldots, x_n)$ may be transformed into n new numbers $(y_1, y_2, \ldots, y_n)$. These relations may be placed in matrix form as follows.

$$Y = AX$$

where

$$Y = \begin{pmatrix} y_1 \\ y_2 \\ \cdot \\ \cdot \\ \cdot \\ y_n \end{pmatrix}, \quad X = \begin{pmatrix} x_1 \\ x_2 \\ \cdot \\ \cdot \\ \cdot \\ x_n \end{pmatrix}, \quad A = \begin{pmatrix} a_{11} & a_{12} & \cdots & a_{1n} \\ a_{21} & a_{22} & \cdots & a_{2n} \\ \cdots & \cdots & \cdots & \cdots \\ \cdots & \cdots & \cdots & \cdots \\ \cdots & \cdots & \cdots & \cdots \\ a_{n1} & a_{n2} & \cdots & a_{nn} \end{pmatrix}$$

Example 5-2

Transform the points $P(1, 1, 1)$ to the new point Q for the system

$$y_1 = 4x_1 - 3x_2 + 2x_3$$
$$y_2 = -2x_1 + 7x_2 + 2x_3$$
$$y_3 = 5x_1 + 2x_2 - x_3$$

The transform for this system is

$$Y = \begin{pmatrix} 4 & -3 & 2 \\ -2 & 7 & 2 \\ 5 & 2 & -1 \end{pmatrix} X$$

For point $P(1, 1, 1)$ the transform is

$$Y = \begin{pmatrix} 4 & -3 & 2 \\ -2 & 7 & 2 \\ 5 & 2 & -1 \end{pmatrix} \begin{pmatrix} 1 \\ 1 \\ 1 \end{pmatrix} = \begin{pmatrix} (4 & -3 & +2) \\ (-2 & +7 & +2) \\ (5 & +2 & -1) \end{pmatrix} = \begin{pmatrix} 3 \\ 7 \\ 6 \end{pmatrix}$$

The transform of $P(1, 1, 1)$ is a new point $Q(3, 7, 6)$. By this procedure point P may be transformed to a new point Q.

5-5. Curvilinear Coordinate Transformations

The advantage of describing relations among geometrical and physical quantities in terms of generalized tensor equations is that these relations are true for all coordinate systems. When it is necessary to consider numerical computations in regard to the solution of problems, it is also necessary to translate vector and generalized tensor equations into specific coordinate systems. For example, in the study of the flow of heat through a spherical shell it is convenient to use spherical coordinates. Cartesian, cylindrical, spherical, ellipsoidal, and bipolar coordinate systems are examples of special cases of curvilinear coordinate systems. If the curvilinear axes are at right angles, the system is called an orthogonal curvilinear system.

A given space V will be referred to the orthogonal Cartesian axes Y_i. The coordinates of any point P in our space V are represented by (y_1, y_2, y_3) as shown in Fig. 5-6. A set of relations connecting the variables (y_1, y_2, y_3) with a new set (x_1, x_2, x_3) are known as equations of transformation of coordinates. Hence

$$x_1 = x_1(y_1, y_2, y_3)$$
$$x_2 = x_2(y_1, y_2, y_3) \tag{5-6}$$
$$x_3 = x_3(y_1, y_2, y_3)$$

These equations are assumed to be single-valued and continuously differentiable at all points throughout space V. It is also assumed

Multilinear Analysis

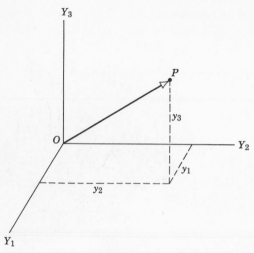

Fig. 5-6.

that these equations can be solved to yield the inverse transformation equations in which the functions are single-valued and continuously differentiable with respect to x_i. The equations are

$$y_1 = y_1(x_1, x_2, x_3)$$
$$y_2 = y_2(x_1, x_2, x_3)$$
$$y_3 = y_3(x_1, x_2, x_3)$$

In equations (5-6) let $x_1 = C_1$, $x_2 = C_2$, $x_3 = C_3$, where C_1, C_2, and C_3 are constants. These equations are

$$x_1(y_1, y_2, y_3) = C_1$$
$$x_2(y_1, y_2, y_3) = C_2$$
$$x_3(y_1, y_2, y_3) = C_3$$

and they represent three surfaces S_1, S_2, and S_3 as shown in Fig. 5-7. The surfaces intersect at point P whose Cartesian coordinates are (y_1, y_2, y_3). The surfaces are called coordinate surfaces and their intersections two at a time form coordinate lines or curves X_1, X_2, X_3. Hence the line of intersection of $X_2 = C_2$ and $X_3 = C_3$ is the coordinate line X_1, that is, a curve along which only x_1 varies. The values x_1, x_2, x_3 which correspond to the point $P(y_1, y_2, y_3)$ will be defined as the curvilinear coordinates of P. The equations $x_i = x_i(y_1, y_2, y_3)$, etc., represent a curvilinear coordinate system x_1, x_2, x_3.

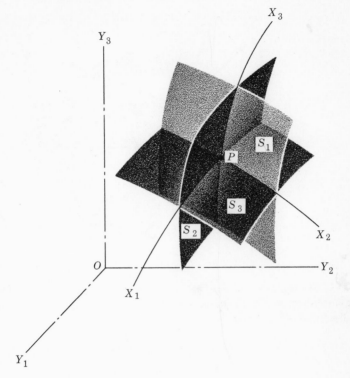

Fig. 5-7.

If the equations reduce to

$$y_1 = x_1$$
$$y_2 = x_2$$
$$y_3 = x_3$$

the coordinate surfaces are planes and their intersections two at a time are straight lines parallel to the coordinate axes.

If the equations are

$$y_1 = r \cos \theta$$
$$y_2 = r \sin \theta$$
$$y_3 = z$$

the system is recognized as a curvilinear system r, θ, z which is called a cylindrical coordinate system such as that shown in Fig. 5-8.

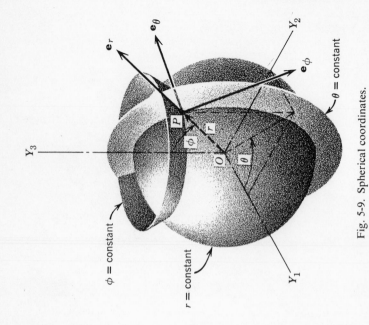

Fig. 5-9. Spherical coordinates.

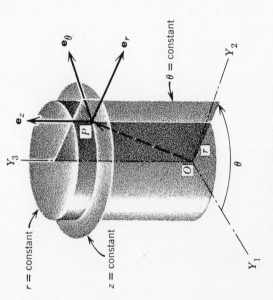

Fig. 5-8. Cylindrical coordinates.

A system having the relations

$$y_1 = r \sin \phi \cos \theta$$
$$y_2 = r \sin \phi \sin \theta$$
$$y_3 = r \cos \phi$$

is the curvilinear system known as the spherical coordinate system. This system is shown in Fig. 5-9.

Consider a system of general curvilinear coordinates Z_1, Z_2, Z_3. These axes may be represented by the symbol Z_s where $s = 1$, 2, and 3. It is desired to express these values in terms of a new coordinate system X_r.

The x and the z coordinates are related by the equations

$$x_1 = x_1(z_1, z_2, z_3)$$
$$x_2 = x_2(z_1, z_2, z_3)$$
$$x_3 = x_3(z_1, z_2, z_3)$$

The coordinates x_1, x_2, and x_3 are mutually independent.

Differentiating these equations gives the following important transformation equations for the differentials of the coordinates.

$$dx_1 = \frac{\partial x_1}{\partial z_1} dz_1 + \frac{\partial x_1}{\partial z_2} dz_2 + \frac{\partial x_1}{\partial z_3} dz_3$$

$$dx_2 = \frac{\partial x_2}{\partial z_1} dz_1 + \frac{\partial x_2}{\partial z_2} dz_2 + \frac{\partial x_2}{\partial z_3} dz_3$$

$$dx_3 = \frac{\partial x_3}{\partial z_1} dz_1 + \frac{\partial x_3}{\partial z_2} dz_2 + \frac{\partial x_3}{\partial z_3} dz_3$$

The Jacobian for these relations is defined as follows.

$$J = \begin{vmatrix} \dfrac{\partial x_1}{\partial z_1} & \dfrac{\partial x_1}{\partial z_2} & \dfrac{\partial x_1}{\partial z_3} \\[2mm] \dfrac{\partial x_2}{\partial z_1} & \dfrac{\partial x_2}{\partial z_2} & \dfrac{\partial x_2}{\partial z_3} \\[2mm] \dfrac{\partial x_3}{\partial z_1} & \dfrac{\partial x_3}{\partial z_2} & \dfrac{\partial x_3}{\partial z_3} \end{vmatrix} = \begin{vmatrix} \dfrac{\partial x_r}{\partial z_s} \end{vmatrix} \tag{5-7}$$

The ranges for r and s are both 3.

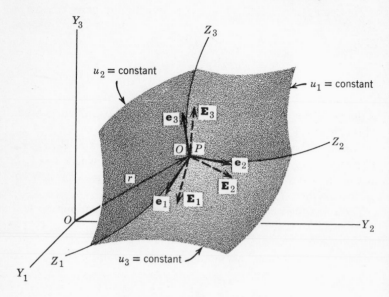

Fig. 5-10. Curvilinear coordinates.

The Jacobian cannot vanish identically, since we have assumed the independence of z_1, z_2, z_3. The equations

$$x_r = x_r(z_1, z_2, z_3)$$

may be inverted to give

$$z_s = z_s(x_1, x_2, x_3)$$

Taking the derivative of the expression results in

$$dx_r = \sum_{s=1}^{3} \frac{\partial x_r}{\partial z_s} dz_s \qquad (r = 1, 2, 3)$$

Employing our short-hand summation convention gives

$$dx_r = \frac{\partial x_r}{\partial z_s} dz_s \qquad (5\text{-}8)$$

The suffix s implies the summation and eliminates the necessity for writing the summation sign.

Consider the rectangular Cartesian coordinate system Y_1, Y_2, Y_3 and the general curvilinear system Z_1, Z_2, Z_3 as shown in Fig. 5-10.

The rectangular coordinates (y_1, y_2, y_3) for the point P may be expressed as functions of z_1, z_2, z_3 in the curvilinear coordinates as follows.

$$y_1 = y_1(z_1, z_2, z_3)$$
$$y_2 = y_2(z_1, z_2, z_3)$$
$$y_3 = y_3(z_1, z_2, z_3)$$

Solving for $z_1, z_2,$ and z_3 in terms of y_1, y_2, y_3 gives

$$z_1 = z_1(y_1, y_2, y_3)$$
$$z_2 = z_2(y_1, y_2, y_3)$$
$$z_3 = z_3(y_1, y_2, y_3)$$

These functions must all be single-valued and must have continuous derivatives so that a unique correspondence exists between y_1, y_2, y_3 and z_1, z_2, z_3.

The position vector $\mathbf{r}$ for point P in Cartesian coordinates is

$$\mathbf{r} = y_1\mathbf{i} + y_2\mathbf{j} + y_3\mathbf{k}$$

This could be written

$$\mathbf{r} = \mathbf{r}(z_1, z_2, z_3)$$

expressed in terms of curvilinear coordinates. A unit vector tangent to the Z_1 curve at P is given by

$$\mathbf{e}_1 = \frac{\partial \mathbf{r}/\partial z_1}{|\partial \mathbf{r}/\partial z_1|} \tag{5-9}$$

Let h_1 represent $|\partial \mathbf{r}/\partial z_1|$; then

$$h_1\mathbf{e}_1 = \frac{\partial \mathbf{r}}{\partial z_1} \tag{5-10}$$

The term h_1 is called a scale factor. In a similar manner values for $h_2\mathbf{e}_2$ and $h_3\mathbf{e}_3$ may be obtained. These unit vectors are so oriented as to be in the direction of increasing values of $z_1, z_2,$ and z_3.

The relation

$$\nabla z_1 = \frac{\partial z_1}{\partial y_1}\mathbf{i} + \frac{\partial z_1}{\partial y_2}\mathbf{j} + \frac{\partial z_1}{\partial y_3}\mathbf{k} \tag{5-11}$$

represents a vector at P normal to the surface $z_1 = c_1$. A unit vector in the same direction is

$$\mathbf{E}_1 = \frac{\nabla z_1}{|\nabla z_1|} \tag{5-12}$$

In a similar manner the unit vectors $\mathbf{E}_2$ and $\mathbf{E}_3$ may be written. At each point P there are two sets of unit vectors, one tangent to the coordinate curves and the other normal to the coordinate surfaces. These two sets of unit vectors are identical if the curvilinear coordinate system is orthogonal.

The vector $\mathbf{r}$ may be represented in terms of the unit base vectors $\mathbf{e}_1, \mathbf{e}_2, \mathbf{e}_3$ or $\mathbf{E}_1, \mathbf{E}_2, \mathbf{E}_3$ as follows.

$$\mathbf{r} = r_1\mathbf{e}_1 + r_2\mathbf{e}_2 + r_3\mathbf{e}_3 = R_1\mathbf{E}_1 + R_2\mathbf{E}_2 + R_3\mathbf{E}_3$$

Here r_1, r_2, r_3 and R_1, R_2, R_3 are the respective components in each system.

The vector $\mathbf{r}$ may also be referred to the base vectors

$$\partial\mathbf{r}/\partial z_1, \; \partial\mathbf{r}/\partial z_2, \; \partial\mathbf{r}/\partial z_3 \quad \text{or} \quad \nabla z_1, \; \nabla z_2, \; \nabla z_3$$

These, in general, are not unit vectors. We may write the expression for $\mathbf{r}$ as

$$\mathbf{r} = C^1 \frac{\partial\mathbf{r}}{\partial z_1} + C^2 \frac{\partial\mathbf{r}}{\partial z_2} + C^3 \frac{\partial\mathbf{r}}{\partial z_3} \tag{5-13}$$

The components C^1, C^2, C^3 are the contravariant components. Also

$$\mathbf{r} = C_1\nabla z_1 + C_2\nabla z_2 + C_3\nabla z_3 \tag{5-14}$$

Here C_1, C_2, C_3 are the covariant components.

From the relation $\mathbf{r} = \mathbf{r}(z_1, z_2, z_3)$ we may write

$$d\mathbf{r} = \frac{\partial\mathbf{r}}{\partial z_1} dz_1 + \frac{\partial\mathbf{r}}{\partial z_2} dz_2 + \frac{\partial\mathbf{r}}{\partial z_3} dz_3$$

But $\partial\mathbf{r}/\partial z_1 = h_1\mathbf{e}_1$, etc.; hence

$$d\mathbf{r} = h_1 \, dz_1\mathbf{e}_1 + h_2 \, dz_2\mathbf{e}_2 + h_3 \, dz_3\mathbf{e}_3$$

The differential arc length is

$$ds^2 = d\mathbf{r} \cdot d\mathbf{r} \tag{5-15}$$

For an orthogonal system $\mathbf{e}_1 \cdot \mathbf{e}_2 = \mathbf{e}_2 \cdot \mathbf{e}_3 = \mathbf{e}_3 \cdot \mathbf{e}_1 = 0$. Hence

$$ds^2 = (h_1 \, dz_1)^2 + (h_2 \, dz_2)^2 + (h_3 \, dz_3)^2 \tag{5-16}$$

For non-orthogonal systems the expression is more complicated and its presentation will be delayed until we discuss tensors.

Example 5-3

Transform the vector $\mathbf{A} = 2y_3\mathbf{i} + 3y_1\mathbf{j} + 5\mathbf{k}$ to cylindrical coordinates.

For cylindrical coordinates (r, θ, z) the relations between y_1, y_2, y_3 and r, θ, z are

$$y_1 = r \cos \theta$$

$$y_2 = r \sin \theta$$

$$y_3 = z$$

Substituting gives the expression for the position vector in cylindrical coordinates for any point P.

$$\mathbf{r} = r \cos \theta \mathbf{i} + r \sin \theta \mathbf{j} + z\mathbf{k}$$

Now

$$\mathbf{e}_1 = \mathbf{e}_r = \frac{\partial \mathbf{r}/\partial r}{|\partial \mathbf{r}/\partial r|} = \frac{\cos \theta \mathbf{i} + \sin \theta \mathbf{j}}{\sqrt{\cos^2 \theta + \sin^2 \theta}} = \cos \theta \mathbf{i} + \sin \theta \mathbf{j}$$

$$\mathbf{e}_2 = \mathbf{e}_\theta = \frac{\partial \mathbf{r}/\partial \theta}{|\partial \mathbf{r}/\partial \theta|} = \frac{-r \sin \theta \mathbf{i} + r \cos \theta \mathbf{j}}{r\sqrt{\cos^2 \theta + \sin^2 \theta}} = -\sin \theta \mathbf{i} + \cos \theta \mathbf{j}$$

$$\mathbf{e}_3 = \mathbf{e}_z = \frac{\partial \mathbf{r}/\partial z}{|\partial \mathbf{r}/\partial z|} = \frac{\mathbf{k}}{1} = \mathbf{k}$$

Solving for $\mathbf{i}$ and $\mathbf{j}$ gives

$$\mathbf{i} = \cos \theta \mathbf{e}_r - \sin \theta \mathbf{e}_\theta$$

$$\mathbf{j} = \sin \theta \mathbf{e}_r + \cos \theta \mathbf{e}_\theta$$

Substituting results in

$$\mathbf{A} = (2z \cos \theta + 3r \cos \theta \sin \theta)\mathbf{e}_r + 3r \cos^2 \theta \mathbf{e}_\theta + 5\mathbf{e}_z$$

5-6. Problems

5-1. Transform the vector $\mathbf{A} = x\mathbf{i} + y\mathbf{j} + z\mathbf{k}$ into cylindrical coordinates.

5-2. Transform the vector $\mathbf{A} = A_r\mathbf{e}_r + A_\theta\mathbf{e}_\theta + A_z\mathbf{e}_z$ expressed in cylindrical coordinates into Cartesian coordinates.

5-3. Transform the vector

$$\mathbf{A} = \frac{\tan \theta}{r} \mathbf{e}_r + \frac{1}{r} \mathbf{e}_\theta$$

in cylindrical coordinates to Cartesian coordinates.

5-4. Transform the vector $\mathbf{A} = x\mathbf{i} + y\mathbf{j} + z\mathbf{k}$ into spherical coordinates.

5-5. Transform the vector $\mathbf{A} = (1/r)\mathbf{e}_r$ in spherical coordinates into Cartesian coordinates.

5-6. Show that a cylindrical coordinate system is orthogonal.

5-7. Show that a spherical coordinate system is orthogonal.

5-8. Determine the square of the element of arc length for cylindrical coordinates.

5-9. Repeat Problem 5-8 using a spherical coordinate system.

5-7. Suggested References

5-1. *Vector Analysis with an Introduction to Tensor Analysis*, A. P. Wills, Dover Publications, Inc.

5-2. *Theory and Problems of Vector Analysis*, Murray R. Spiegel, Schaum Publishing Company.

5-3. *Vector and Tensor Analysis*, G. E. Hay, Dover Publications, Inc.

5-4. *Engineering Electromagnetics*, W. H. Hayt, Jr., McGraw-Hill Book Company.

5-5. *Elementary Analysis*, H. C. Trimble and F. W. Lott, Jr., Prentice-Hall, Inc.

5-6. *Mathematics of Physics and Modern Engineering*, I. S. Sokolnikoff and R. M. Redheffer, McGraw-Hill Book Company.

5-7. *Caiculus and Analytic Geometry*, G. B. Thomas, Jr., Addison-Wesley Publishing Company.

5-8. *Advanced Calculus*, W. Kaplan, Addison-Wesley Publishing Company.

5-9. *Mathematical Handbook for Scientists and Engineers*, G. A. Korn and T. M. Korn, McGraw-Hill Book Company.

6

Vectors and Tensors

6-1. Contravariant Vectors

To introduce the subject, let x^i represent the coordinates of a point M in space, and $x^i + dx^i$ the coordinates of point N. The infinitesimal quantity dx^i is the displacement of N from M. The displacement vector **MN** will be called an infinitesimal contravariant vector. The components are dx^i.

The components of the displacement vector in a new set of coordinates x'^i may be found from the transformation equation which follows directly from the chain rule of the calculus.

$$dx'^j = \frac{\partial x'^j}{\partial x^i} \, dx^i$$

The following transformation relation is used to define a contravariant vector.

$$A'^r = \frac{\partial z'^r}{\partial z^s} A^s \tag{6-1}$$

In general terms, a contravariant vector is defined as one which transforms according to the relation (6-1).

The transformation equation (6-1) may be written in matrix form. Hence

$$
\begin{pmatrix} A'^1 \\ A'^2 \\ A'^3 \end{pmatrix} =
\begin{pmatrix}
\dfrac{\partial z'^1}{\partial z^1} & \dfrac{\partial z'^1}{\partial z^2} & \dfrac{\partial z'^1}{\partial z^3} \\[2mm]
\dfrac{\partial z'^2}{\partial z^1} & \dfrac{\partial z'^2}{\partial z^2} & \dfrac{\partial z'^2}{\partial z^3} \\[2mm]
\dfrac{\partial z'^3}{\partial z^1} & \dfrac{\partial z'^3}{\partial z^2} & \dfrac{\partial z'^3}{\partial z^3}
\end{pmatrix}
\begin{pmatrix} A^1 \\ A^2 \\ A^3 \end{pmatrix}
$$

6-2. Contravariant Tensors

Let B^i and C^j represent two contravariant vectors. The product $B^i C^j$ may be represented by an $n \times n$ matrix whose elements will be denoted by A^{ij}, that is,

$$A^{ij} = B^i C^j$$

In another (primed) coordinate system the elements of the matrix would be

$$\acute{A}^{ij} = \acute{B}^i \acute{C}^j$$

However, we may substitute for $\acute{B}^i$ and $\acute{C}^j$ the transformation equation (6-1) as previously developed; thus

$$\acute{A}^{ij} = \left(\frac{\partial \acute{z}^i}{\partial z^k} B^k \right) \left(\frac{\partial \acute{z}^j}{\partial z^l} C^l \right)$$

But $B^k C^l$ is equal to A^{kl}, hence

$$\acute{A}^{ij} = \left(\frac{\partial \acute{z}^i}{\partial z^k} \frac{\partial \acute{z}^j}{\partial z^l} \right) A^{kl} \tag{6-2}$$

This is the defining equation for a contravariant tensor of the second order; that is, a set of quantities A^{rs} is a contravariant tensor of the second order it if transforms according to the relation (6-2).

Contravariant tensors of higher order are defined in a similar manner.

A contravariant vector is a contravariant tensor of the first order.

The transformation equation (6-2) for i, j, k each equal to 1, 2, and 3 in matrix form is

$$\begin{pmatrix} \acute{A}^{11} & \acute{A}^{12} & \acute{A}^{13} \\ \acute{A}^{21} & \acute{A}^{22} & \acute{A}^{23} \\ \acute{A}^{31} & \acute{A}^{32} & \acute{A}^{33} \end{pmatrix}$$

$$= \begin{pmatrix} \dfrac{\partial \acute{z}^1}{\partial z^1} & \dfrac{\partial \acute{z}^1}{\partial z^2} & \dfrac{\partial \acute{z}^1}{\partial z^3} \\[2ex] \dfrac{\partial \acute{z}^2}{\partial z^1} & \dfrac{\partial \acute{z}^2}{\partial z^2} & \dfrac{\partial \acute{z}^2}{\partial z^3} \\[2ex] \dfrac{\partial \acute{z}^3}{\partial z^1} & \dfrac{\partial \acute{z}^3}{\partial z^2} & \dfrac{\partial \acute{z}^3}{\partial z^3} \end{pmatrix} \begin{pmatrix} A^{11} & A^{12} & A^{13} \\ A^{21} & A^{22} & A^{23} \\ A^{31} & A^{32} & A^{33} \end{pmatrix} \begin{pmatrix} \dfrac{\partial \acute{z}^1}{\partial z^1} & \dfrac{\partial \acute{z}^2}{\partial z^1} & \dfrac{\partial \acute{z}^3}{\partial z^1} \\[2ex] \dfrac{\partial \acute{z}^1}{\partial z^2} & \dfrac{\partial \acute{z}^2}{\partial z^2} & \dfrac{\partial \acute{z}^3}{\partial z^2} \\[2ex] \dfrac{\partial \acute{z}^1}{\partial z^3} & \dfrac{\partial \acute{z}^2}{\partial z^3} & \dfrac{\partial \acute{z}^3}{\partial z^3} \end{pmatrix}$$

6-3. An Invariant

A tensor of order zero is one which is unaltered by a change of coordinates. The transformation equation in this case may be expressed as

$$\overset{'}{A} = A \tag{6-3}$$

Because the tensor of order zero is not affected by a change in coordinates, it is called an invariant, or a scalar.

6-4. Covariant Vectors

As already indicated, a covariant vector is defined as one whose components transform according to the relation

$$A_r' = \frac{\partial z^s}{\partial z'^r} A_s \tag{6-4}$$

It is important to note again that a superscript will be used to indicate contravariant vectors and tensors, and a subscript to indicate covariant vectors and tensors.

6-5. Covariant Tensors

In a similar manner covariant tensors of the second order are those which transform according to the relation

$$A_{rs}' = \frac{\partial z^t}{\partial z'^r} \frac{\partial z^u}{\partial z'^s} A_{tu} \tag{6-5}$$

A covariant vector is a covariant tensor of order one.

Similar expressions for the transformation from one set of coordinates to another may be written for higher-order covariant tensors.

6-6. Mixed Tensors

If a set of quantities such as $A_{st}{}^r$ transforms according to the relation

$$A_{st}^{'\,r} = \frac{\partial z'^r}{\partial z^u} \frac{\partial z^v}{\partial z'^s} \frac{\partial z^w}{\partial z'^t} A_{vw}{}^u \qquad (6\text{-}6)$$

it will be defined as a mixed tensor.

This particular mixed tensor is of the third order, having one contravariant index and two covariant indices. The order of a tensor is determined by the number of free indices.

6-7. The Tensor Character of the Kronecker Delta

The Kronecker delta $\delta_s{}^r$ may be transformed according to the relation

$$\delta_s^{'\,r} = \frac{\partial z'^r}{\partial z^t} \frac{\partial z^u}{\partial z'^s} \delta_u{}^t \qquad (6\text{-}7)$$

From this relation the tensor character of the Kronecker delta is seen to be the same as that indicated by its indices, namely, one contravariant and one covariant.

That (6-7) is true follows by observing that

$$\frac{\partial z^u}{\partial z'^s} \delta_u{}^t$$

is non-zero only when $t = u$; otherwise $\delta_u{}^t$ is zero. Therefore

$$\frac{\partial z^u}{\partial z'^s} \delta_u{}^t = \frac{\partial z^t}{\partial z'^s}$$

Substituting into (6-7) gives

$$\delta_s^{'\,r} = \frac{\partial z'^r}{\partial z^t} \frac{\partial z^t}{\partial z'^s} = \frac{\partial z'^r}{\partial z'^s} \qquad (6\text{-}8)$$

which is a known relation for the Kronecker delta.

6-8. Outer Multiplication of Tensors

The outer product of two tensors is defined as the set of quantities obtained by multiplication of each component of the first tensor by each component of the second tensor.

Before performing outer multiplication of tensors it is imperative to change the index symbols so that there are no repeating indices at the same level.

In a three-dimensional space the outer product of $A_t{}^r$ and $B_{uv}{}^s$ is a set of 243 quantities expressed as

$$C_{tuv}^{rs} = A_t{}^r B_{uv}{}^s$$

In outer multiplication each particular suffix must be maintained at the same level on both sides of the relation. The tensor character of the outer product is determined by the position and number of suffixes. C_{tuv}^{rs} is classed as a mixed tensor of the fifth order.

Example 6-1

(a) Find the outer product of A_{ij} and $B_l{}^k$.

$$C_{ijl}^k = A_{ij} B_l{}^k$$

(b) Find the outer product of $A_s{}^r$ and $B_{st}{}^r$. Since these quantities have the same indices on both the upper and lower levels, it will be necessary to change indices to avoid repetition at the same level. The s in $A_s{}^r$ will be changed to u, and the r in $B_{st}{}^r$ to v. Hence $A_s{}^r$ is changed to $A_u{}^r$ and $B_{st}{}^r$ is changed to $B_{st}{}^v$. The outer product is

$$A_u{}^r B_{st}{}^v = C_{ust}^{rv}$$

6-9. Contraction

Suppose we are dealing with a mixed tensor having contravariant rank s and covariant rank r. Contraction is the operation whereby a contravariant and covariant index are equated and the sum taken with respect to that index. The resulting mixed tensor is of contravariant rank $s - 1$ and covariant rank $r - 1$.

Consider the mixed tensor B^i_{jkl}. The transformation equation for this tensor between two curvilinear coordinate systems z^i and z'^i is

$$B'^i_{jkl} = \frac{\partial z'^i}{\partial z^\alpha} \frac{\partial z^\beta}{\partial z'^j} \frac{\partial z^\gamma}{\partial z'^k} \frac{\partial z^\delta}{\partial z'^l} B^\alpha_{\beta\gamma\delta}$$

The $B^\alpha_{\beta\gamma\delta}$ terms are the components of B^i_{jkl} in the unprimed system. The indices i and k will be equated and the sum taken.

$$B'^i_{jil} = \frac{\partial z'^i}{\partial z^\alpha} \frac{\partial z^\beta}{\partial z'^j} \frac{\partial z^\gamma}{\partial z'^i} \frac{\partial z^\delta}{\partial z'^l} B^\alpha_{\beta\gamma\delta}$$

Also

$$\frac{\partial z'^i}{\partial z^\alpha} \frac{\partial z^\gamma}{\partial z'^i} = \frac{\partial z^\gamma}{\partial z^\alpha} = \delta_\alpha{}^\gamma$$

Substituting gives

$$B'^i_{jil} = \frac{\partial z^\beta}{\partial z'^j} \frac{\partial z^\delta}{\partial z'^l} \delta_\alpha{}^\gamma B^\alpha_{\beta\gamma\delta}$$

If $\gamma = \alpha$, then $\delta_\alpha{}^\gamma = 1$; hence

$$B'^i_{jil} = \frac{\partial z^\beta}{\partial z'^j} \frac{\partial z^\delta}{\partial z'^l} B^\alpha_{\beta\alpha\delta}$$

This is the form of the transformation equation for a second-order tensor; hence we shall drop the repeated indices.

$$B'_{jl} = \frac{\partial z^\beta}{\partial z'^j} \frac{\partial z^\delta}{\partial z'^l} B_{\beta\delta}$$

We may therefore conclude that when B'^i_{jil} is contracted the result is a second-order tensor B'_{jl} or

$$B'^i_{jil} = B'_{jl}$$

A tensor such as A^i_{jkl} may be contracted in three different ways to yield $A^\alpha_{\alpha kl}$, $A^\alpha_{j\alpha l}$, and $A^\alpha_{jk\alpha}$. The contraction of A^i_j yields a scalar.

6-10. Inner Multiplication of Tensors

When the operation of contraction is applied to an outer product, the result is called the inner product.

To obtain the inner product of two tensors, the first step is to form the outer product. A contraction is then performed by equating a contravariant index on one tensor to a covariant index on the other tensor and then summing.

The inner product of two tensors $A_s{}^u$ and B_{rt} will be considered. Outer multiplication gives

$$C^u_{srt} = A_s{}^u B_{rt}$$

One of the two possible contractions is obtained by equating the u and r indices and summing:

$$C_{st} = C^r_{srt} = A_s{}^r B_{rt}$$

In summary, the process of multiplying tensors, or outer multiplication, and then contracting is called inner multiplication and the final result is the inner product.

Consider the outer product of two vectors A^p and B_q. Since these vectors are tensors they must transform as follows.

$$\acute{A}^j = \frac{\partial \acute{x}^j}{\partial x^p} A^p \quad \text{and} \quad \acute{B}_k = \frac{\partial x^q}{\partial \acute{x}^k} B_q$$

Hence

$$\acute{A}^j \acute{B}_k = \frac{\partial \acute{x}^j}{\partial x^p} \frac{\partial x^q}{\partial \acute{x}^k} A^p B_q$$

Contracting, that is, putting $j = k$ and summing, gives

$$\acute{A}^j \acute{B}_j = \frac{\partial \acute{x}^j}{\partial x^p} \frac{\partial x^q}{\partial \acute{x}^j} A^p B_q = \delta_p{}^q A^p B_q = A^p B_p$$

This shows that $A^p B_p$ is an invariant or a scalar. The term $A^p B_p$, being a scalar, is called the scalar or dot product of the two vectors.

6-11. Tests of Tensor Character

The tensor character of two-index quantities may be established in the following manner: If the symbol A^{pq} represents a set of nine quantities such that $A^{pq} x_q$ is a contravariant vector where x_q is an arbitrary covariant vector, then A^{pq} is a second-order contravariant tensor. To see this we note that, since $A^{pq}x_q$ is a contravariant vector, it must transform as follows.

$$\overset{'}{A}{}^{rs}\overset{'}{x}_s = \frac{\partial \overset{'}{z}{}^r}{\partial z^p} A^{pq}x_q$$

In like manner, x_q must transform according to the equation

$$x_q = \frac{\partial \overset{'}{z}{}^t}{\partial z^q} \overset{'}{x}_t$$

Substituting for x_q gives

$$\overset{'}{A}{}^{rs}\overset{'}{x}_s = \frac{\partial \overset{'}{z}{}^r}{\partial z^p} \frac{\partial \overset{'}{z}{}^t}{\partial z^q} A^{pq}\overset{'}{x}_t$$

Changing the dummy index s to t and rearranging results in

$$\left(\overset{'}{A}{}^{rt} - \frac{\partial \overset{'}{z}{}^r}{\partial z^p} \frac{\partial \overset{'}{z}{}^t}{\partial z^q} A^{pq} \right) \overset{'}{x}_t = 0$$

Since x_q is arbitrary, so is $\overset{'}{x}_t$; hence the terms in parentheses must vanish or

$$\overset{'}{A}{}^{rt} = \frac{\partial \overset{'}{z}{}^r}{\partial z^p} \frac{\partial \overset{'}{z}{}^t}{\partial z^q} A^{pq}$$

This is the transformation equation for a second-order contravariant tensor; hence A^{pq} must be a second-order contravariant tensor.

A second test is covered in the following statement. If the quantity $A_{rs}x^r y^s$ represents an invariant where x^r and y^s are both arbitrary contravariant vectors, A_{rs} is a covariant tensor of second order. To see this we note that, since $A_{rs}x^r y^s$ is an invariant, the following relationship exists.

$$\overset{'}{A}_{ij}\overset{'}{x}{}^i\overset{'}{y}{}^j = A_{rs}x^r y^s$$

The transformation relations for the vectors x^r and y^s are

$$x^r = \frac{\partial z^r}{\partial \overset{'}{z}{}^i} \overset{'}{x}{}^i$$

$$y^s = \frac{\partial z^s}{\partial \overset{'}{z}{}^j} \overset{'}{y}{}^j$$

Substituting gives

$$\overset{'}{A}_{ij}\overset{'}{x}{}^i\overset{'}{y}{}^j = A_{rs} \frac{\partial z^r}{\partial \overset{'}{z}{}^i} \frac{\partial z^s}{\partial \overset{'}{z}{}^j} \overset{'}{x}{}^i\overset{'}{y}{}^j$$

Rearranging gives

$$\left(\acute{A}_{ij} - \frac{\partial z^r}{\partial z'^i} \frac{\partial z^s}{\partial z'^j} A_{rs} \right) \acute{x}^i \acute{y}^j = 0$$

Since x^r, $\acute{x}^s$, y^i, $\acute{y}^j$ are arbitrary vectors, the terms in parentheses vanish and

$$\acute{A}_{ij} = \frac{\partial z^r}{\partial z'^i} \frac{\partial z^s}{\partial z'^j} A_{rs}$$

This is the transformation equation for a second-order covariant tensor; thus the tensor character of A_{rs} is established.

6-12. Some Properties of Tensors

The important fact about tensors is that tensor equations, if valid for one coordinate system, are true for all other systems. Thus tensor equations are true in all coordinate systems.

Consider the transformation

$$\acute{A}_{rs} = \frac{\partial z^t}{\partial z'^r} \frac{\partial z^u}{\partial z'^s} A_{tu}$$

If A_{tu} is zero, then $\acute{A}_{rs}$ is zero in any other coordinate system.

Assume that two quantities A_{ij} and B_{ij} are equal. Are they equal if transformed to another system of coordinates? Now we have $A_{ij} = B_{ij}$ and

$$\acute{A}_{ij} = \frac{\partial z^t}{\partial z'^i} \frac{\partial z^u}{\partial z'^j} A_{tu}$$

$$\acute{B}_{ij} = \frac{\partial z^t}{\partial z'^i} \frac{\partial z^u}{\partial z'^j} B_{tu}$$

Subtracting gives

$$\acute{A}_{ij} - \acute{B}_{ij} = \left(\frac{\partial z^t}{\partial z'^i} \frac{\partial z^u}{\partial z'^j} \right) (A_{tu} - B_{tu}) = 0$$

Therefore

$$\acute{A}_{ij} = \acute{B}_{ij}$$

We shall now discuss the commonness of tensors or the property of being transitive. Assume that a set of quantities A_{rs} are transformed into a new coordinate system $\acute{A}_{rs}$, and then to still another system $\overset{\prime\prime}{A}_{rs}$. Is the transfer directly from A_{rs} to $\overset{\prime\prime}{A}_{rs}$ a tensorial transformation?

Now

$$\overset{\prime}{A}_{rs} = \frac{\partial z^t}{\partial z'^r}\frac{\partial z^u}{\partial z'^s} A_{tu}$$

$$\overset{\prime\prime}{A}_{rs} = \frac{\partial z'^t}{\partial z''^r}\frac{\partial z'^u}{\partial z''^s} \overset{\prime}{A}_{tu}$$

Rewriting $\overset{\prime}{A}_{rs}$ as $\overset{\prime}{A}_{tu}$ gives

$$\overset{\prime}{A}_{tu} = \frac{\partial z^m}{\partial z'^t}\frac{\partial z^n}{\partial z'^u} A_{mn}$$

Substituting this term in $\overset{\prime\prime}{A}_{rs}$ gives

$$\overset{\prime\prime}{A}_{rs} = \frac{\partial z'^t}{\partial z''^r}\frac{\partial z'^u}{\partial z''^s}\frac{\partial z^m}{\partial z'^t}\frac{\partial z^n}{\partial z'^u} A_{mn}$$

which reduces to

$$\overset{\prime\prime}{A}_{rs} = \frac{\partial z^m}{\partial z''^r}\frac{\partial z^n}{\partial z''^s} A_{mn}$$

This is a second-order tensor transformation.

A transitive tensor relation is one which has the property that, if $A_t{}^{rs}$ bears a relation to $\overset{\prime}{A}_t{}^{rs}$ and $\overset{\prime}{A}_t{}^{rs}$ bears the same relation to $\overset{\prime\prime}{A}_t{}^{rs}$, $A_t{}^{rs}$ bears a relation to $\overset{\prime\prime}{A}_t{}^{rs}$.

6-13. Addition and Subtraction of Tensors

Consider tensors $A_{st}{}^r$ and $B_{st}{}^r$ of the same type and rank. The transformation equations are

$$\overset{\prime}{A}_{vw}{}^u = \frac{\partial z'^u}{\partial z^r}\frac{\partial z^s}{\partial z'^v}\frac{\partial z^t}{\partial z'^w} A_{st}{}^r$$

and

$$\overset{\prime}{B}_{vw}{}^u = \frac{\partial z'^u}{\partial z^r}\frac{\partial z^s}{\partial z'^v}\frac{\partial z^t}{\partial z'^w} B_{st}{}^r$$

Subtracting or adding these equations gives

$$(\overset{\prime}{A}_{vw}{}^u \pm \overset{\prime}{B}_{vw}{}^u) = \left(\frac{\partial z'^u}{\partial z^r}\frac{\partial z^s}{\partial z'^v}\frac{\partial z^t}{\partial z'^w}\right)(A_{st}{}^r \pm B_{st}{}^r)$$

This is the transformation equation for third-order tensors; hence

$$A_{st}{}^{r} \pm B_{st}{}^{r} = C_{st}{}^{r}$$

and

$$\acute{A}_{vw}{}^{u} \pm \acute{B}_{vw}{}^{u} = \acute{C}_{vw}{}^{u}$$

Therefore the sum or difference of two tensors which are of the same rank and type is a tensor of the same rank and type as the original tensors.

6-14. Problems

6-1. Evaluate $\delta_r{}^r$, $\delta_s{}^r\delta_r{}^s$, and $\delta_s{}^r\delta_t{}^s\delta_r{}^t$.

6-2. A skewed coordinate system consists of a set of orthogonal Cartesian axes $\acute{X}^i$ and a set of skewed axes resulting from rotating $\acute{X}^1$ and $\acute{X}^2$ axes through the angles α and β. The X^3 axis coincides with the $\acute{X}^3$ axis. Show that the vector **A** has contravariant components A^i which are the parallel projections of **A** on the axes X^i and that the covariant components A_i are the orthogonal projections of **A** on the $\acute{X}^i$ axes.

6-3. Write the law of transformation for the tensors

$$(a)\ A_{ijk}, \quad (b)\ A_{jk}{}^{i}, \quad (c)\ A_{ijk}^{nm}, \quad (d)\ A^n, \quad (e)\ A_{lm}{}^{ij}$$

6-4. Show that the following relations are true.

(a)
$$\delta_s{}^r A_{rt} = A_{st}$$

(b)
$$\delta_s{}^r \delta_t{}^u A_r{}^t = A_s{}^u$$

6-5. The components of a covariant tensor are xy, $2y - z^2$, xz in rectangular coordinates. Determine the covariant components in spherical coordinates.

6-6. Prove that

$$\frac{\partial^2 z'^r}{\partial z^s \partial z^t} = -\frac{\partial z'^r}{\partial z^u}\frac{\partial z'^v}{\partial z^s}\frac{\partial z'^w}{\partial z^t}\frac{\partial^2 z^u}{\partial z'^v \partial z'^w}$$

by differentiating

$$\delta_t{}^r = \frac{\partial z^r}{\partial z'^k}\frac{\partial z'^k}{\partial z^t} \quad \text{with respect to } z^s$$

6-7. Determine whether or not the following are tensors.

$$(a)\ dx^k, \quad (b)\ \frac{\partial \phi(x^1, \ldots, x^n)}{\partial x^k}, \quad \phi \text{ is an invariant}$$

6-8. Prove that

$$(A_{rs} + A_{sr})z^r z^s = 2A_{rs}z^r z^s$$

if A_{rs} is symmetric.

6-9. A_i is a covariant tensor of rank one. Show that $\partial A^i / \partial x^j$ is or is not a tensor.

6-10. Show that a tensor such as $A_{tu}{}^{rs}$ is transitive.

6-11. Show that the contraction of tensor $A_j{}^i$ is a scalar.

6-12. A_{rst} is a set of quantities such that $A_{rst} X^t$ is a second-order covariant tensor. X^t is an arbitrary contravariant vector. What is the tensor character of A_{rst}?

6-13. Show that the contraction of the outer product of tensors A^i and B_j is an invariant.

6-14. If $n = 3$, express in matrix notation the transformation equations for a covariant vector and a contravariant tensor of rank two.

6-15. Is $A_{rt}{}^r$ a tensor if $A_{st}{}^r$ is a tensor?

6-16. $A_s{}^r$ is a set of nine terms such that $A_s{}^r X_r{}^s$ is an invariant. $X_r{}^s$ is a mixed tensor of the second order. Show that $A_s{}^r$ is a mixed tensor of second order.

6-15. Suggested References

6-1. *Vector and Tensor Analysis*, G. E. Hay, Dover Publications, Inc.

6-2. *Tensor Analysis: Theory and Applications*, I. S. Sokolnikoff, John Wiley and Sons, Inc.

6-3. *Vector Analysis with an Introduction to Tensor Analysis*, A. P. Wills, Dover Publications, Inc.

6-4. *Application of Tensor Analysis*, A. J. McConnell, Dover Publications, Inc.

6-5. *Vector and Tensor Analysis*, Louis Brand, The Macmillan Company.

6-6. *Vector and Tensor Analysis*, Nathaniel Coburn, The Macmillan Company.

6-7. *Vector and Tensor Analysis*, Harry Lass, McGraw-Hill Book Company.

6-8. *Matrix and Tensor Calculus, with Applications to Mechanics, Elasticity, and Aeronautics*, A. D. Michal, John Wiley and Sons, Inc.

6-9. *Tensors for Circuits*, Gabriel Kron, Dover Publications, Inc.

6-10. *An Introduction to Tensor Analysis*, Leonard L. Barrett, The National Press, Palo Alto, Calif.

6-11. *Nonlinear Theory of Continuous Media*, A. Cemal Eringen, McGraw-Hill Book Company.

The Metric Tensor

7-1. The Fundamental or Metric Tensor

Figure 7-1 represents a portion of space referred to the rectangular Cartesian coordinates axes X^1, X^2, X^3. The distance between the points P and Q is ds. To find ds we need only take the square root of the sums of the squares of dx^1, dx^2, dx^3. Thus

$$(ds)^2 = (dx^1)^2 + (dx^2)^2 + (dx^3)^2 = dx^r \, dx^r = \sum_{r=1}^{3}(dx^r)^2 \quad (7\text{-}1)$$

Let Z^1, Z^2, Z^3 be a set of curvilinear coordinate axes such that

$$x^1 = f^1(z^1, z^2, z^3); \quad x^2 = f^2(z^1, z^2, z^3); \quad x^3 = f^3(z^1, z^2, z^3)$$

or, in general,

$$x^r = f^r(z^1, z^2, z^3) = f^r(z^s) = X^r(z^s)$$

According to the general transformation equation,

$$dx^r = \frac{\partial f^r}{\partial z^s} dz^s$$

Since $(ds)^2 = dx^r \, dx^r$ we may write the following, changing the dummy indices to avoid confusion.

$$(ds)^2 = \left(\frac{\partial f^r}{\partial z^i} dz^i\right)\left(\frac{\partial f^r}{\partial z^j} dz^j\right) = \left(\frac{\partial f^r}{\partial z^i} \frac{\partial f^r}{\partial z^j}\right) dz^i \, dz^j$$

This represents a homogeneous quadratic form in the variable dz^i. Now let

$$b_{(ij)} = \frac{\partial f^r}{\partial z^i} \frac{\partial f^r}{\partial z^j} \quad \text{where} \begin{array}{l} i = 1, 2, 3 \\ j = 1, 2, 3 \end{array}$$

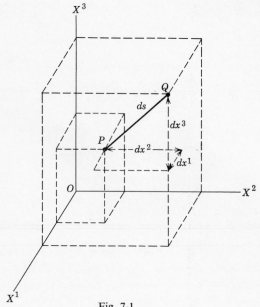

Fig. 7-1.

Then

$$(ds)^2 = b_{(ij)} \, dz^i \, dz^j \tag{7-2}$$

The parentheses are introduced to indicate that at this time $b_{(ij)}$ has not been established as a tensor.

The $b_{(ij)}$ terms for $n = 3$ are

$$\begin{pmatrix} b_{(11)} & b_{(12)} & b_{(13)} \\ b_{(21)} & b_{(22)} & b_{(23)} \\ b_{(31)} & b_{(32)} & b_{(33)} \end{pmatrix}$$

The quadratic equation (7-2), in expanded form, is

$$\begin{aligned} (ds)^2 = {} & b_{(11)} \, dz^1 \, dz^1 + b_{(12)} \, dz^1 \, dz^2 + b_{(13)} \, dz^1 \, dz^3 \\ & + b_{(21)} \, dz^2 \, dz^1 + b_{(22)} \, dz^2 \, dz^2 + b_{(23)} \, dz^2 \, dz^3 \\ & + b_{(31)} \, dz^3 \, dz^1 + b_{(32)} \, dz^3 \, dz^2 + b_{(33)} \, dz^3 \, dz^3 \end{aligned}$$

Rearranging gives

$$\begin{aligned} (ds)^2 = {} & b_{(11)} \, (dz^1)^2 + b_{(22)} \, (dz^2)^2 + b_{(33)} \, (dz^3)^2 \\ & + (b_{(12)} + b_{(21)}) \, dz^1 \, dz^2 + (b_{(13)} + b_{(31)}) \, dz^1 \, dz^3 \\ & + (b_{(23)} + b_{(32)}) \, dz^2 \, dz^3 \end{aligned} \tag{7-3}$$

In general form, the quadratic equation can be expressed as

$$(ds)^2 = \left(\frac{b_{(ij)} + b_{(ji)}}{2}\right) dz^i \, dz^j \tag{7-4}$$

In order to simplify the equation let $g_{(ij)}$ represent the term in parentheses on the right side of equation (7-4); that is,

$$g_{(ij)} = \frac{b_{(ij)} + b_{(ji)}}{2} \tag{7-5}$$

Hence

$$(ds)^2 = g_{(ij)} \, dz^i \, dz^j$$

The $g_{(ij)}$ terms for $n = 3$ are

$$(g_{(ij)}) = \frac{1}{2}\begin{pmatrix} b_{(11)} + b_{(11)} & b_{(12)} + b_{(21)} & b_{(13)} + b_{(31)} \\ b_{(21)} + b_{(12)} & b_{(22)} + b_{(22)} & b_{(23)} + b_{(32)} \\ b_{(31)} + b_{(13)} & b_{(32)} + b_{(23)} & b_{(33)} + b_{(33)} \end{pmatrix}$$

By interchanging the i and j subscripts in equation (7-5), the following equality is easily verified.

$$g_{(ij)} = g_{(ji)}$$

Since dz^i is an arbitrary contravariant vector and ds is an invariant, we may conclude that $g_{(ij)}$ is a tensor, g_{ij}, according to the tests established in Chapter 6. This covariant second-order tensor, g_{ij}, is called the fundamental or metric tensor. The $g_{(ij)}$ terms are the symmetric components of the tensor $b_{(ij)}$. The skew part of b_{ij} contributes nothing to the sum, $b_{ij} \, dz^i \, dz^j$. Consequently the general form for ds in terms of the metric tensor is

$$(ds)^2 = g_{ij} \, dz^i \, dz^j \tag{7-6}$$

7-2. The Base Vectors g_1, g_2, and g_3

Various aspects of the rectangular coordinate system X^i and the curvilinear coordinate system Z^i as shown in Fig. 7-2 will be considered. The unit vectors, i_j's are base vectors associated with the Cartesian coordinates X^i.

The transformation equations are represented as follows:

$$z^i = z^i(x^1, x^2, x^3) \qquad (i = 1, 2, 3)$$

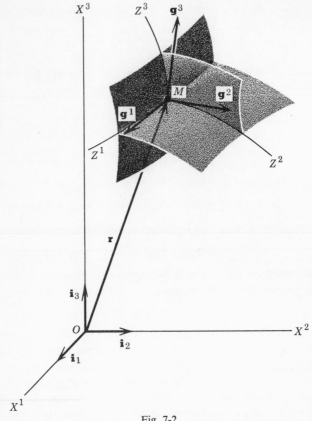

Fig. 7-2.

The inverse equations are

$$x^i = x^i(z^1, z^2, z^3)$$

Let $M(x^1, x^2, x^3)$ be a point in space referred to the Cartesian axes X^i, whose position vector, $\mathbf{r}$, is expressed as

$$\mathbf{r} = x^1\mathbf{i}_1 + x^2\mathbf{i}_2 + x^3\mathbf{i}_3 = x^j\mathbf{i}_j \tag{7-7}$$

The expression for the element of arc ds is

$$(ds)^2 = d\mathbf{r} \cdot d\mathbf{r} = (dx^1)^2 + (dx^2)^2 + (dx^3)^2$$
$$= dx^i\, dx^i = \sum_{i=1}^{3}(dx^i)^2 \tag{7-8}*$$

* Also equation (5-15).

The following expression may be written for $d\mathbf{r}$.

$$d\mathbf{r} = \frac{\partial \mathbf{r}}{\partial z^1} dz^1 + \frac{\partial \mathbf{r}}{\partial z^2} dz^2 + \frac{\partial \mathbf{r}}{\partial z^3} dz^3$$

$$= \sum_{i=1}^{3} \frac{\partial \mathbf{r}}{\partial z^i} dz^i = \frac{\partial \mathbf{r}}{\partial z^i} dz^i \tag{7-9}$$

The term $\partial \mathbf{r}/\partial z^1$ implies that during the differentiation the values for z^2 and z^3 are constant, or z^2 and z^3 are fixed by setting both equal to constants. Under this condition $\mathbf{r}$ is only a function of z^1. The terminus of $\mathbf{r}$ can only move along the z^1 coordinate line in the $z^i = z^i(x^1, z^2, x^3)$ system; hence the term $\partial \mathbf{r}/\partial z^1$ is tangent to the coordinate line z^1. The tangent equation is

$$\frac{\partial \mathbf{r}}{\partial z^1} = \lim_{\Delta z^1 \to 0} \frac{\Delta \mathbf{r}}{\Delta z^1}$$

By similar analysis $\partial \mathbf{r}/\partial z^2$ and $\partial \mathbf{r}/\partial z^3$ are tangents to the coordinate lines z^2 and z^3, respectively. These tangent vectors are designated by the symbol $\mathbf{g}_i$ in Fig. 7-2. In general terms the vectors $\mathbf{g}_i$ are

$$\mathbf{g}_i = \frac{\partial \mathbf{r}}{\partial z^i} \tag{7-10}$$

Employing the relation $\mathbf{r} = x^j \mathbf{i}_j$ gives the relation between the base vectors $\mathbf{i}$'s and $\mathbf{g}$'s; that is,

$$\mathbf{g}_i = \frac{\partial \mathbf{r}}{\partial z^i} = \frac{\partial x^j}{\partial z^i} \mathbf{i}_j \tag{7-11}$$

Substituting in equation (7-9) gives

$$d\mathbf{r} = \sum_{i=1}^{3} \frac{\partial \mathbf{r}}{\partial z^i} dz^i = \sum_{i=1}^{3} \mathbf{g}_i dz^i = \mathbf{g}_i dz^i \tag{7-12}$$

Substituting equation (7-12) into equation (7-8) gives

$$(ds)^2 = d\mathbf{r} \cdot d\mathbf{r} = \left(\sum_{i=1}^{3} \mathbf{g}_i dz^i \right) \cdot \left(\sum_{i=1}^{3} \mathbf{g}_i dz^i \right)$$

Rearranging and replacing the i index in the extreme right hand term by j gives

$$(ds)^2 = \sum_{i=1}^{3} \sum_{j=1}^{3} \mathbf{g}_i \cdot \mathbf{g}_j \, dz^i \, dz^j$$

Let

$$\mathbf{g}_i \cdot \mathbf{g}_j = g_{ij} \tag{7-13}$$

Since

$$\mathbf{g}_i \cdot \mathbf{g}_j = \mathbf{g}_j \cdot \mathbf{g}_i, \quad g_{ij} = g_{ji} \tag{7-14}$$

and the g_{ij} terms are symmetric, the expression for the square of the arc length, ds, is

$$(ds)^2 = \sum_{i=1}^{3} \sum_{j=1}^{3} g_{ij}\, dz^i\, dz^j = g_{ij}\, dz^i\, dz^j \tag{7-15}$$

Comparing (7-15) and (7-6), we see that the g_{ij}'s are the same. Therefore equation (7-13) gives a geometric interpretation of the previously defined metric tensor in terms of the dot product of the base vectors $\mathbf{g}_i$.

The value of dx_k in terms of the Z^j coordinate system may be written

$$dx_k = \frac{\partial x_k}{\partial z^1}\, dz^1 + \frac{\partial x_k}{\partial z^2}\, dz^2 + \frac{\partial x_k}{\partial z^3}\, dz^3 = \frac{\partial x_k}{\partial z^j}\, dz^j \tag{7-16}$$

Inserting this relation into equation (7-1) gives

$$(ds)^2 = \frac{\partial x^k}{\partial z^i}\, dz^i\, \frac{\partial x^k}{\partial z^j}\, dz^j = \frac{\partial x^k}{\partial z^i}\frac{\partial x^k}{\partial z^j}\, dz^i\, dz^j \tag{7-17}$$

Equations (7-15) and (7-17) imply that

$$g_{ij} = \frac{\partial x^k}{\partial z^i}\frac{\partial x^k}{\partial z^j} \tag{7-18}$$

For $k = 1, 2, 3$ we obtain

$$g_{ij} = \frac{\partial x^1}{\partial z^i}\frac{\partial x^1}{\partial z^j} + \frac{\partial x^2}{\partial z^i}\frac{\partial x^2}{\partial z^j} + \frac{\partial x^3}{\partial z^i}\frac{\partial x^3}{\partial z^j} \qquad (i, j = 1, 2, 3)$$

When $i = j$,

$$g_{ii} = \frac{\partial x^k}{\partial z^i}\frac{\partial x^k}{\partial z^i} = \left(\frac{\partial x^k}{\partial z^i}\right)^2 \qquad \begin{pmatrix} \text{No summation on } i \\ \text{Summation on } k \end{pmatrix} \tag{7-19}$$

Using the Kronecker delta, equation (7-18) may be written

$$g_{ij} = \frac{\partial x^m}{\partial z^i}\frac{\partial x^n}{\partial z^j}\, \delta_{mn} \tag{7-20}$$

If and only if $m = n$, will $\delta_{mn} = 1$.

A curvilinear system is said to be orthogonal if the tangent vectors at each point form a triple of mutually perpendicular vectors.

For an orthogonal system the relation for $(ds)^2$ reduces to

$$(ds)^2 = g_{11}\,(dz^1)^2 + g_{22}\,(dz^2)^2 + g_{33}\,(dz^3)^2 \tag{7-21}$$

Another common system of notation uses the symbol h, where

$$g_{11} = h_1{}^2, \quad g_{22} = h_2{}^2, \quad g_{33} = h_3{}^2$$

According to this nomenclature the following equation may be written for $(ds)^2$.

$$(ds)^2 = (h_1\,dz^1)^2 + (h_2\,dz^2)^2 + (h_3\,dz^3)^2 \tag{7-22}$$

Using the equations already developed (see also 5-16), we shall now study several coordinate systems.

CARTESIAN COORDINATE SYSTEMS

The square of the arc length is expressed by the relation

$$(ds)^2 = (dx^1)^2 + (dx^2)^2 + (dx^3)^2 = \sum_{r=1}^{3}(dx^r)^2$$

Consequently

$$g_{11} = 1, \quad g_{22} = 1, \quad g_{33} = 1$$
$$h_1 = 1, \quad h_2 = 1, \quad h_3 = 1$$
$$g_{ij} = \delta_{ij}$$

$$g_{ij} = \begin{pmatrix} 1 & 0 & 0 \\ 0 & 1 & 0 \\ 0 & 0 & 1 \end{pmatrix}$$

CYLINDRICAL COORDINATE SYSTEMS

We now consider the cylindrical coordinate system shown in Fig. 7-3. The Cartesian coordinates x^1, x^2, x^3 are related to the cylindrical coordinates r, θ, z by the equations

$$x^1 = r \cos \theta = z^1 \cos z^2$$
$$x^2 = r \sin \theta = z^1 \sin z^2$$
$$x^3 = z \quad\quad\; = z^3$$

It is often convenient to replace the symbols used for cylindrical coordinates, r, θ, z, by others such as z^1, z^2, z^3. For our purpose we shall use them interchangeably.

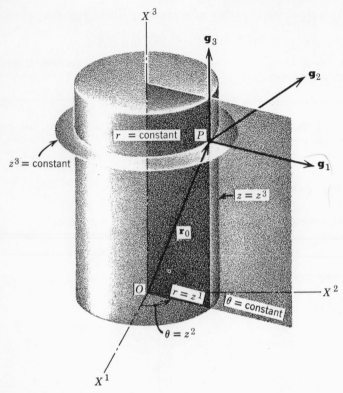

Fig. 7-3. $X^1 = z^1 \cos z^2 = r \cos \theta; \quad X^2 = z^1 \sin z^2 = r \sin \theta; \quad X^3 = z^3 = z.$

Employing the general relation (7-18) for g_{ij} gives

$$g_{ij} = \frac{\partial r \cos \theta}{\partial z^i} \frac{\partial r \cos \theta}{\partial z^j} + \frac{\partial r \sin \theta}{\partial z^i} \frac{\partial r \sin \theta}{\partial z^j} + \frac{\partial z}{\partial z^i} \frac{\partial z}{\partial z^j}$$

If $i = 1 = j$,

$$g_{11} = \frac{\partial r \cos \theta}{\partial r} \frac{\partial r \cos \theta}{\partial r} + \frac{\partial r \sin \theta}{\partial r} \frac{\partial r \sin \theta}{\partial r} + \frac{\partial z}{\partial r} \frac{\partial z}{\partial r}$$

$$= \cos^2 \theta + \sin^2 \theta + 0 = 1$$

If $i = 2 = j$,

$$g_{22} = \frac{\partial r \sin \theta}{\partial \theta} \frac{\partial r \sin \theta}{\partial \theta} + \frac{\partial r \cos \theta}{\partial \theta} \frac{\partial r \cos \theta}{\partial \theta} + \frac{\partial z}{\partial \theta} \frac{\partial z}{\partial \theta}$$

$$= r^2 \cos^2 \theta + r^2 \sin^2 \theta + 0 = r^2$$

If $i = 3 = j$,

$$g_{33} = \frac{\partial r \cos \theta}{\partial z} \frac{\partial r \cos \theta}{\partial z} + \frac{\partial r \sin \theta}{\partial z} \frac{\partial r \sin \theta}{\partial z} + \frac{\partial z}{\partial z} \frac{\partial z}{\partial z}$$

$$= \qquad 0 \qquad + \qquad 0 \qquad + \quad 1 \quad = 1$$

If $i = 1$ and $j = 2$,

$$g_{12} = \frac{\partial r \cos \theta}{\partial r} \frac{\partial r \cos \theta}{\partial \theta} + \frac{\partial r \sin \theta}{\partial r} \frac{\partial r \sin \theta}{\partial \theta} + \frac{z}{\partial r} \frac{\partial z}{\partial \theta}$$

$$= -\cos \theta r \sin \theta + \sin \theta r \cos \theta + 0 = 0$$

All other values are also zero; hence

$$g_{12} = g_{21} = g_{13} = g_{31} = g_{32} = g_{23} = 0$$

Employing the fundamental equation for $(ds)^2$ gives

$$(ds)^2 = g_{ij} \, dz^i \, dz^j$$

or

$$(ds)^2 = g_{11} \, dz^1 \, dz^1 + g_{22} \, dz^2 \, dz^2 + g_{33} \, dz^3 \, dz^3 + 0 + 0 + \cdots$$

Substituting gives

$$(ds)^2 = dr^2 + r^2 \, d\theta^2 + (dz)^2$$

For cylindrical coordinates we may conclude that

$$(ds)^2 = dr^2 + r^2 \, d\theta^2 + (dz)^2$$

$$g_{11} = 1, \quad g_{22} = r^2, \quad g_{33} = 1$$

An alternative procedure consists in employing the unit vectors $\mathbf{i}_1$, $\mathbf{i}_2$, and $\mathbf{i}_3$.

The general relation between the base vectors $\mathbf{g}_i$ and $\mathbf{i}_j$ is

$$\mathbf{g}_i = \frac{\partial x^j}{\partial z^i} \mathbf{i}_j$$

For $i = 1$,

$$\mathbf{g}_1 = \frac{\partial x^j}{\partial z^1} \mathbf{i}_j$$

Summing on j gives

$$\mathbf{g}_1 = \frac{\partial x^1}{\partial z^1} \mathbf{i}_1 + \frac{\partial x^2}{\partial z^1} \mathbf{i}_2 + \frac{\partial x^3}{\partial z^1} \mathbf{i}_3$$

$$= \frac{\partial r \cos \theta}{\partial r} \mathbf{i}_1 + \frac{\partial r \sin \theta}{\partial r} \mathbf{i}_2 + \frac{\partial z^3}{\partial r} \mathbf{i}_3$$

$$= \cos \theta \mathbf{i}_1 + \sin \theta \mathbf{i}_2 + 0$$

For $i = 2$ and $j = 1, 2, 3$,

$$\mathbf{g}_2 = \frac{\partial r \cos \theta}{\partial \theta} \mathbf{i}_1 + \frac{\partial r \sin \theta}{\partial \theta} \mathbf{i}_2 + \frac{\partial z^3}{\partial \theta} \mathbf{i}_3$$

$$= -r \sin \theta \mathbf{i}_1 + r \cos \theta \mathbf{i}_2 + 0$$

For $i = 3$ and $j = 1, 2, 3$,

$$\mathbf{g}_3 = \frac{\partial r \cos \theta}{\partial z^3} \mathbf{i}_1 + \frac{\partial r \sin \theta}{\partial z^3} \mathbf{i}_2 + \frac{\partial z^3}{\partial z^3} \mathbf{i}_3$$

$$= 0 + 0 + \mathbf{i}_3$$

Now

$$g_{ij} = \mathbf{g}_i \cdot \mathbf{g}_j$$

$$g_{11} = \mathbf{g}_1 \cdot \mathbf{g}_1 = \cos^2 \theta + \sin^2 \theta = 1$$

$$g_{12} = \mathbf{g}_1 \cdot \mathbf{g}_2 = -r \sin \theta \cos \theta + r \sin \theta \cos \theta = 0$$

$$g_{22} = \mathbf{g}_2 \cdot \mathbf{g}_2 = r^2 \sin^2 \theta + r^2 \cos^2 \theta = r^2$$

$$g_{33} = \mathbf{g}_3 \cdot \mathbf{g}_3 = 1$$

In summary, for cylindrical coordinates

$$g_{ij} = \begin{pmatrix} 1 & 0 & 0 \\ 0 & r^2 & 0 \\ 0 & 0 & 1 \end{pmatrix}$$

SPHERICAL COORDINATE SYSTEMS

Consider the spherical coordinate system shown in Fig. 7-4. The general equations relating the two coordinate systems are

$$x^1 = r \sin \phi \cos \theta = z^1 \sin z^2 \cos z^3$$

$$x^2 = r \sin \phi \sin \theta = z^1 \sin z^2 \sin z^3$$

$$x^3 = r \cos \phi \qquad = z^1 \cos z^2$$

The general expression, equation (7-18), for g_{ij} is

$$g_{ij} = \frac{\partial x^1}{\partial z^i} \frac{\partial x^1}{\partial z^j} + \frac{\partial x^2}{\partial z^i} \frac{\partial x^2}{\partial z^j} + \frac{\partial x^3}{\partial z^i} \frac{\partial x^3}{\partial z^j}$$

Let $i = j = 1$. Then

$$g_{11} = (\sin \phi \cos \theta)^2 + (\sin \phi \sin \theta)^2 + (\cos \phi)^2$$

$$= \sin^2 \phi \cos^2 \theta + \sin^2 \phi \sin^2 \theta + \cos^2 \phi$$

$$= \sin^2 \phi (\cos^2 \theta + \sin^2 \theta) + \cos^2 \phi = 1$$

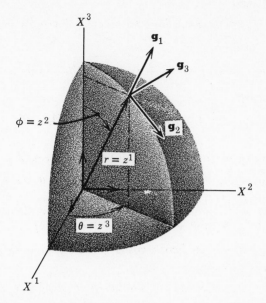

Fig. 7-4. $X^1 = z^1 \sin z^2 \cos z^3 = r \sin \phi \cos \theta$; $X^2 = z^1 \sin z^2 \sin z^3 = r \sin \phi \sin \theta$; $X^3 = z^1 \cos z^2 = r \cos \phi$.

Let $i = 2, j = 2$; then

$$g_{22} = (r \cos \phi \cos \theta)^2 + (r \cos \phi \sin \theta)^2 + (-r \sin \phi)^2$$
$$= r^2 \cos^2 \phi \cos^2 \theta + r^2 \cos^2 \phi \sin^2 \theta + r^2 \sin^2 \phi$$
$$= r^2 \cos^2 \phi (\cos^2 \theta + \sin^2 \theta) + r^2 \sin^2 \phi = r^2$$

Let $i = 3, j = 3$; then

$$g_{33} = (-r \sin \phi \sin \theta)^2 + (r \sin \phi \cos \theta)^2$$
$$= r^2 \sin^2 \phi \sin^2 \theta + r^2 \sin^2 \phi \cos^2 \theta$$
$$= r^2 \sin^2 \phi (\sin^2 \theta + \cos^2 \theta) = r^2 \sin^2 \phi$$

In a similar manner the other values for g_{ij} may be shown to be zero.

An alternative method for evaluating g_{ij} involves the use of the unit vectors $\mathbf{i}_j$. The basic relation for $\mathbf{g}_i$ is

$$\mathbf{g}_i = \frac{\partial \mathbf{r}}{\partial z^i} = \frac{\partial(x^j \mathbf{i}_j)}{\partial z^i} = \frac{\partial x^j}{\partial z^i} \mathbf{i}_j \qquad (j = 1, 2, 3) \qquad (7\text{-}11)$$

Let $i = 1$; then
$$\mathbf{g}_1 = \sin \phi \cos \theta \mathbf{i}_1 + \sin \phi \sin \theta \mathbf{i}_2 + \cos \phi \mathbf{i}_3$$

Let $i = 2$; then
$$\mathbf{g}_2 = r \cos \phi \cos \theta \mathbf{i}_1 + r \cos \phi \sin \theta \mathbf{i}_2 - r \sin \phi \mathbf{i}_3$$

Let $i = 3$; then
$$\mathbf{g}_3 = -r \sin \phi \sin \theta \mathbf{i}_1 + r \sin \phi \cos \theta \mathbf{i}_2 + 0$$

Now

$$g_{11} = \mathbf{g}_1 \cdot \mathbf{g}_1 = \sin^2 \phi \cos^2 \theta + \sin^2 \phi \sin^2 \theta + \cos^2 \phi = 1$$

$$\begin{aligned} g_{22} &= \mathbf{g}_2 \cdot \mathbf{g}_2 = r^2 \cos^2 \phi \cos^2 \theta + r^2 \cos^2 \phi \sin^2 \theta + r^2 \sin^2 \phi \\ &= r^2 \cos^2 \phi \, (\cos^2 \theta + \sin^2 \theta) + r^2 \sin^2 \phi = r^2 \end{aligned}$$

$$g_{33} = r^2 \sin^2 \phi \sin^2 \theta + r^2 \sin^2 \phi \cos^2 \theta = r^2 \sin^2 \phi$$

$$\begin{aligned} g_{12} &= \mathbf{g}_1 \cdot \mathbf{g}_2 = r \sin \phi \cos \phi \cos^2 \theta + r \sin^2 \phi \cos \theta \sin^2 \theta \\ &\quad - r \cos \phi \sin \phi \\ &= r \cos \phi \sin \phi (\cos^2 \theta + \sin^2 \theta) - r \cos \phi \sin \phi = 0 \end{aligned}$$

All other g_{ij} values are zero.

Now
$$(ds)^2 = g_{11} \, dz^1 \, dz^1 + g_{22} \, dz^2 \, dz^2 + g_{33} \, dz^3 \, dz^3 + 0 + 0 \cdots + 0$$

Substituting gives
$$(ds)^2 = dr^2 + r^2 \, d\phi^2 + r^2 \sin^2 \phi \, d\theta^2$$

Summarizing for spherical coordinates,

$$g_{ij} = \begin{pmatrix} 1 & 0 & 0 \\ 0 & r^2 & 0 \\ 0 & 0 & r^2 \sin^2 \phi \end{pmatrix}$$

Our results for rectangular, cylindrical, and spherical coordinate systems are summarized in the accompanying table.

Coordinate System	g_{11}	g_{22}	g_{33}	All Others	Differential Quadratic
Rectangular	1	1	1	0	$(ds)^2 = dx^k \, dx^k$
Cylindrical	1	r^2	1	0	$(ds)^2 = dr^2 + r^2 \, d\theta^2 + dz^2$
Spherical	1	r^2	$r^2 \sin^2 \phi$	0	$(ds)^2 = dr^2 + r^2 \, d\phi^2 + r^2 \sin^2 \phi \, d\theta^2$

7-3. The Direction Cosines of the Base Vectors

The angle between the base vectors, $\mathbf{g}_i$, may be found by the dot product, for example,

$$\mathbf{g}_1 \cdot \mathbf{g}_2 = |\mathbf{g}_1| \, |\mathbf{g}_2| \cos(\mathbf{g}_1, \mathbf{g}_2)$$

Hence the cosine of the angle between $\mathbf{g}_1$ and $\mathbf{g}_2$ is

$$\cos(\mathbf{g}_1, \mathbf{g}_2) = \frac{\mathbf{g}_1 \cdot \mathbf{g}_2}{|\mathbf{g}_1| \, |\mathbf{g}_2|} \tag{7-23}$$

The procedure for determining the values for the direction cosines between the $\mathbf{i}_i$ and $\mathbf{g}_i$ vectors will now be considered. The $\mathbf{i}_i$ are unit vectors, whereas the $\mathbf{g}_i$ may not be unit vectors.

$$\mathbf{g}_i \cdot \mathbf{i}_j = |\mathbf{g}_i| \, |\mathbf{i}_j| \cos(\mathbf{g}_i, \mathbf{i}_j) = \sqrt{\mathbf{g}_i \cdot \mathbf{g}_i} \cos(\mathbf{g}_i, \mathbf{i}_j)$$
$$= \sqrt{g_{ii}} \cos(\mathbf{g}_i, \mathbf{i}_j)$$

or

$$\cos(\mathbf{g}_i, \mathbf{i}_j) = \frac{\mathbf{g}_i \cdot \mathbf{i}_j}{\sqrt{g_{ii}}} \qquad \text{(no summation on } i) \tag{7-24}$$

For the spherical coordinate system shown in Fig. 7-4 we can use the results of Section 7-2 for the base vector $\mathbf{g}$ in equation (7-24) to obtain

$$\cos(\mathbf{g}_1, \mathbf{i}_1) = \frac{(\sin\phi\cos\theta\,\mathbf{i}_1 + \sin\phi\sin\theta\,\mathbf{i}_2 + \cos\phi\,\mathbf{i}_3) \cdot \mathbf{i}_1}{1}$$
$$= \sin\phi\cos\theta$$

In a similar manner the other direction cosines may be found.

$$
\cos(\mathbf{g}_i, \mathbf{i}_j) = \begin{array}{c} \\ \mathbf{g} \\ \downarrow \end{array}
\begin{array}{c} 1 \\ 2 \\ 3 \end{array}
\begin{pmatrix}
\sin\phi\cos\theta & \sin\phi\sin\theta & \cos\phi \\
\cos\phi\cos\theta & \sin\theta\cos\phi & -\sin\phi \\
-\sin\theta & \cos\theta & 0
\end{pmatrix}
$$

$$\mathbf{i} \rightarrow \qquad 1 \qquad\qquad 2 \qquad\qquad 3$$

A slight variation in this procedure is now considered. Substituting into equation (7-24) the expressions

$$g_{ii} = \frac{\partial x^m}{\partial z^i} \frac{\partial x^n}{\partial z^i} \delta_{mn} \quad \text{and} \quad \mathbf{g}_i = \frac{\partial x^j}{\partial z^i} \mathbf{i}_j$$

gives

$$\cos(\mathbf{g}_i, \mathbf{i}_j) = \frac{\mathbf{g}_i \cdot \mathbf{i}_j}{\sqrt{g_{ii}}} = \frac{\partial x^j/\partial z^i}{\sqrt{g_{ii}}} = \frac{\partial x^j/\partial z^i}{\sqrt{(\partial x^m/\partial z^i)(\partial x^n/\partial z^i)\,\delta_{mn}}} \tag{7-25}$$

The spherical coordinate system will again be used to illustrate the steps. The transformation equations are

$$x^1 = z^1 \sin z^2 \cos z^3 = r \sin \phi \cos \theta$$
$$x^2 = z^1 \sin z^2 \sin z^3 = r \sin \phi \sin \theta$$
$$x^3 = z^1 \cos z^2 \qquad\quad = r \cos \phi$$

The values for $\partial x^j / \partial z^i$ are presented in the accompanying tabulation.

$$
\left(\frac{\partial x^j}{\partial z^i} \right) =
\begin{array}{c}
\\
j \to \\
i \\
\downarrow 1 \\
2 \\
3
\end{array}
\begin{pmatrix}
1 & 2 & 3 \\
\dfrac{\partial x^1}{\partial r} = \sin \phi \cos \theta & \dfrac{\partial x^2}{\partial r} = \sin \phi \sin \theta & \dfrac{\partial x^3}{\partial r} = \cos \phi \\
\dfrac{\partial x^1}{\partial \phi} = r \cos \phi \cos \theta & \dfrac{\partial x^2}{\partial \phi} = r \sin \theta \cos \phi & \dfrac{\partial x^3}{\partial \phi} = -r \sin \phi \\
\dfrac{\partial x^1}{\partial \theta} = -r \sin \phi \sin \theta & \dfrac{\partial x^2}{\partial \theta} = r \sin \phi \cos \theta & \dfrac{\partial x^3}{\partial \theta} = 0
\end{pmatrix}
$$

To obtain the direction cosines we need only divide the value of $\partial x^j / \partial z^i$ by the proper value of $\sqrt{g_{ii}}$. For spherical coordinates $\sqrt{g_{11}} = 1$, $\sqrt{g_{22}} = r$, $\sqrt{g_{33}} = r \sin \phi$.

$$\cos (\mathbf{g}_1, \mathbf{i}_1) = \frac{\partial x^1 / \partial z^1}{\sqrt{g_{11}}} = \frac{\sin \phi \cos \theta}{1} = \sin \phi \cos \theta$$

$$\cos (\mathbf{g}_1, \mathbf{i}_2) = \frac{\sin \phi \sin \theta}{1} = \sin \phi \sin \theta$$

$$\cos (\mathbf{g}_1, \mathbf{i}_3) = \frac{\cos \phi}{1} = \cos \phi$$

These values check those previously computed.

7-4. Problems

7-1. The components for a vector **A** in rectangular Cartesian coordinates is designated by the symbol a_j. Find the covariant components of this vector in (*a*) cylindrical coordinates (r, θ, z) and (*b*) in spherical coordinates (r, θ, ϕ).

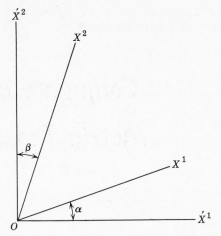

Problem 7-2.

7-2. $\acute{X}^i$ represents a set of orthogonal Cartesian axes and X^i a skewed set resulting from the rotation of $\acute{X}^1$ and $\acute{X}^2$ through the angles α and β as shown in the figure. The X^3 axes coincides with $\acute{X}^3$. Establish the transformation relations in the forms

$$x^i = f^i(\acute{x}^1, \acute{x}^2, \acute{x}^3)$$
$$\acute{x}^i = f'^i(x^1, x^2, x^3)$$

Calculate the metric tensor.

7-3. Develop the following equations from the relation for a vector referred to its base vectors.

$$\acute{A}^j = A^i \frac{\partial \acute{x}^j}{\partial x^i} \quad \text{and} \quad \acute{A}_j = A_i \frac{\partial x^i}{\partial \acute{x}^j}$$

7-5. Suggested References

7-1. *Vector and Tensor Analysis*, G. E. Hay, Dover Publications, Inc.
7-2. *Mathematics of Physics and Modern Engineering*, I. S. Sokolnikoff and R. M. Redheffer, McGraw-Hill Book Company.
7-3. *Vector Analysis with an Introduction to Tensor Analysis*, A. P. Wills, Dover Publications, Inc.
7-4. *Advanced Calculus*, W. Kaplan, Addison-Wesley Publishing Company.
7-5. *Vector Analysis*, L. Brand, John Wiley and Sons, Inc.
7-6. *Nonlinear Theory of Continuous Media*, A. Cemal Eringen, McGraw-Hill Book Company.

8

Conjugate and Metric Tensors

8-1. Conjugate Tensors

In Chapter 2 it was shown that the sum of the products of the elements of a row or a column of a determinant and their respective cofactors equals the product of the determinant and the Kronecker delta, which is expressed in equation form as follows.

$$a_j{}^i A_k{}^j = a\delta_k{}^i = |a_j{}^i|\, \delta_k{}^i \qquad (2\text{-}1)$$

or

$$a_{ij}A^{jk} = a\delta_i{}^k = |a_{ij}|\, \delta_i{}^k$$

or

$$a^{ij}A_{jk} = a\delta_k{}^i = |a^{ij}|\, \delta_k{}^i$$

The metric tensor and its cofactors will be represented by the symbols g_{ij} and G^{ji}, respectively. Employing equation (2-1) gives

$$g_{ij}G^{jk} = g\delta_i{}^k \qquad (8\text{-}1)$$

A new term will be defined:

$$g^{(jk)} = \frac{G^{jk}}{g} \qquad (8\text{-}2)$$

Substituting this expression into equation (8-1) gives

$$g_{ij}g^{(jk)} = \delta_i{}^k \qquad (8\text{-}3)$$

or,

$$g_{ij}g^{(ki)} = \delta_j{}^k$$

The tensor character of $g^{(ki)}$ will now be determined. Let D^j represent an arbitrary contravariant vector. Now we may express an arbitrary covariant vector u_i as

$$u_i = g_{ij} D^j$$

Multiplying the relation by $g^{(ki)}$ gives

$$g^{(ki)}u_i = g_{ij}g^{(ki)} D^j$$

But $g_{ij}g^{(ki)} = \delta_j{}^k$; hence

$$g^{(ki)}u_i = \delta_j{}^k D^j$$

If and only if $j = k$ will $\delta_j{}^k =$ unity; hence

$$g^{(ki)}u_i = D^k$$

This establishes the fact that $g^{(ki)}$ is a second-order contravariant tensor. Hence

$$g^{(ki)} = g^{ki}$$

This tensor is called the conjugate metric tensor. It is the inverse matrix of the g_{ij} matrix. We may now write several important relations by replacing $g^{(jk)}$ by g^{jk} in equations (8-2) and (8-3).

$$g_{ij}g^{jk} = \delta_i{}^k \tag{8-4}$$

or

$$g_{ji}g^{kj} = \delta_i{}^k$$

and

$$g^{jk} = \frac{G^{jk}}{g} \tag{8-5}$$

Taking the determinant of both sides of equation (8-4) gives

$$|g_{ji}| \, |g^{ik}| = |\delta_j{}^k|$$

When $k = j$, $\delta_j{}^k = 1$. Therefore

$$|g_{ji}| \, |g^{ij}| = 1$$

but $|g_{ij}| = |g_{ji}| = g$; hence

$$|g^{ij}| = \frac{1}{g} \tag{8-6}$$

Example 8-1

If G_{ij} is the cofactor of g^{ij}, show that $g_{ij} = gG_{ij} = |g_{ij}| \, G_{ij}$.
According to equation (2-1) the following equation may be written.

$$g^{ij}G_{jk} = |g^{ij}| \, \delta_k{}^i$$

Substituting $1/g$ for $|g^{ij}|$ from equation (8-6) gives

$$g^{ij}G_{jk} = \frac{1}{g}\,\delta_k{}^i$$

Multiplying each side by $g\,g_{il}$ and summing over i,

$$g\,g_{il}g^{ij}G_{jk} = g_{il}\delta_k{}^i$$

But $g_{il}g^{ij}$ is equal to $\delta_l{}^j$; hence

$$gG_{jk}\delta_l{}^j = g_{il}\delta_k{}^i$$

Summing on j,

$$gG_{lk} = g_{il}\delta_k{}^i$$

Summing on i,

$$gG_{lk} = g_{kl} \quad \text{or} \quad g_{ij} = gG_{ij}$$

Example 8-2

Show that

$$\frac{\partial g}{\partial g_{ij}} = g\,g^{ji}$$

Equation (2-1) is valid for any matrix; hence it may be written

$$g_{ij}G^{ki} = g\delta_j{}^k$$

If $j = k = 1$, then $\delta_j{}^k$ equals unity and

$$g_{il}G^{li} = g$$

Expanding gives

$$g = g_{11}G^{11} + g_{21}G^{12} + g_{31}G^{13} + \cdots + g_{(n)1}G^{1(n)}$$

In this expression the g_{ij} terms are explicit and do not occur in the G^{ji} terms; hence differentiation gives

$$\frac{\partial g}{\partial g_{11}} = G^{11} + 0 + 0 + \cdots = G^{11}$$

$$\frac{\partial g}{\partial g_{21}} = 0 + G^{12} + 0 + \cdots = G^{12}$$

$$\frac{\partial g}{\partial g_{31}} = 0 + 0 + G^{13} + \cdots = G^{13}$$

These relations may be expressed as follows.

$$\frac{\partial g}{\partial g_{ij}} = G^{ji}$$

However,

$$\frac{G^{ji}}{g} = g^{ji}$$

Substitution gives

$$\frac{\partial g}{\partial g_{ij}} = g\,g^{ji}$$

Another useful relation will be developed by taking the derivative of $\ln g$ with respect to x^k. Hence

$$\frac{\partial}{\partial x^k} (\ln g) = \frac{1}{g} \frac{\partial g}{\partial x^k}$$

It was also shown in the section on differentiation of determinants (equation 2-4) that

$$\frac{\partial g}{\partial x^k} = G^{ij} \frac{\partial g_{ij}}{\partial x^k}$$

Substituting this into the preceding equation gives

$$\frac{\partial}{\partial x^k} (\ln g) = \frac{G^{ij}}{g} \frac{\partial g_{ij}}{\partial x^k} \tag{8-7}$$

According to equation 8-5, G^{ij}/g may be replaced by g^{ij}; hence we finally have the relationship

$$\frac{\partial}{\partial x^k} (\ln g) = g^{ij} \frac{\partial g_{ij}}{\partial x^k} \tag{8-8}$$

8-2. A Summary of Relations for Metric and Conjugate Tensors

1. The components of the Euclidean metric and conjugate metric tensors are symmetric.

$$g_{ij} = g_{ji} \quad \text{and} \quad g^{ij} = g^{ji} \tag{8-9}$$

2. The dot or scalar product of two vectors $\mathbf{a}$ and $\mathbf{b}$ in rectangular coordinates may be calculated by the relations

$$\mathbf{a} \cdot \mathbf{b} = a^i b_i = a_i b^i = g_{ij} a^i b^j = g^{ij} a_i b_j \tag{8-10}$$

3. The square of the length of vector $\mathbf{a}$ and the cosine $(\mathbf{a}, \mathbf{b})$ may be expressed as

$$|\mathbf{a}^2| = \mathbf{a} \cdot \mathbf{a} = a_i a^i = g_{ij} a^i a^j = g^{ij} a_i a_j \tag{8-11}$$

$$\cos (\mathbf{a}, \mathbf{b}) = \frac{g^{ij} a_i b_j}{(g^{kl} a_k a_l)^{1/2} (g^{mn} b_m b_n)^{1/2}} \tag{8-12}$$

4. The covariant and contravariant components of vector **a** are related to each other as follows.

$$\left.\begin{array}{l} a_i = g_{ij}a^j \\ a^i = g^{ij}a_j \end{array}\right\} \tag{8-13}$$

5. Reciprocal base vectors **e** are related to each other according to the equations

$$\begin{array}{l} \mathbf{e}_i = g_{ij}\mathbf{e}^j \\ \mathbf{e}^i = g^{ij}\mathbf{e}_j \end{array} \tag{8-14}$$

The proof for these equations may be established in the following manner.

The vector **a** may be expressed in terms of the base vectors, $\mathbf{e}^j$, as follows.

$$\mathbf{a} = a_j\mathbf{e}^j$$

Also

$$\mathbf{a} \cdot \mathbf{e}_j = a_j$$

Hence substituting gives

$$\mathbf{a} = (\mathbf{a} \cdot \mathbf{e}_j)\mathbf{e}^j$$

Replacing **a** by $\mathbf{e}_i$ results in

$$\mathbf{e}_i = (\mathbf{e}_i \cdot \mathbf{e}_j)\mathbf{e}^j$$

But

$$\mathbf{e}_i \cdot \mathbf{e}_j = g_{ij}$$

and hence

$$\mathbf{e}_i = g_{ij}\mathbf{e}^j$$

In a similar manner

$$\mathbf{e}^i = g^{ij}\mathbf{e}_j$$

6. The contravariant components of the conjugate tensor, g^{ji}, and the components of the metric tensor, g_{ij}, are related to each other in accordance with the equations

$$\begin{array}{l} g_{ik}g^{kj} = \delta_i{}^j \\ g^{jk}g_{ki} = \delta_i{}^j \end{array} \tag{8-15}$$

7. The relationship between the metric and conjugate tensors for orthogonal systems is

$$g_{ij} = \frac{1}{g^{ij}} \tag{8-16}$$

8. The conjugate tensor and cofactor are related by

$$g^{ji} = \frac{G^{ji}}{g} \tag{8-17}$$

8-3. Raising and Lowering of Indices

At this time, in order to illustrate the raising and lowering of indices we adopt the system of placing only one superior and one inferior suffix in a vertical line. Dots will be used to designate vacant spaces. The mixed tensor A_s^r will then be represented by $A_{.s}^{\ r}$. Likewise the tensor C_t^{rs} may be represented by $C_{..t}^{\ \ rs}$. In general, in the superscripts a letter ends the series.

If the inner products are formed with the metric or conjugate tensors and a given tensor, other tensor forms are generated. Let us form the inner product of the metric tensor g_{li} and the tensor $A_{.jk}^{\ \ \ i}$.

$$g_{li}A_{.jk}^{\ \ \ i} = A_{ljk}$$

It is evident that the index i has been removed from the superscript position related to A. This is called lowering the index. Suppose we wish to lower the index t in the tensor A^{rt}. Multiplying by g_{st} gives

$$g_{st}A^{rt} = A_{.s}^{\ r}$$

Other examples follow.

$$g_{rt}A^{ts} = A_r^{\ \cdot s}$$

$$g_{rt}g_{su}A^{tu} = A_{rs}$$

It is customary to use the same capital letter to designate all tensors generated from a given tensor by lowering the indices.

Raising the index involves forming the inner product of the conjugate tensor with the given tensor. Examples follow.

$$g^{rt}B_{ts} = B_{.s}^{\ r}$$

$$g^{st}B_{rt} = B_r^{\ \cdot s}$$

$$g^{rt}g^{su}B_{tu} = B^{rs}$$

If a certain index of a tensor is lowered and then raised, the tensor is the same as the original one. For example,

$$g_{st}A^{rt} = A_{.s}^{\ r}$$

$$g^{st}A_{.s}^{\ r} = A^{rt}$$

8-4. Magnitude of a Vector

The magnitude of a vector **a** may be expressed as

$$|\mathbf{a}|^2 = \mathbf{a} \cdot \mathbf{a} = a_i a^i$$

However,

$$a^i = g^{ij} a_j$$

Substituting gives

$$|\mathbf{a}|^2 = a_i a_j g^{ij} = a^i a^j g_{ij}$$

Therefore

$$|\mathbf{a}| = \sqrt{a_i a^i} = \sqrt{g_{ij} a^i a^j} = \sqrt{g^{ij} a_i a_j} \qquad (8\text{-}18)$$

If the coordinates are rectangular Cartesian coordinates,

$$g_{ij} = \delta_{ij}$$

and

$$|\mathbf{a}| = \sqrt{\delta_{ij} a^i a^j}$$

For $i = j$ and $i = 1, 2, 3$ we obtain the familiar relation

$$\mathbf{a} = \sqrt{(a^1)^2 + (a^2)^2 + (a^3)^2}$$

8-5. Angle between Two Vectors

The angle between two unit vectors $\mathbf{e}_1$ and $\mathbf{e}_2$ may be found by use of the dot product; thus

$$\cos \theta = \frac{\mathbf{e}_1 \cdot \mathbf{e}_2}{|\mathbf{e}_1| \, |\mathbf{e}_2|} = \mathbf{e}_1 \cdot \mathbf{e}_2$$

An equivalent expression according to equation (8-10) gives

$$\cos \theta = g_{ij} e_1{}^i e_2{}^j \qquad (8\text{-}19)$$

Another, more roundabout method is now also presented. Consider two curves passing through a point M as shown in Fig. 8-1. The distances from M to points $B_{(1)}$ and $B_{(2)}$ are $ds_{(1)}$ and $ds_{(2)}$, respectively.

According to the cosine law the angle θ between the direction of the curves at M may be expressed as

$$\cos \theta = \frac{(ds_{(1)})^2 + (ds_{(2)})^2 - (B_{(1)} - B_{(2)})^2}{2 \, ds_{(1)} \, ds_{(2)}}$$

The coordinates of the points M, $B_{(1)}$, and $B_{(2)}$ are x^i, $x^i + dx^i_{(1)}$, $x^i + dx^i_{(2)}$, respectively. Also

$$(ds_{(1)})^2 = g_{ij}\, dx^i_{(1)}\, dx^j_{(1)}$$
$$(ds_{(2)})^2 = g_{ij}\, dx^i_{(2)}\, dx^j_{(2)}$$
$$(B_{(1)} - B_{(2)})^2 = g_{ij}\, (dx^i_{(2)} - dx^i_{(1)})\,(dx^j_{(2)} - dx^j_{(1)})$$

Hence

$$\cos\theta = \frac{g_{ij}(dx^i_{(2)}\, dx^j_{(1)} + dx^j_{(2)}\, dx^i_{(1)})}{2\, ds_{(1)}\, ds_{(2)}}$$

Since g_{ij} is symmetric,

$$g_{ij}\, dx^i_{(2)}\, dx^j_{(1)} = g_{ij}\, dx^i_{(1)}\, dx^j_{(2)}$$

The numerator may be written

$$2g_{ij}\, dx^i_{(1)}\, dx^j_{(2)}$$

Rewriting the expression for $\cos\theta$ gives

$$\cos\theta = \frac{g_{ij}\, dx^i_{(1)}\, dx^j_{(2)}}{ds_{(1)}\, ds_{(2)}} = g_{ij}\left(\frac{dx^i_{(1)}}{ds_{(1)}}\right)\left(\frac{dx^j_{(2)}}{ds_{(2)}}\right)$$

Now $(dx^i_{(1)}/ds_{(1)})$ and $(dx^j_{(2)}/ds_{(2)})$ are unit contravariant vectors tangent to the curves at point M. Let $e^i_{(1)}$ and $e^j_{(2)}$ represent these vectors. Substituting gives

$$\cos\theta = g_{ij}\, e_1{}^i e_2{}^j \qquad (8\text{-}19)$$

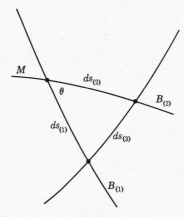

Fig. 8-1.

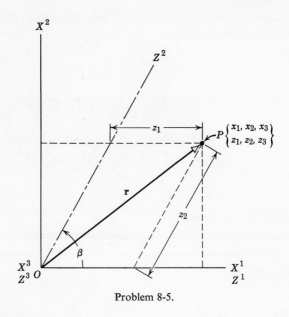

Problem 8-5.

8-6. Problems

8-1. Find the components of g^{rs} in cylindrical coordinates.

8-2. Find the components of g_{ij} and g^{ij} in spherical coordinates.

8-3. If $g_{mn} = 0$ for $m \neq n$, show that $g^{22} = 1/g_{22}$ and $g^{12} = 0$.

8-4. Evaluate $g_{mn}g^{mn}$ for a range of 3.

8-5. Consider the X^1, X^2, X^3 and Z^1, Z^2, Z^3 coordinate systems shown in the figure. The axes X^1, X^2, and Z^1, Z^2 are all in the same plane. Axis Z^2 is at an angle β with Z^1, and X^1 and Z^1 coincide as well as X^3 and Z^3. Determine the g_{rs} and g^{rs} values.

8-7. Suggested References

See references at end of Chapter 7.

9

Geodesics and the
Christoffel Symbols

9-1. Geodesics

The general equation for the line element $(ds)^2$ for space is the quadratic form

$$(ds)^2 = g_{\alpha\beta}\, dz^\alpha\, dz^\beta \qquad (7\text{-}15)$$

The term $g_{\alpha\beta}$ represents the components of the metric tensor. This quadratic differential form is referred to as the Riemannian metric. Any space for which $g_{\alpha\beta}$ is positive definite is known as a Riemannian space.

The study of tensors now leads to the problem of finding curves of minimum length joining two points on a given surface in space. Curves of this type are called geodesics. On a spherical surface a geodesic between two points is a portion of a great circle. On a plane surface the geodesic between two points is a section of a straight line. Relations developed which are based on n-dimensional Riemannian space are important because they are applicable to the geometry of surfaces and to dynamical trajectories in space.

The differential equations for the geodesic lines will be developed for a surface having two dimensions. These equations will be used later to establish equations for use in an n-dimensional space.

Let M and N represent two points on a surface S in a two-dimensional space. The length of the curve MP_1P_2N is designated L,

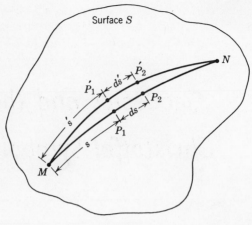

Fig. 9-1.

and *ds* represents an element of this curve as shown in Fig. 9-1. The length of the curve MP_1P_2N may be expressed in equation form as

$$L = \int_M^N ds \qquad (9\text{-}1)$$

The curve $MP_1'P_2'N$ is infinitesimally near curve MP_1P_2N, and its length is $L + \delta L$. The curve MP_1P_2N will be a geodesic if and only if

$$\delta L = \delta \int_M^N ds = 0 \qquad (9\text{-}2)$$

We may then conclude that the length of a geodesic line must be a minimum with regard to all curves connecting the same two points. The determination of the geodesic lines is somewhat analogous to finding the maximum and minimum values of algebraic functions. For geodesics the process is more complicated because it is necessary to find the minimum of arc lengths instead of considering points as in algebraic functions.

The distances measured along curve MP_1P_2N from M to P_1 and P_2 are s and $s + ds$, respectively. The corresponding distances along curve $MP_1'P_2'N$ are s' and $s' + ds'$. In the following discussions it is essential to remember that points P_1 and P_1' and P_2 and P_2' are infinitesimally close to each other. It is also assumed that the correspondence between ds and $d\acute{s}$ is one to one. The symbol δ is an operator used to denote minute differences in corresponding quantities for lines MP_1P_2N and $M\acute{P_1}\acute{P_2}N$.

The change in arc length, ds may be represented as

$$\delta \, ds = d\acute{s} - ds = d(\acute{s} - s) = d \, \delta s \qquad (9\text{-}3)$$

The expressions for the square of the arc length are

$$\delta \, (ds)^2 = (d\acute{s})^2 - (ds)^2 = (d\acute{s} + ds)(d\acute{s} - ds)$$
$$= (\delta \, ds + ds + ds)(\delta \, ds + ds - ds) = (\delta \, ds + 2 \, ds)(\delta \, ds)$$
$$= (\delta \, ds)^2 + 2 \, ds \, \delta \, ds = 2 \, ds \, \delta \, ds \qquad (9\text{-}4)$$

The final result neglects the small quantity $(\delta \, ds)^2$. The operator δ is now applied to equation (7-15).

$$\delta \, (ds)^2 = \delta \, (g_{ij} \, dz^i \, dz^j)$$

In this equation the coefficients g_{ij} are, in general, functions of the coordinates z^1 and z^2.

Carrying out the operation gives

$$2 \, ds \, \delta \, ds = dz^i \, dz^j \, \delta \, g_{ij} + g_{ij} \, dz^i \, \delta \, dz^j + g_{ij} \, dz^j \, \delta \, dz^i \qquad (9\text{-}5)$$

Since $\delta g_{ij} = (\partial g_{ij}/\partial z^k) \, \delta z^k$ the first term on the right side may be altered as follows.

$$dz^i \, dz^j \, \delta g_{ij} = \frac{\partial g_{ij}}{\partial z^k} \, dz^i \, dz^j \, \delta z^k = \frac{\partial g_{ik}}{\partial z^j} \, dz^i \, dz^k \, \delta z^j$$

Substituting this term into equation (9-5) and dividing by $2 \, ds$ gives

$$\delta \, ds = \frac{1}{2} \frac{\partial g_{ik}}{\partial z^j} \frac{dz^i}{ds} \frac{dz^k}{ds} \, \delta z^j \, ds + \frac{1}{2} g_{ij} \frac{dz^i}{ds} \, d \, \delta z^j$$
$$+ \frac{1}{2} g_{ij} \frac{dz^j}{ds} \, d \, \delta z^i \qquad (9\text{-}6)$$

Note that $\delta \, dz^j = d \, \delta z^j$.

In general form equation (9-2) may be expressed as

$$\delta L = \delta \int ds = \int d\acute{s} - \int ds = \int (d\acute{s} - ds)$$
$$= \int d(\acute{s} - s) = \int d \, \delta s = \int \delta \, ds \qquad (9\text{-}7)$$

Remember that $d\,\delta s = \delta\,ds$ from Equation (9-4).

Substituting for $\delta\,ds$ from equation (9-6) into (9-7) gives

$$\delta L = \int_M^N \frac{1}{2}\frac{\partial g_{ik}}{\partial z^j}\frac{dz^i}{ds}\frac{dz^k}{ds}\,\delta z^j\,ds + \int_M^N \frac{1}{2}\,g_{ij}\frac{dz^i}{ds}\,d\,\delta z^j$$

$$+ \int_M^N \frac{1}{2}\,g_{ij}\frac{dz^j}{ds}\,d\,\delta z^i \tag{9-8}$$

Since considerable manipulation is required in the solution of this equation, the last two terms on the right will be dealt with first. These terms will be designated by the symbol T. If the dummy indices i and j are interchanged in the extreme right term, the two terms are equal, since $g_{ji} = g_{ij}$. Hence

$$T = \int_M^N g_{ij}\frac{dz^i}{ds}\,d\,\delta z^j$$

Integrating by parts gives

$$T = \left(g_{ij}\frac{dz^i}{ds}\,\delta z^j\right)_M^N - \int_M^N d\left(g_{ij}\frac{dz^i}{ds}\right)\delta z^j$$

The first term on the right side of the equation must vanish, since at M and N the δz^j terms vanish. The integral may be split into two parts as follows.

$$T = -\int_M^N g_{ij}\frac{d^2 z^i}{ds^2}\,\delta z^j\,ds - \int_M^N dg_{ij}\frac{dz^i}{ds}\,\delta z^j$$

The expression in the extreme right integral may be represented by

$$dg_{ij}\frac{dz^i}{ds}\,\delta z^j = \frac{1}{2}\left(\frac{\partial g_{ij}}{\partial z^k}\,dz^k\frac{dz^i}{ds}\,\delta z^j + \frac{\partial g_{kj}}{\partial z^i}\,dz^i\frac{dz^k}{ds}\,\delta z^j\right)$$

The equivalence of these two expressions can easily be established by interchanging the dummy indices i and k in the right-hand term. The expression can then be rearranged as

$$dg_{ij}\frac{dz^i}{ds}\,\delta z^i = \frac{1}{2}\left(\frac{\partial g_{ij}}{\partial z^k} + \frac{\partial g_{kj}}{\partial z^i}\right)\frac{dz^i}{ds}\frac{dz^k}{ds}\,\delta z^j\,ds$$

Substituting this relation back into the equation for T and then substituting T in equation (9-7) gives

$$\delta L = \int_M^N \frac{1}{2}\frac{\partial g_{ik}}{\partial z^j}\frac{dz^i}{ds}\frac{dz^k}{ds}\,\delta z^j\,ds - \int_M^N g_{ij}\frac{d^2 z^i}{ds^2}\,\delta z^j\,ds$$

$$- \int_M^N \frac{1}{2}\left[\frac{\partial g_{ij}}{\partial z^k} + \frac{\partial g_{kj}}{\partial z^i}\right]\frac{dz^i}{ds}\frac{dz^k}{ds}\,\delta z^j\,ds$$

On rearranging,

$$\delta L = -\int_M^N \left\{ \frac{1}{2} \left(\frac{\partial g_{ij}}{\partial z^k} + \frac{\partial g_{kj}}{\partial z^i} - \frac{\partial g_{ik}}{\partial z^j} \right) \frac{dz^i}{ds} \frac{dz^k}{ds} + g_{ij} \frac{d^2 z^i}{ds^2} \right\} \delta z^j \, ds$$

The three partial derivative terms will be replaced by the following symbol.

$$[ik, j] = \frac{1}{2} \left(\frac{\partial g_{ij}}{\partial z^k} + \frac{\partial g_{kj}}{\partial z^i} - \frac{\partial g_{ik}}{\partial z^j} \right) \tag{9-9}$$

This relation is symmetrical in so far as i and k are concerned. The symbol $[ik, j]$ is termed the Christoffel symbol of the first kind.

The equation for δL becomes

$$\delta L = -\int_M^N \left([ik, j] \frac{dz^i}{ds} \frac{dz^k}{ds} + g_{ij} \frac{d^2 z^i}{ds^2} \right) \delta z^j \, ds \tag{9-10}$$

According to equation (9-2) the curve is a geodesic if δL vanishes. Because of the arbitrary nature of the δz's, the terms within the brackets must be zero; hence

$$g_{ij} \frac{d^2 z^i}{ds^2} + [ik, j] \frac{dz^i}{ds} \frac{dz^k}{ds} = 0 \tag{9-11}$$

Since we are dealing with a two-dimensional space, equation (9-11) represents two ordinary differential equations of the second order ($j = 1, 2$). A summation around i is needed in the first term and one around i and k in the second term.

Multiplying equation (9-11) by g^{lj} and summing on j gives

$$g_{ij} g^{lj} \frac{d^2 z^i}{ds^2} + g^{lj}[ik, j] \frac{dz^i}{ds} \frac{dz^k}{ds} = 0$$

However, $g_{ij} g^{lj} = \delta_i{}^l$. If $i = l$, then $\delta_i{}^l = 1$. Hence

$$\frac{d^2 z^l}{ds^2} + g^{lj}[ik, j] \frac{dz^i}{ds} \frac{dz^k}{ds} = 0 \tag{9-12}$$

Let

$$g^{lj}[ik, j] = \left\{ \begin{matrix} l \\ i \ k \end{matrix} \right\} = \{ik, l\}$$

It then follows that

$$[ik, j] = g_{lj} \left\{ \begin{matrix} l \\ i \ k \end{matrix} \right\} = g_{lj}\{ik, l\} \tag{9-13}$$

The new symbols are called the Christoffel symbols of the second kind. Both forms

$$\begin{Bmatrix} l \\ i\,k \end{Bmatrix} \quad \text{and} \quad \{ik, l\}$$

are used in the literature and are symmetrical in i and k.

Using the Christoffel symbol of the second kind, equation (9-13) may now be written as

$$\frac{d^2 z^l}{ds^2} + \begin{Bmatrix} l \\ i\,k \end{Bmatrix} \frac{dz^i}{ds} \frac{dz^k}{ds} = 0 \qquad (i, k, l = 1, 2) \qquad (9\text{-}14)$$

Although the discussion has been limited to a two-dimensional space, the equations may be extended to n-dimensional space. Hence

$$\frac{d^2 z^l}{ds^2} + \begin{Bmatrix} l \\ i\,k \end{Bmatrix} \frac{dz^i}{ds} \frac{dz^k}{ds} = 0 \qquad (i, k, l = 1, 2, 3, \ldots, n)$$

This expression represents n differential equations, which when integrated give the parametric equations for the geodesic line.

We have thus obtained the equations of the geodesic line in the following forms.

$$g_{ij} \frac{d^2 z^i}{ds^2} + [ik, j] \frac{dz^i}{ds} \frac{dz^k}{ds} = 0 \qquad (9\text{-}11)$$

and

$$\frac{d^2 z^l}{ds^2} + \begin{Bmatrix} l \\ i\,k \end{Bmatrix} \frac{dz^i}{ds} \frac{dz^k}{ds} = 0 \qquad (9\text{-}14)$$

Example 9-1

Determine the expressions for the Christoffel symbols of the first and second kind for a space where $g_{ij} = 0$ if $i \neq j$.

Refer to equation (9-9).

$$[ij, k] = \frac{1}{2} \left(\frac{\partial g_{ik}}{\partial z^j} + \frac{\partial g_{jk}}{\partial z^i} - \frac{\partial g_{ij}}{\partial z^k} \right)$$

If $i = j = k$, then, suspending the summation convention,

$$[ii, i] = \frac{1}{2} \left(\frac{\partial g_{ii}}{\partial z^i} + \frac{\partial g_{ii}}{\partial z^i} - \frac{\partial g_{ii}}{\partial z^i} \right) = \frac{1}{2} \frac{\partial g_{ii}}{\partial z^i}$$

If $i = j \neq k$, then

$$[ii, k] = \frac{1}{2} \left(\frac{\partial g_{ik}}{\partial z^i} + \frac{\partial g_{ik}}{\partial z^i} - \frac{\partial g_{ii}}{\partial z^k} \right) = -\frac{1}{2} \frac{\partial g_{ii}}{\partial z^k}$$

(Since $i \neq k, g_{ik} = 0$ in accordance with the original requirement.)

If $i = k \neq j$,

$$[ij, i] = \frac{1}{2}\left(\frac{\partial g_{ii}}{\partial z^j} + \frac{\partial g_{ji}}{\partial z^i} - \frac{\partial g_{ij}}{\partial z^i}\right) = \frac{1}{2}\frac{\partial g_{ii}}{\partial z^j}$$

If i, j, and k are distinct, the Christoffel symbol of the first kind is zero, or $[ij, k] = 0$.

According to equation (9-13),

$$\begin{Bmatrix} l \\ i\,j \end{Bmatrix} = g^{lk}[ij, k]$$

If $k \neq l$,

$$\begin{Bmatrix} l \\ i\,j \end{Bmatrix} = g^{lk}[ij, k] = 0$$

(This is true since $g^{lk} = 0$ in accordance with the original requirement that $g_{ij} = 0$ if $i \neq j$.)

If $k = l$, then, dropping the summation convention,

$$\begin{Bmatrix} l \\ i\,j \end{Bmatrix} = g^{ll}[ij, l] = \frac{1}{g_{ll}}[ij, l]$$

If $i = j = l$,

$$\begin{Bmatrix} i \\ i\,i \end{Bmatrix} = \frac{1}{g_{ii}}[ii, i] = \frac{1}{2g_{ii}}\frac{\partial g_{ii}}{\partial z_i} = \frac{1}{2}\frac{\partial \ln g_{ii}}{\partial z^i}$$

If $i = j \neq l$,

$$\begin{Bmatrix} l \\ i\,i \end{Bmatrix} = \frac{1}{g_{ll}}[ii, l] = -\frac{1}{2g_{ll}}\frac{\partial g_{ii}}{\partial z^l}$$

If $i = l \neq j$,

$$\begin{Bmatrix} i \\ i\,j \end{Bmatrix} = \frac{1}{g_{ii}}[ij, i] = \frac{1}{2g_{ii}}\frac{\partial g_{ii}}{\partial z^j} = \frac{1}{2}\frac{\partial \ln g_{ii}}{\partial z^j}$$

If i, j, and l are distinct,

$$\begin{Bmatrix} l \\ i\,j \end{Bmatrix} = 0$$

Example 9-2

Determine the Christoffel symbols of the first and second kinds for rectangular Cartesian, cylindrical, and spherical coordinates.

Cartesian Rectangular Coordinates. The criteria of $g_{ij} = \delta_{ij}$ describes a Cartesian rectangular coordinate system. For this type of system $g_{ii} = 1$ as shown in Section 7-1. Because this is the same system used in Example 9-1 the relations developed there may be used. Substituting $g_{ij} = \delta_{ij}$ gives

$$[ij, k] = 0 \quad \text{and} \quad \begin{Bmatrix} l \\ i\,j \end{Bmatrix} = 0$$

In other words, the Christoffel symbols of the first and second kinds are zero for a rectangular Cartesian coordinate system.

Cylindrical Coordinates. The Cartesian coordinates x^1, x^2, x^3 are related to the cylindrical coordinates r, θ, z by the equations

$$
\begin{aligned}
x^1 &= r \cos \theta = z^1 \cos z^2, & r &= z^1 \\
x^2 &= r \sin \theta = z^1 \sin z^2, & \theta &= z^2 \\
x^3 &= z = z^3, & z &= z^3
\end{aligned}
$$

In Section 7-1 the values for g_{ij} were found to be $g_{11} = 1$, $g_{22} = r^2$, $g_{33} = 1$, and all others zero. Hence we may use the results of Example 9-1 to find the values for the Christoffel symbols because the criteria $g_{ij} = 0$ if $i \neq j$ is also valid for cylindrical coordinates.

The Christoffel symbols of the first kind having values other than zero are

$$
[22, 1] = -\frac{1}{2} \frac{\partial r^2}{\partial r} = -r
$$

$$
[21, 2] = [12, 2] = \frac{1}{2} \frac{\partial r^2}{\partial r} = r
$$

The Christoffel symbols of the second kind having values other than zero are

$$
\left\{ \begin{matrix} 2 \\ 2\ 1 \end{matrix} \right\} = \left\{ \begin{matrix} 2 \\ 1\ 2 \end{matrix} \right\} = \frac{1}{g_{22}} [21, 2] = \frac{r}{r^2} = \frac{1}{r}
$$

$$
\left\{ \begin{matrix} 1 \\ 2\ 2 \end{matrix} \right\} = \frac{1}{g_{11}} [22, 1] = \frac{-r}{1} = -r
$$

Spherical Coordinates. The Cartesian coordinates x^1, x^2, x^3 are related to the spherical coordinates r, ϕ, θ by the equations

$$
\begin{aligned}
x^1 &= r \sin \phi \cos \theta = z^1 \sin z^2 \cos z^3, & r &= z^1 \\
x^2 &= r \sin \phi \sin \theta = z^1 \sin z^2 \sin z^3, & \phi &= z^2 \\
x^3 &= r \cos \phi = z^1 \cos z^2, & \theta &= z^3
\end{aligned}
$$

In Section 7-1 the values for g_{ij} were found to be $g_{11} = 1$, $g_{22} = r^2$, $g_{33} = r^2 \sin^2 \phi$.

Again the results in Example 9-1 may be used because $g_{ij} = 0$ if $i \neq j$.

The Christoffel symbols of the first kind having values other than zero are

$$
[22, 1] = -\frac{1}{2} \frac{\partial r^2}{\partial r} = -r
$$

$$
[33, 2] = -\frac{1}{2} \frac{\partial r^2 \sin^2 \phi}{\partial \phi} = -r^2 \sin \phi \cos \phi
$$

$$
[23, 3] = [32, 3] = \frac{1}{2} \frac{\partial r^2 \sin^2 \phi}{\partial \phi} = r^2 \sin \phi \cos \phi
$$

$$
[33, 1] = -\frac{1}{2} \frac{\partial r^2 \sin^2 \phi}{\partial r} = -r \sin^2 \phi
$$

$$
[12, 2] = [21, 2] = \frac{1}{2} \frac{\partial r^2}{\partial r} = r
$$

$$
[31, 3] = [13, 3] = \frac{1}{2} \frac{\partial r^2 \sin^2 \phi}{\partial r} = r \sin^2 \phi
$$

The Christoffel symbols of the second kind having values other than zero are

$$\begin{Bmatrix} 1 \\ 2\ 2 \end{Bmatrix} = \frac{1}{g_{11}} [22, 1] \qquad = -r$$

$$\begin{Bmatrix} 2 \\ 3\ 3 \end{Bmatrix} = \frac{1}{g_{22}} [33, 2] \qquad = -\sin \phi \cos \phi$$

$$\begin{Bmatrix} 3 \\ 3\ 2 \end{Bmatrix} = \begin{Bmatrix} 3 \\ 2\ 3 \end{Bmatrix} = \frac{1}{g_{33}} [32, 3] = \cot \phi$$

$$\begin{Bmatrix} 1 \\ 3\ 3 \end{Bmatrix} = \frac{1}{g_{11}} [33, 1] \qquad = -r \sin^2 \phi$$

$$\begin{Bmatrix} 2 \\ 2\ 1 \end{Bmatrix} = \begin{Bmatrix} 2 \\ 1\ 2 \end{Bmatrix} = \frac{1}{g_{22}} [21, 2] = \frac{1}{r}$$

$$\begin{Bmatrix} 3 \\ 3\ 1 \end{Bmatrix} = \begin{Bmatrix} 3 \\ 1\ 3 \end{Bmatrix} = \frac{1}{g_{33}} [31, 3] = \frac{1}{r}$$

Example 9-3

Using polar coordinates, show that the geodesics in a plane are straight lines. The point P is represented on the two-dimensional surface as shown in Fig. 9-2.

$$i = 1, 2 \quad \text{and} \quad j = 1, 2$$

Hence

$$(ds)^2 = g_{ij}\, dz^i\, dz^j = g_{11}\, dz^1\, dz^1 + g_{22}\, dz^2\, dz^2 + g_{12}\, dz^1\, dz^2 + g_{21}\, dz^2\, dz^1$$

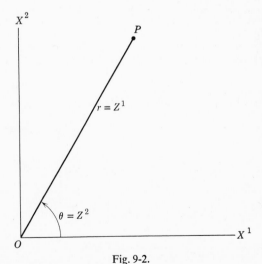

Fig. 9-2.

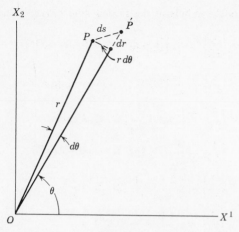

Fig. 9-3.

Considering the polar coordinates (see Fig. 9-3) the value for $(ds)^2$ may be expressed as

$$(ds)^2 = (dr)^2 + r^2 (d\theta)^2$$

Comparing these relations for ds, we see that $g_{11} = 1, g_{22} = r^2, g_{12} = 0$, and $g_{21} = 0$. Hence

$$|g_{ij}| = \begin{vmatrix} g_{11} & g_{12} \\ g_{21} & g_{22} \end{vmatrix} = \begin{vmatrix} 1 & 0 \\ 0 & r^2 \end{vmatrix} = r^2$$

The Christoffel symbols of the first kind will be obtained by use of equation (9-9). In this problem $z^1 = r$ and $z^2 = \theta$.

Substituting gives

$$[11, 1] = \frac{1}{2} \left(\frac{\partial g_{11}}{\partial z^1} + \frac{\partial g_{11}}{\partial z^1} - \frac{\partial g_{11}}{\partial z^1} \right) = \frac{1}{2} \frac{\partial g_{11}}{\partial z^1} = 0$$

$$[11, 2] = \frac{1}{2} \left(\frac{\partial g_{21}}{\partial z^1} + \frac{\partial g_{21}}{\partial z^1} - \frac{\partial g_{11}}{\partial z^2} \right) = 0$$

$$[12, 1] = [21, 1] = \frac{1}{2} \left(\frac{\partial g_{12}}{\partial z^1} + \frac{\partial g_{11}}{\partial z^2} - \frac{\partial g_{12}}{\partial z^1} \right) = 0$$

$$[12, 2] = [21, 2] = \frac{1}{2} \left(\frac{\partial g_{22}}{\partial z^1} + \frac{\partial g_{21}}{\partial z^2} - \frac{\partial g_{12}}{\partial z^2} \right) = \frac{1}{2} \frac{\partial r^2}{\partial r} = r$$

$$[22, 1] = \frac{1}{2} \left(\frac{\partial g_{12}}{\partial z^2} + \frac{\partial g_{12}}{\partial z^2} - \frac{\partial g_{22}}{\partial z^1} \right) = -\frac{1}{2} \frac{\partial r^2}{\partial r} = -r$$

$$[22, 2] = \frac{1}{2} \left(\frac{\partial g_{22}}{\partial z^2} + \frac{\partial g_{22}}{\partial z^2} - \frac{\partial g_{22}}{\partial z^2} \right) = 0$$

The Christoffel symbols of the second kind will be obtained from equation (9-13).

Since we are dealing with a two-dimensional system, the i's will be summed over 1 and 2.

$$\left\{ {1 \atop 1\,1} \right\} = g^{11}[11,1] + g^{12}[11,2] = 0$$

$$\left\{ {2 \atop 1\,1} \right\} = g^{21}[11,1] + g^{22}[11,2] = 0$$

$$\left\{ {1 \atop 1\,2} \right\} = \left\{ {1 \atop 2\,1} \right\} = g^{11}[12,1] + g^{12}[12,2] = 0$$

$$\left\{ {2 \atop 1\,2} \right\} = \left\{ {2 \atop 2\,1} \right\} = g^{21}[12,1] + g^{22}[12,2] = \frac{1}{r}$$

$$\left\{ {1 \atop 2\,2} \right\} = g^{11}[22,1] + g^{12}[22,2] = -r$$

$$\left\{ {2 \atop 2\,2} \right\} = g^{21}[22,1] + g^{22}[22,2] = 0$$

Substituting in equation (9-14) results in the following equations, wherein $\ddot{z}$ and $\dot{z}$ represent the second and first derivatives with respect to s, For $l = 1$,

$$\ddot{z}^1 + \left\{ {1 \atop j\,k} \right\} \dot{z}^j \dot{z}^k = 0$$

$$\ddot{z}^1 + \left\{ {1 \atop 1\,1} \right\} \dot{z}^1 \dot{z}^1 + \left\{ {1 \atop 2\,2} \right\} \dot{z}^2 \dot{z}^2 + \left\{ {1 \atop 1\,2} \right\} \dot{z}^1 \dot{z}^2 + \left\{ {1 \atop 2\,1} \right\} \dot{z}^1 \dot{z}^2 = 0$$

$$\ddot{z}^1 + \left\{ {1 \atop 2\,2} \right\} \dot{z}^2 \dot{z}^2 = 0$$

For $l = 2$,

$$\ddot{z}^2 + \left\{ {2 \atop 1\,1} \right\} \dot{z}^1 \dot{z}^1 + \left\{ {2 \atop 2\,2} \right\} \dot{z}^2 \dot{z}^2 + \left\{ {2 \atop 1\,2} \right\} \dot{z}^1 \dot{z}^2 + \left\{ {2 \atop 2\,1} \right\} \dot{z}^2 \dot{z}^1 = 0$$

$$\ddot{z}^{12} + \left\{ {2 \atop 1\,2} \right\} \dot{z}^1 \dot{z}^2 + \left\{ {2 \atop 2\,1} \right\} \dot{z}^2 \dot{z}^1 = 0$$

Thus

(a)
$$\ddot{z}^1 - r(\dot{z}^2)^2 = 0$$

and

(b)
$$\ddot{z}^2 + \frac{2}{r} \dot{z}^1 \dot{z}^2 = 0$$

or

(c)
$$\ddot{r} - r(\dot{\theta})^2 = 0$$

and

(d)
$$\ddot{\theta} + \frac{2}{r} \dot{r}\dot{\theta} = 0$$

Multiplying equation (*d*) by r^2 gives

$$r^2\ddot{\theta} + 2r\dot{r}\dot{\theta} = 0$$

or

$$\frac{d}{ds}\left(r^2\dot{\theta}\right) = 0$$

Solving gives

$$r^2\dot{\theta} = \text{constant} = \alpha$$

Let $V = 1/r$. Then

$$\dot{\theta} = \alpha V^2$$

Now

$$\dot{r} = \frac{dr}{d\theta}\frac{d\theta}{ds} = \frac{dr}{d\theta}\dot{\theta} = \dot{\theta}\frac{d}{d\theta}\left(\frac{1}{V}\right) = -V^{-2}\frac{dV}{d\theta}\alpha V^2 = -\alpha\frac{dV}{d\theta}$$

$$\ddot{r} = \frac{d}{ds}\left(-\alpha\frac{dV}{d\theta}\right) = -\alpha\frac{d^2V}{d\theta^2}\dot{\theta} = -\alpha^2 V^2\frac{d^2V}{d\theta^2}$$

Substituting these relations in equation (*c*) gives

$$-\alpha^2 V^2\frac{d^2V}{d\theta^2} - \frac{1}{V}\alpha^2 V^4 = 0$$

or

$$\frac{d^2V}{d\theta^2} + V = 0$$

The solution of the equation is

$$V = a^{-1}\cos\left(\theta - \beta\right)$$

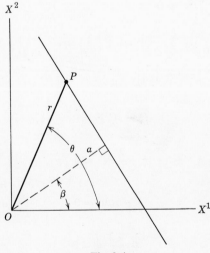

Fig. 9-4.

where a is the perpendicular distance from the origin to the line and β is the angle between a and the X^1 axis.

$$r = a \sec (\theta - \beta)$$

This is the equation of a straight line as shown in Fig. 9-4.

9-2. Transformation of the Christoffel Symbols

The symbols z^r and $\acute{z}^r$ will be considered as two sets of curvilinear coordinates. The geodesics equation (9-14) in terms of these coordinates may be written

$$\frac{d^2z^r}{ds^2} + \left\{ \begin{matrix} r \\ m\,n \end{matrix} \right\} \frac{dz^m}{ds} \frac{dz^n}{ds} = 0 \tag{9-15}$$

and

$$\frac{d^2\acute{z}^s}{ds^2} + \left\{ \begin{matrix} \acute{s} \\ p\,q \end{matrix} \right\} \frac{d\acute{z}^p}{ds} \frac{d\acute{z}^q}{ds} = 0 \tag{9-16}$$

Now

$$\frac{dz^r}{ds} = \frac{\partial z^r}{\partial \acute{z}^p} \frac{d\acute{z}^p}{ds}$$

and

$$\frac{d^2z^r}{ds^2} = \frac{\partial z^r}{\partial \acute{z}^p} \frac{d^2\acute{z}^p}{ds^2} + \frac{d\acute{z}^p}{ds} \frac{d}{ds}\left(\frac{\partial z^r}{\partial \acute{z}^p} \right)$$

Using the chain rule for differentiation,

$$\frac{d^2z^r}{ds^2} = \frac{\partial z^r}{\partial \acute{z}^p} \frac{d^2\acute{z}^p}{ds^2} + \frac{\partial^2 z^r}{\partial \acute{z}^p \partial \acute{z}^q} \frac{d\acute{z}^q}{ds} \frac{d\acute{z}^p}{ds}$$

Substituting in equation (9-15) gives

$$\frac{\partial z^r}{\partial \acute{z}^p} \frac{d^2\acute{z}^p}{ds^2} + \left(\frac{\partial^2 z^r}{\partial \acute{z}^p \partial \acute{z}^q} + \left\{ \begin{matrix} r \\ m\,n \end{matrix} \right\} \frac{\partial z^m}{\partial \acute{z}^p} \frac{\partial z^n}{\partial \acute{z}^q} \right) \frac{d\acute{z}^p}{ds} \frac{d\acute{z}^q}{ds} = 0$$

Multiplying by $\partial \acute{z}^s / \partial z^r$ and summing on r gives

$$\frac{\partial \acute{z}^s}{\partial z^r} \frac{\partial z^r}{\partial \acute{z}^p} \frac{d^2\acute{z}^p}{ds^2} + \left(\frac{\partial \acute{z}^s}{\partial z^r} \frac{\partial^2 z^r}{\partial \acute{z}^p \partial \acute{z}^q} + \left\{ \begin{matrix} r \\ m\,n \end{matrix} \right\} \frac{\partial \acute{z}^s}{\partial z^r} \frac{\partial z^m}{\partial \acute{z}^p} \frac{\partial z^n}{\partial \acute{z}^q} \right) \frac{d\acute{z}^p}{ds} \frac{d\acute{z}^q}{ds} = 0$$

Now

$$\frac{\partial \acute{z}^s}{\partial z^r} \frac{\partial z^r}{\partial \acute{z}^p} = \delta_p{}^s$$

Substituting gives

$$\frac{d^2 z'^s}{ds^2} + \left(\frac{\partial z'^s}{\partial z^r}\frac{\partial^2 z^r}{\partial z'^p \partial z'^q} + \left\{\begin{matrix} r \\ m\ n \end{matrix}\right\}\frac{\partial z'^s}{\partial z^r}\frac{\partial z^m}{\partial z'^p}\frac{\partial z^n}{\partial z'^q}\right)\frac{dz'^p}{ds}\frac{dz'^q}{ds} = 0$$

A comparison of this relation and equation (9-16) shows that

$$\left\{\begin{matrix} s \\ p\ q \end{matrix}\right\} = \frac{\partial z'^s}{\partial z^r}\frac{\partial z^m}{\partial z'^p}\frac{\partial z^n}{\partial z'^q}\left\{\begin{matrix} r \\ m\ n \end{matrix}\right\} + \frac{\partial z'^s}{\partial z^r}\frac{\partial^2 z^r}{\partial z'^p \partial z'^q} \tag{9-17}$$

This then represents the transformation equation of the Christoffel symbols of the second kind. These symbols are not tensors, since they do not follow a tensor transformation.

We now develop the relation for the transformation of the Christoffel symbols of the first kind.

Consider the relations previously established equation (9-13).

$$[mn,\ l]g^{rl} = \left\{\begin{matrix} r \\ m\ n \end{matrix}\right\}$$

$$[mn,\ l] = g_{rl}\left\{\begin{matrix} r \\ m\ n \end{matrix}\right\}$$

$$[p'q',\ j] = g'_{sj}\left\{\begin{matrix} s \\ p\ q \end{matrix}\right\}$$

$$[pq',\ j]g'^{sj} = \left\{\begin{matrix} s \\ p\ q \end{matrix}\right\}$$

Substituting in equation (9-17) gives

$$[pq',\ j]g'^{sj} = \frac{\partial z'^s}{\partial z^r}\frac{\partial z^m}{\partial z'^p}\frac{\partial z^n}{\partial z'^q}\,g^{rl}[mn,\ l] + \frac{\partial z'^s}{\partial z^r}\frac{\partial^2 z^r}{\partial z'^p \partial z'^q}$$

Multiply both sides of this equation by g'_{st},

$$[pq',\ j]g'_{st}g'^{sj} = \frac{\partial z'^s}{\partial z^r}\frac{\partial z^m}{\partial z'^p}\frac{\partial z^n}{\partial z'^q}\,g^{rl}g'_{st}[mn,\ l] + g'_{st}\frac{\partial z'^s}{\partial z^r}\frac{\partial^2 z^r}{\partial z'^p \partial z'^q}$$

$g'_{st}g'^{sj}$ will be replaced by its equivalent, $\delta_t^{\ j}$. Summing on j gives

$$[p'q',\ j] = \frac{\partial z'^s}{\partial z^r}\frac{\partial z^m}{\partial z'^p}\frac{\partial z^n}{\partial z'^q}\,g'_{sj}g^{rl}[mn,\ l] + g'_{sj}\frac{\partial z'^s}{\partial z^r}\frac{\partial^2 z^r}{\partial z'^p \partial z'^q}$$

According to the transformation equation,

$$g'_{sj} = \frac{\partial z^a}{\partial z'^s}\frac{\partial z^b}{\partial z'^j}\,g_{ab}$$

Substituting yields

$$[p\acute{q},j] = \frac{\partial z'^s}{\partial z^r}\frac{\partial z^m}{\partial z'^p}\frac{\partial z^n}{\partial z'^q}\frac{\partial z^a}{\partial z'^s}\frac{\partial z^b}{\partial z'^j}\,g_{ab}g^{rl}[mn,\,l] + \frac{\partial z'^s}{\partial z^r}\frac{\partial^2 z^r}{\partial z'^p\,\partial z'^q}\frac{\partial z^a}{\partial z'^s}\frac{\partial z^b}{\partial z'^j}\,g_{ab}$$

or

$$[p\acute{q},j] = \frac{\partial z^m}{\partial z'^p}\frac{\partial z^n}{\partial z'^q}\frac{\partial z^b}{\partial z'^j}\,g_{rb}g^{rl}[mn,\,l] + g_{rb}\frac{\partial z^b}{\partial z'^j}\frac{\partial^2 z^r}{\partial z'^p\,\partial z'^q}$$

but

$$g_{rb}g^{rl} = \delta_b{}^l$$

If $b = l$, $\delta = 1$. Therefore

$$[p\acute{q},j] = \frac{\partial z^m}{\partial z'^p}\frac{\partial z^n}{\partial z'^q}\frac{\partial z^l}{\partial z'^j}\,[mn,\,l] + g_{rb}\frac{\partial z^b}{\partial z'^j}\frac{\partial^2 z^r}{\partial z'^p\,\partial z'^q} \qquad (9\text{-}18)$$

This is the transformation relation for the Christoffel symbols of the first kind.

9-3. Base Vectors and the Christoffel Symbols

The covariant components of the Euclidean metric tensor, g_{ij}, are related to the base vectors $\mathbf{g}_i$ by the relation

$$g_{ij} = \mathbf{g}_i \cdot \mathbf{g}_j \qquad (1\text{-}23)$$

Taking the derivative of this expression with respect to z^k gives

$$\frac{\partial g_{ij}}{\partial z^k} = \frac{\partial \mathbf{g}_i}{\partial z^k}\cdot \mathbf{g}_j + \frac{\partial \mathbf{g}_j}{\partial z^k}\cdot \mathbf{g}_i \qquad (9\text{-}19)$$

By changing the order of the indices (permuting), the following relations may be written.

$$ijk \rightarrow ikj$$

$$\frac{\partial g_{ik}}{\partial z^j} = \frac{\partial \mathbf{g}_i}{\partial z^j}\cdot \mathbf{g}_k + \frac{\partial \mathbf{g}_k}{\partial z^j}\cdot \mathbf{g}_i \qquad (9\text{-}20)$$

and

$$ijk \rightarrow jki$$

$$\frac{\partial g_{jk}}{\partial z^i} = \frac{\partial \mathbf{g}_j}{\partial z^i}\cdot \mathbf{g}_k + \frac{\partial \mathbf{g}_k}{\partial z^i}\cdot \mathbf{g}_j \qquad (9\text{-}21)$$

If **r** represents the position vector, the vector $\partial\mathbf{r}/\partial z^i$ is the base vector $\mathbf{g}_i$ directed tangentially to the z^i coordinate curves.

The derivative of the base vector $\mathbf{g}_i$ with respect to z^j is

$$\frac{\partial\mathbf{g}_i}{\partial z^j} = \frac{\partial}{\partial z^j}\left(\frac{\partial\mathbf{r}}{\partial z^i}\right) = \frac{\partial}{\partial z^i}\left(\frac{\partial\mathbf{r}}{\partial z^j}\right) = \frac{\partial\mathbf{g}_j}{\partial z^i} \qquad (9\text{-}22)$$

Therefore

$$\frac{\partial\mathbf{g}_i}{\partial z^j} = \frac{\partial\mathbf{g}_j}{\partial z^i} \qquad (9\text{-}23)$$

Adding equations (9-20) and (9-21) and subtracting equation (9-19) gives

$$\frac{\partial g_{ik}}{\partial z^j} + \frac{\partial g_{jk}}{\partial z^i} - \frac{\partial g_{ij}}{\partial z^k} = \frac{\partial\mathbf{g}_i}{\partial z^j}\cdot\mathbf{g}_k + \frac{\partial\mathbf{g}_k}{\partial z^j}\cdot\mathbf{g}_i$$

$$+ \frac{\partial\mathbf{g}_j}{\partial z^i}\cdot\mathbf{g}_k + \frac{\partial\mathbf{g}_k}{\partial z^i}\cdot\mathbf{g}_j - \frac{\partial\mathbf{g}_i}{\partial z^k}\cdot\mathbf{g}_j - \frac{\partial\mathbf{g}_j}{\partial z^k}\cdot\mathbf{g}_i$$

According to equation (9-23),

$$\frac{\partial\mathbf{g}_j}{\partial z^i} = \frac{\partial\mathbf{g}_i}{\partial z^j}, \quad \frac{\partial\mathbf{g}_i}{\partial z^k} = \frac{\partial\mathbf{g}_k}{\partial z^i} \quad \text{and} \quad \frac{\partial\mathbf{g}_k}{\partial z^j} = \frac{\partial\mathbf{g}_j}{\partial z^k}$$

Substituting gives

$$\frac{\partial\mathbf{g}_i}{\partial z^j}\cdot\mathbf{g}_k = \frac{1}{2}\left(\frac{\partial g_{ik}}{\partial z^j} + \frac{\partial g_{jk}}{\partial z^i} - \frac{\partial g_{ij}}{\partial z^k}\right)$$

But the right-hand term is the Christoffel symbol, $[ij, k]$. Therefore

$$\frac{\partial\mathbf{g}_i}{\partial z^j}\cdot\mathbf{g}_k = [ij, k] \qquad (9\text{-}24)$$

Equation (9-24) will now be transformed into another expression. Let **a** represent the vector $\partial\mathbf{g}_i/\partial z^j$. Then

$$\mathbf{a}\cdot\mathbf{g}_k = [ij, k]$$

The vector **a** will be replaced by the following equivalent expressions.

$$\mathbf{a} = \beta_m\mathbf{g}^m = \beta_k\mathbf{g}^k$$

Substituting gives

$$\beta_m\mathbf{g}^m\cdot\mathbf{g}_k = \beta_m\,\delta_k{}^m = \beta_k = [ij, k]$$

Therefore

$$\mathbf{a} = \frac{\partial\mathbf{g}_i}{\partial z^j} = \beta_k\mathbf{g}^k = [ij, k]\mathbf{g}^k \qquad (9\text{-}25)$$

Now

$$\mathbf{g}^k = g^{mk}\mathbf{g}_m$$

so

$$\frac{\partial \mathbf{g}_i}{\partial z^j} = [ij, k]g^{mk}\mathbf{g}_m$$

also

$$[ij, k]g^{mk} = \begin{Bmatrix} m \\ i \ j \end{Bmatrix}$$

Hence we may write

$$\frac{\partial \mathbf{g}_i}{\partial z^j} = \begin{Bmatrix} m \\ i \ j \end{Bmatrix} \mathbf{g}_m \tag{9-26}$$

In terms of $\mathbf{g}^i$ the analogous relation becomes

$$\frac{\partial \mathbf{g}^i}{\partial z^j} = - \begin{Bmatrix} i \\ m \ j \end{Bmatrix} \mathbf{g}^m \tag{9-26a}$$

9-4. Partial Derivative of the Fundamental Tensor g_{ij} in Terms of the Christoffel Symbols

Let us first write the Christoffel symbols of the first kind as follows (see equation 9-9).

$$[ik, j] = \frac{1}{2}\left(\frac{\partial g_{ij}}{\partial z^k} + \frac{\partial g_{kj}}{\partial z^i} - \frac{\partial g_{ik}}{\partial z^j}\right)$$

$$[jk, i] = \frac{1}{2}\left(\frac{\partial g_{ji}}{\partial z^k} + \frac{\partial g_{ki}}{\partial z^j} - \frac{\partial g_{jk}}{\partial z^i}\right)$$

Since $g_{ik} = g_{ki}$, $g_{ij} = g_{ji}$, and $g_{jk} = g_{kj}$, it is apparent that when these equations are added the following expressions result.

$$\frac{\partial g_{ij}}{\partial z^k} = [ik, j] + [jk, i] \tag{9-27}$$

or

$$\frac{\partial g_{ij}}{\partial z^k} = g_{\alpha j}\begin{Bmatrix} \alpha \\ i \ k \end{Bmatrix} + g_{\alpha i}\begin{Bmatrix} \alpha \\ j \ k \end{Bmatrix} \tag{9-28}$$

The analogous expression for the contravariant tensor g^{ij} may be found by first differentiating the following identity with respect to z^k.

$$g_{i\alpha}g^{\alpha j} = \delta_i{}^j$$

Differentiating gives

$$g^{\alpha j} \frac{\partial g_{i\alpha}}{\partial z^k} + g_{i\alpha} \frac{\partial g^{\alpha j}}{\partial z^k} = 0$$

or

$$g_{i\alpha} \frac{\partial g^{\alpha j}}{\partial z^k} = -g^{\alpha j} \frac{\partial g_{i\alpha}}{\partial z^k}$$

Multiplying both sides by $g^{i\beta}$ and summing on i gives

$$g^{i\beta} g_{i\alpha} \frac{\partial g^{\alpha j}}{\partial z^k} = -g^{i\beta} g^{\alpha j} \frac{\partial g_{i\alpha}}{\partial z^k}$$

However, $g^{i\beta} g_{i\alpha} = \delta_\alpha{}^\beta$. If $\alpha = \beta$, the Kronecker delta equals unity.

$$\frac{\partial g^{\beta j}}{\partial z^k} = -g^{i\beta} g^{\alpha j} \frac{\partial g_{i\alpha}}{\partial z^k}$$

It has been shown that

$$\frac{\partial g_{i\alpha}}{\partial z^k} = [ik, \alpha] + [\alpha k, i] \qquad (9\text{-}27)$$

Hence

$$\frac{\partial g^{\beta j}}{\partial z^k} = -g^{i\beta} g^{\alpha j} [ik, \alpha] - g^{i\beta} g^{\alpha j} [\alpha k, i]$$

But

$$g^{j\alpha}[ik, \alpha] = \begin{Bmatrix} j \\ i\ k \end{Bmatrix} \quad \text{and} \quad g^{\beta i}[\alpha k, i] = \begin{Bmatrix} \beta \\ \alpha\ k \end{Bmatrix}$$

Hence

$$\frac{\partial g^{\beta j}}{\partial z^k} = -g^{i\beta} \begin{Bmatrix} j \\ i\ k \end{Bmatrix} - g^{\alpha j} \begin{Bmatrix} \beta \\ \alpha\ k \end{Bmatrix}$$

Now we change i to α in the first term on the right-hand side of the equation and β to i in all terms.

$$\frac{\partial g^{ij}}{\partial z^k} = -g^{\alpha i} \begin{Bmatrix} j \\ \alpha\ k \end{Bmatrix} - g^{\alpha j} \begin{Bmatrix} i \\ \alpha\ k \end{Bmatrix} \qquad (9\text{-}28a)$$

With this result we can further refine some of the relations derived in Chapter 8. From Example 8-2 we saw that

$$\frac{\partial g}{\partial g_{\alpha\beta}} = g g^{\alpha\beta} = G^{\alpha\beta}$$

but, since the $g_{\alpha\beta}$'s are functions of the z^i's, we may employ the chain rule to write

$$\frac{\partial g}{\partial z^i} = \frac{\partial g}{\partial g_{\alpha\beta}} \frac{\partial g_{\alpha\beta}}{\partial z^i}$$

But $\partial g/\partial g_{\alpha\beta} = G^{\alpha\beta}$ as previously shown; hence

$$\frac{\partial g}{\partial z^i} = G^{\alpha\beta} \frac{\partial g_{\alpha\beta}}{\partial z^i} \tag{9-29}$$

Using the results of Example 8-2, p. 122, for $\partial g/\partial g_{\alpha\beta}$ gives

$$\frac{\partial g}{\partial z^i} = g g^{\alpha\beta} \frac{\partial g_{\alpha\beta}}{\partial z^i} \tag{9-30}$$

We now insert for $\partial g_{\alpha\beta}/\partial z^i$ its equivalent (see equation 9-28).

$$\frac{\partial g}{\partial z^i} = g g^{\alpha\beta} \left(g_{\gamma\beta} \begin{Bmatrix} \gamma \\ \alpha\ i \end{Bmatrix} + g_{\gamma\alpha} \begin{Bmatrix} \gamma \\ \beta\ i \end{Bmatrix} \right)$$

$$= g \left(g^{\alpha\beta} g_{\gamma\beta} \begin{Bmatrix} \gamma \\ \alpha\ i \end{Bmatrix} + g^{\alpha\beta} g_{\gamma\alpha} \begin{Bmatrix} \gamma \\ \beta\ i \end{Bmatrix} \right)$$

But $g^{\alpha\beta} g_{\gamma\beta} = \delta_\gamma{}^\alpha$ and $g^{\alpha\beta} g_{\gamma\alpha} = \delta_\gamma{}^\beta$.
If $\gamma = \alpha$, then $\delta_\gamma{}^\alpha = 1$; and, if $\gamma = \beta$, then $\delta_\gamma{}^\beta = 1$; hence

$$\frac{\partial g}{\partial z^i} = g \left(\begin{Bmatrix} \alpha \\ \alpha\ i \end{Bmatrix} + \begin{Bmatrix} \beta \\ \beta\ i \end{Bmatrix} \right)$$

Changing the dummy indices β to α gives

$$\frac{\partial g}{\partial z^i} = 2g \begin{Bmatrix} \alpha \\ \alpha\ i \end{Bmatrix} \tag{9-31}$$

Therefore

$$\frac{1}{2g} \frac{\partial g}{\partial z^i} = \begin{Bmatrix} \alpha \\ \alpha\ i \end{Bmatrix} = \begin{Bmatrix} \alpha \\ i\ \alpha \end{Bmatrix}$$

or

$$\frac{\partial \ln \sqrt{g}}{\partial z^i} = \begin{Bmatrix} \alpha \\ i\ \alpha \end{Bmatrix} \tag{9-32}$$

or

$$\frac{1}{\sqrt{g}} \frac{\partial \sqrt{g}}{\partial z^i} = \begin{Bmatrix} \alpha \\ i\ \alpha \end{Bmatrix} \tag{9-33}$$

9-5. Riemannian Coordinates

A Riemannian space has been defined as a space of points $(z_1, z_2, z_3, \ldots, z_n)$ whose element of arc length, ds, is represented by a positive definite quadratic differential having the form

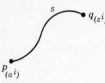

Fig. 9-5.

$$(ds)^2 = g_{ij}(z^1, z^2, \ldots, z^n)\, dz^i\, dz^j \quad (7\text{-}15)$$

Consider a point p having coordinates of a^i in a Riemannian space. A second point q having coordinates of z^i is located near p as shown in Fig. 9-5. Let the symbol s represent the length of the geodesic from point p to point q. According to a Taylor series expansion we may express z^i as

$$z^i = a^i + \left(\frac{dz^i}{ds}\right)_p s + \frac{1}{2!}\left(\frac{d^2z^i}{ds^2}\right)_p s^2 + \frac{1}{3!}\left(\frac{d^3z^i}{ds^3}\right)_p s^3 + \cdots \quad (9\text{-}34)$$

The differential equation of the geodesic line through point p is

$$\left(\frac{d^2z^i}{ds^2}\right) + \left\{{i \atop j\,k}\right\}\left(\frac{dz^j}{ds}\right)\left(\frac{dz^k}{ds}\right) = 0 \quad (9\text{-}14)$$

Let (dz^j/ds) be represented by ξ^j. Then

$$\left(\frac{d^2z^i}{ds^2}\right) = -\left\{{i \atop j\,k}\right\}\xi^j\xi^k \quad (9\text{-}35)$$

Differentiating equation (9-14) with respect to s gives

$$\left(\frac{d^3z^i}{ds^3}\right) + \left(\frac{dz^j}{ds}\right)\left(\frac{dz^k}{ds}\right)\frac{d\left\{{i \atop j\,k}\right\}}{ds} + \left\{{i \atop j\,k}\right\}\left(\frac{dz^k}{ds}\right)\left(\frac{d^2z^j}{ds^2}\right)$$
$$+ \left\{{i \atop j\,k}\right\}\left(\frac{dz^j}{ds}\right)\left(\frac{d^2z^k}{ds^2}\right) = 0$$

or

$$\left(\frac{d^3z^i}{ds^3}\right) + \left(\frac{dz^l}{ds}\right)\left(\frac{dz^j}{ds}\right)\left(\frac{dz^k}{ds}\right)\frac{d\left\{{i \atop j\,k}\right\}}{dz^l} + \left\{{i \atop j\,k}\right\}\left(\frac{dz^k}{ds}\right)\left(\frac{d^2z^j}{ds^2}\right)$$
$$+ \left\{{i \atop j\,k}\right\}\left(\frac{dz^j}{ds}\right)\left(\frac{d^2z^k}{ds^2}\right) = 0$$

Evaluating the above at point p and employing the ξ symbol gives

$$\left(\frac{d^3z^i}{ds^3}\right)_p + \left[\frac{\partial}{\partial z^l}\left\{{i \atop j\ k}\right\}\right]_p \xi^j\xi^k\xi^l + \left\{{i \atop j\ k}\right\}_p\left(\frac{d^2z^j}{ds^2}\right)_p\xi^k$$
$$+ \left\{{i \atop j\ k}\right\}_p\left(\frac{d^2z^k}{ds^2}\right)_p\xi^j = 0$$

Equation (9-35) enables us to eliminate the second derivative terms.

$$\left(\frac{d^3z^i}{ds^3}\right)_p + \left[\frac{\partial}{\partial z^l}\left\{{i \atop j\ k}\right\}\right]_p \xi^j\xi^k\xi^l - \left\{{i \atop j\ k}\right\}_p\left\{{j \atop l\ n}\right\}_p \xi^l\xi^n\xi^k$$
$$- \left\{{i \atop j\ k}\right\}_p\left\{{k \atop l\ n}\right\}_p \xi^l\xi^n\xi^j = 0$$

Interchanging the dummy indices n and j in the third term and interchanging the dummy indices n and k in the last term gives

$$\left(\frac{d^3z^i}{ds^3}\right)_p = -\left[\frac{\partial}{\partial z^l}\left\{{i \atop j\ k}\right\}_p\right]\xi^j\xi^k\xi^l + \left\{{i \atop n\ k}\right\}_p\left\{{n \atop l\ j}\right\}_p \xi^j\xi^k\xi^l$$
$$+ \left\{{i \atop j\ n}\right\}_p\left\{{n \atop l\ k}\right\}_p \xi^j\xi^k\xi^l$$

Let the symbol $\Gamma\left({i \atop j\ k\ l}\right)_p$ represent the expression

$$\Gamma\left({i \atop j\ k\ l}\right)_p = \left[-\frac{\partial}{\partial z^l}\left\{{i \atop j\ k}\right\} + \left\{{i \atop n\ k}\right\}\left\{{n \atop l\ j}\right\} + \left\{{i \atop j\ n}\right\}\left\{{n \atop l\ k}\right\}\right]_p \qquad (9\text{-}36)$$

Then

$$\left(\frac{d^3z^i}{ds^3}\right)_p = \left[\Gamma\left({i \atop j\ k\ l}\right)\right]_p \xi^j\xi^k\xi^l \qquad (9\text{-}37)$$

Substituting in equation (9-34) gives

$$z^i = a^i + s\xi^i - \frac{1}{2!}s^2\left\{{i \atop j\ k}\right\}_p\xi^j\xi^k + \frac{1}{3!}s^3\left[\Gamma\left({i \atop j\ k\ l}\right)\right]_p\xi^j\xi^k\xi^l + \cdots \qquad (9\text{-}38)$$

We now consider a coordinate system z'^i defined as

$$z'^i = \left(\frac{dz^i}{ds}\right)_p s = s\xi^i \quad \text{or} \quad \xi^i = \frac{z'^i}{s} \qquad (9\text{-}39)$$

z'^i are the new coordinates for q.

Substituting equation (9-39) into equation (9-38) and changing the dummy indices j to m gives

$$z^i = a^i + z'^i - \frac{1}{2!}\left\{{i \atop m\ k}\right\}_p z'^m z'^k + \frac{1}{3!}\left[\Gamma\left({i \atop m\ k\ l}\right)\right]_p z'^m z'^k z'^l + \cdots \qquad (9\text{-}40)$$

The z'^i terms are known as the Riemannian coordinates. It will now be shown that the determinant $|\partial z^i/\partial z'^j|$ does not vanish or become infinite in the region near p; terms of higher order than the first in z' are neglected.

Differentiating equation (9-40) with respect to z'^j gives

$$\frac{\partial z^i}{\partial z'^j} = \delta_j{}^i - \frac{1}{2!}\begin{Bmatrix} i \\ m\ k \end{Bmatrix} z'^k \delta_j{}^m - \frac{1}{2!}\begin{Bmatrix} i \\ m\ k \end{Bmatrix}_p z'^m \delta_j{}^k + \cdots$$

Interchanging the dummy indices m and k in the last term on the right gives

$$\frac{\partial z^i}{\partial z'^j} = \delta_j{}^i - \frac{1}{2!}\begin{Bmatrix} i \\ m\ k \end{Bmatrix}_p z'^k \delta_j{}^m - \frac{1}{2!}\begin{Bmatrix} i \\ k\ m \end{Bmatrix}_p z'^k \delta_j{}^m + \cdots$$

Because

$$\begin{Bmatrix} i \\ m\ k \end{Bmatrix} \text{ is symmetric,} \quad \begin{Bmatrix} i \\ m\ k \end{Bmatrix} = \begin{Bmatrix} i \\ k\ m \end{Bmatrix}$$

Hence

$$\frac{\partial z^i}{\partial z'^j} = \delta_j{}^i - \begin{Bmatrix} i \\ j\ k \end{Bmatrix} z'^k \tag{9-41}$$

The same result is obtained if additional terms in the series are employed.

Thus, at p, z'^k is zero; therefore

$$\left| \frac{\partial z^i}{\partial z'^j} \right|_p = |\delta_j{}^i| = 1 \tag{9-42}$$

We shall now prove that

$$\left(\frac{\partial g'_{ij}}{\partial z'^k} \right)_p = 0$$

We know that

$$g'_{ij} = \frac{\partial z^m}{\partial z'^i} \frac{\partial z^n}{\partial z'^j} g_{mn}$$

Thus by differentiation with respect to z'^k we obtain

$$\frac{\partial g'_{ij}}{\partial z'^k} = \frac{\partial^2 z^m}{\partial z'^i \partial z'^k} \frac{\partial z^n}{\partial z'^j} g_{mn} + \frac{\partial z^m}{\partial z'^i} \frac{\partial^2 z^n}{\partial z'^j \partial z'^k} g_{mn}$$
$$+ \frac{\partial z^m}{\partial z'^i} \frac{\partial z^n}{\partial z'^j} \left(\frac{\partial g_{mn}}{\partial z^l} \frac{\partial z^l}{\partial z'^k} \right) \tag{9-43}$$

Replacing the dummy index m by j and then differentiating equation (9-41) with respect to z'^m gives

$$\frac{\partial^2 z^i}{\partial z'^j \partial z'^m} = -\left\{\begin{matrix} i \\ j\ k \end{matrix}\right\} \frac{dz'^k}{dz'^m} - z'^k \frac{\partial \left\{\begin{matrix} i \\ j\ k \end{matrix}\right\}}{\partial z'^m} + \cdots$$

At point p this reduces to

$$\left(\frac{\partial^2 z^i}{\partial z'^j \partial z'^m}\right)_p = -\left\{\begin{matrix} i \\ j\ k \end{matrix}\right\} \delta_m{}^k$$

Summing on k gives

$$\left(\frac{\partial^2 z^i}{\partial z'^j \partial z'^m}\right)_p = -\left\{\begin{matrix} i \\ j\ m \end{matrix}\right\} \tag{9-44}$$

From equation (9-41) at p we obtain

$$\left(\frac{\partial z^i}{\partial z'^j}\right)_p = \delta_j{}^i \tag{9-45}$$

Substituting equations (9-44) and (9-45) into the equation (9-43) gives

$$\left(\frac{\partial g'_{ij}}{\partial z'^k}\right)_p = -\left\{\begin{matrix} m \\ i\ k \end{matrix}\right\}_p \delta_j{}^n (g_{mn})_p - \left\{\begin{matrix} n \\ j\ k \end{matrix}\right\}_p \delta_i{}^m (g_{mn})_p + \delta_i{}^m \delta_j{}^n \left(\frac{\partial g_{mn}}{\partial z^l}\right)_p \delta_k{}^l$$

Employing equation (9-13) we obtain

$$\left(\frac{\partial g'_{ij}}{\partial z'^k}\right)_p = -[ik, j]_p - [jk, i]_p + \left(\frac{\partial g_{ij}}{\partial z^k}\right)_p$$

According to equation (9-9),

$$\left(\frac{\partial g'_{ij}}{\partial z'^k}\right)_p = -\frac{1}{2}\left(\frac{\partial g_{ij}}{\partial z^k} + \frac{\partial g_{kj}}{\partial z^i} - \frac{\partial g_{ik}}{\partial z^j}\right)_p - \frac{1}{2}\left(\frac{\partial g_{ji}}{\partial z^k} + \frac{\partial g_{ki}}{\partial z^j} - \frac{\partial g_{jk}}{\partial z^i}\right)_p$$
$$+ \left(\frac{\partial g_{ij}}{\partial z^k}\right)_p = 0$$

Hence

$$\left(\frac{\partial g'_{ij}}{\partial z'^k}\right)_p = 0, \quad [jk', i]_p = 0, \quad \left\{\begin{matrix} i' \\ j\ k \end{matrix}\right\}_p = 0$$

A less involved procedure may be used to obtain the same general result. If the g'_{ij} are constants, then $\left\{\begin{matrix} i' \\ j\ k \end{matrix}\right\} = [ij', k] = 0$ since the derivative of a constant is zero. If $\left\{\begin{matrix} i' \\ j\ k \end{matrix}\right\}$ is zero for all values of i, j, k, then from equation (9-13) we also have $[ij', k] = 0$. Then, according to equation (9-27), $\partial \acute{g}_{ij} / \partial \acute{z}^{k} = 0$ for all values of i, j, k; hence $\acute{g}_{ij} = \acute{a}_{ij}$ (constants).

9-6. Problems

9-1. For a rectangular Cartesian coordinate system prove that the geodesics in three-dimensional space are straight lines.

9-2. Develop the differential equations of the geodesics for a three-dimensional space in terms of cylindrical coordinates.

9-3. Develop the differential equations of the geodesics for a three-dimensional space in terms of spherical coordinates.

9-4. Compute the Christoffel symbols for cylindrical coordinates by use of the base vectors $\mathbf{g}^{i}$.

9-5. Compute the Christoffel symbols for spherical coordinates by use of base vectors $\mathbf{g}^{i}$.

9-6. Evaluate the Christoffel symbols for the skewed coordinate system shown in the figure.

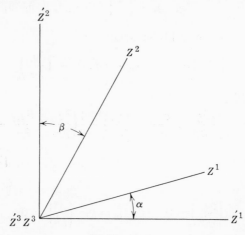

Problem 9-6.

9-7. Verify the equation

$$\frac{1}{2}\left(\frac{\partial \acute{g}_{jk}}{\partial \acute{z}^{i}} + \frac{\partial \acute{g}_{ki}}{\partial \acute{z}^{j}} - \frac{\partial \acute{g}_{ij}}{\partial \acute{z}^{k}}\right)$$
$$= \frac{1}{2}\left(\frac{\partial g_{mn}}{\partial z^{l}} + \frac{\partial g_{nl}}{\partial z^{m}} - \frac{\partial g_{lm}}{\partial z^{n}}\right)\frac{\partial z^{l}}{\partial \acute{z}^{i}}\frac{\partial z^{m}}{\partial \acute{z}^{j}}\frac{\partial z^{n}}{\partial \acute{z}^{k}} + \frac{\partial^{2} z^{m}}{\partial \acute{z}^{i}\,\partial \acute{z}^{j}}\frac{\partial z^{n}}{\partial \acute{z}^{k}}g_{mn}$$

9-8. Show that the following relation is valid.

$$\begin{Bmatrix} h' \\ i j \end{Bmatrix} = \frac{\partial z^l}{\partial z'^i} \frac{\partial z^m}{\partial z'^j} \frac{\partial z'^h}{\partial z^p} \begin{Bmatrix} p \\ l m \end{Bmatrix} + \frac{\partial z'^h}{\partial z^p} \frac{\partial^2 z^p}{\partial z'^i \partial z'^j}$$

9-9. Is the following relation true?

$$\frac{\partial A'_i}{\partial z'^j} - \begin{Bmatrix} m' \\ i j \end{Bmatrix} A'_m = \frac{\partial z^k}{\partial z'^i} \frac{\partial z^l}{\partial z'^j} \left(\frac{\partial A_k}{\partial z^l} - \begin{Bmatrix} m \\ k l \end{Bmatrix} A_m \right)$$

9-10. Show that the following relation is true for an orthogonal system.

$$[rm, n] + [rn, m] = \frac{\partial g_{mn}}{\partial z^r}$$

9-11. Prove that the following equation is true for an orthogonal co-ordinate system.

$$[mn, r] = g_{rt} \begin{Bmatrix} t \\ m n \end{Bmatrix}$$

9-12. Given

$$\frac{\partial g}{\partial g_{mn}} = g g^{mn}$$

prove that

$$\begin{Bmatrix} s \\ r s \end{Bmatrix} = \frac{1}{\sqrt{g}} \frac{\partial \sqrt{g}}{\partial z^r}$$

9-7. Suggested References

9-1. *Vector and Tensor Analysis*, H. Lass, McGraw-Hill Book Company.
9-2. *Tensor Analysis: Theory and Applications*, I. S. Sokolnikoff, John Wiley and Sons, Inc.
9-3. *Vector Analysis with an Introduction to Tensor Analysis*, A. P. Wills, Dover Publications, Inc.
9-4. *Nonlinear Theory of Continuous Media*, A. C. Eringen, McGraw-Hill Book Company.

10

The Inertia Tensor

10-1. Introduction

As an example of the use of tensors we now consider the inertia tensor. A mass M having a density ρ is shown in Fig. 10-1 in a three-dimensional rectangular Cartesian system X_i. A differential portion of mass dm has a direction vector $\mathbf{r}$ from the origin and coordinates x_1, x_2, and x_3. The mass moment of inertia of the body referred to the X_1X_1 axes is defined as

$$I_{X_1X_1} = \iiint_V \rho(x_2{}^2 + x_3{}^2)\, dv \quad \text{or} \quad I_{X_1X_1} = \int (x_2{}^2 + x_3{}^2)\, dm \quad (10\text{-}1)$$

By employing the magnitude of the direction vector, $|\mathbf{r}|^2 = x_1{}^2 + x_2{}^2 + x_3{}^2$, and the Kronecker delta, a general expression for the mass moment of inertia may be written

$$\phi_{X_iX_j} = \phi_{X_jX_i} = \int (r^2\, \delta_{ij} - x_i x_j)\, dm \quad (10\text{-}2)$$

If and only if $i = j$, $\delta_{ij} = 1$. Let $i = j = 1$; then

$$\phi_{X_1X_1} = I_{X_1X_1} = \int [(x_1{}^2 + x_2{}^2 + x_3{}^2) - x_1 x_1]\, dm$$

$$= \int (x_2{}^2 + x_3{}^2)\, dm$$

The mass product of inertia relative to the X_1X_2 plane is defined by

$$I_{X_1X_2} = \iiint_V x_1 x_2 \rho\, dv \quad \text{or} \quad I_{X_1X_2} = \int x_1 x_2\, dm \quad (10\text{-}3)$$

154

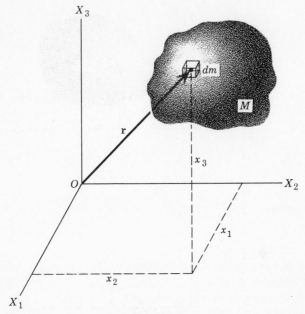

Fig. 10-1.

If $i = 1$ and $j = 2$, equation (10-2) reduces to

$$\phi_{X_1 X_2} = \phi_{X_2 X_1} = \int (0 - x_1 x_2)\, dm = -\int x_1 x_2\, dm = -I_{X_1 X_2}$$

It is apparent that equation (10-2) represents nine terms which may be arranged in the matrix

$$(\phi_{X_i X_j}) = \begin{pmatrix} I_{X_1 X_1} & -I_{X_1 X_2} & -I_{X_1 X_3} \\ -I_{X_2 X_1} & I_{X_2 X_2} & -I_{X_2 X_3} \\ -I_{X_3 X_1} & -I_{X_3 X_2} & I_{X_3 X_3} \end{pmatrix}$$

One can show that the elements in this array obey the transformation laws for second-order tensors between coordinate frames with the same origin; consequently the array is known as the inertia tensor.

10-2. Translation of the Coordinate Axes

The relations for the moments and products of inertia about the translated axes X_1', X_2', and X_3' in terms of the values for X_1, X_2, and X_3

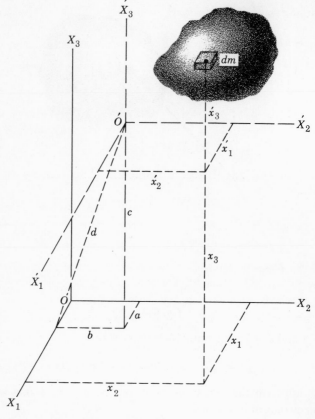

Fig. 10-2.

will be developed. Refer to Fig. 10-2. It will be assumed that the mass moments and products of inertia are known for the $X_1 X_2 X_3$ system.

The transformation equations are

$$\dot{x_1} = x_1 - a$$
$$\dot{x_2} = x_2 - b$$
$$\dot{x_3} = x_3 - c$$

The mass moment of inertia about the $\dot{X_1}\dot{X_1}$ axes is

$$\dot{I}_{\dot{X_1}\dot{X_1}} = \int [(\dot{x_2})^2 + (\dot{x_3})^2]\, dm$$

Substituting for $\dot{x}_2'$ and $\dot{x}_3'$ gives

$$I_{X_1'X_1'}' = \int [(x_2 - b)^2 + (x_3 - c)^2]\, dm$$

$$= \int [x_2{}^2 - 2x_2 b + b^2 + x_3{}^2 - 2x_3 c + c^2]\, dm$$

$$= \int (x_2{}^2 + x_3{}^2)\, dm + \int (b^2 + c^2)\, dm - \int (2bx_2 + 2cx_3)\, dm$$

$$= I_{X_1 X_1} + \int (b^2 + c^2)\, dm - \int (2bx_{2c} + 2cx_{3c})\, dm$$

Here x_{2c} and x_{3c} are the coordinates of the mass center in the $X_1 X_2 X_3$ system.

If the origin O of the $X_1 X_2 X_3$ system falls on the center of mass, $x_{1c} = x_{2c} = x_{3c} = 0$; hence

$$I_{X_1 X_1}' = I_{X_1 X_{1c}} + (b^2 + c^2)M = I_{X_1 X_{1c}} + d^2 M \qquad (10\text{-}4)$$

This is at once recognized as the parallel-axes theorem for the moments of inertia. Here $I_{X_1 X_{1c}}$ indicates that $I_{X_1 X_1}$ is referred to an origin which coincides with the center of mass.

The product of inertia, $I_{X_1 X_2}'$, may be expressed as

$$I_{X_1 X_2}' = \int \dot{x}_1' \dot{x}_2'\, dm = \int (x_1 - a)(x_2 - b)\, dm$$

$$= \int (x_1 x_2 - ax_2 - bx_1 + ab)\, dm$$

$$= \int x_1 x_2\, dm + \int ab\, dm - \int ax_{2c}\, dm - \int bx_{1c}\, dm$$

$$= I_{X_1 X_{2c}} + abM - ax_{2c}M - bx_{1c}M \qquad (10\text{-}5)$$

If the origin coincides with the mass center,

$$I_{X_1 X_2}' = I_{X_1 X_{2c}} + abM \qquad (10\text{-}6)$$

This is the parallel-axes theorem for the product of inertia.

10-3. Rotation of the Coordinate Axes

For purposes of discussion the Cartesian coordinate system X_1, X_2, X_3 as shown in Fig. 10-3 will be rotated to the new position, X_1', X_2', X_3'. The unit base vectors $\mathbf{i}_j$ and $\mathbf{i}_j'$ are indicated in the figure.

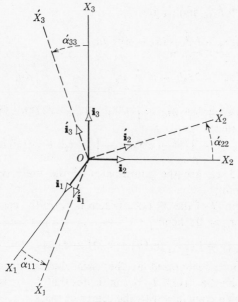

Fig. 10-3.

The symbol α_{ij} is used to represent the direction cosines between the two sets of coordinate axes. The general equation is

$$\alpha_{ij} = \mathbf{i}'_i \cdot \mathbf{i}_j = \cos\left(X'_i, X_j\right) \qquad (10\text{-}7)$$

The direction cosine between X'_1 and X_1 would be

$$\alpha_{11} = \mathbf{i}'_1 \cdot \mathbf{i}_1 = \cos\left(X'_1, X_1\right)$$

The component of one unit base vector in the direction of another is equal to the cosine of the angle between them. Hence α_{12} is the scalar component of $\mathbf{i}_2$ in the direction of $\mathbf{i}'_1$. The unit vector $\mathbf{i}'_i$ may be expressed in terms of the unit vector $\mathbf{i}_j$ as follows.

$$\mathbf{i}'_i = \alpha_{ij}\mathbf{i}_j \qquad (i, j = 1, 2, 3) \qquad (10\text{-}8)$$

The relation for $\mathbf{i}_i$ in terms of $\mathbf{i}'_i$ is

$$\mathbf{i}_j = \alpha_{ij}\mathbf{i}'_i \qquad (i, j = 1, 2, 3) \qquad (10\text{-}9)$$

The dot product of the position vector $\mathbf{r}$ and the terms of equation (10-8) will be formed.

$$\mathbf{r} \cdot \mathbf{i}'_i = \sum_j \alpha_{ij}\mathbf{r} \cdot \mathbf{i}_j$$

But $\mathbf{r} \cdot \mathbf{i}_i' = x_i'$ and $\mathbf{r} \cdot \mathbf{i}_j = x_j$, hence

$$x_i' = \alpha_{ij} x_j \qquad (10\text{-}10)$$

The inverse transformation may be found in a similar manner; thus

$$x_i = \alpha_{ji} x_j' \qquad (10\text{-}11)$$

If, in the general relation for the moments and products of inertia for the coordinate system X_i',

$$I'_{X_i X_j} = \int (r^2\, \delta_{ij} - x_i' x_j')\, dm \qquad (10\text{-}2)$$

we substitute from equation (10-10) for x'^i and we obtain

$$I'_{X_i X_j} = \delta_{ij} \int r^2\, dm - \sum_k \sum_l \alpha_{ik} \alpha_{jl} \int x_k x_l\, dm \qquad (10\text{-}12)$$

According to equation (10-2), $I_{x_k x_l}$ is given by

$$I_{X_k X_l} = \int (r^2\, \delta_{kl} - x_k x_l)\, dm = \int r^2\, \delta_{kl}\, dm - \int x_k x_l\, dm$$

or

$$\int x_k x_l\, dm = -I_{X_k X_l} + \delta_{kl} \int r^2\, dm$$

Substituting the last expression into equation (10-12) gives

$$I'_{X_i X_j} = \delta_{ij} \int r^2\, dm + \sum_k \sum_l \alpha_{ik} \alpha_{jl} \left(I_{X_k X_l} - \delta_{kl} \int r^2\, dm \right)$$

Consider the final term on the right-hand side.

$$-\sum_k \sum_l \alpha_{ik} \alpha_{jl}\, \delta_{kl} \int r^2\, dm$$

If $l = k$, the term equals

$$-\sum_k \alpha_{ik} \alpha_{jk} \int r^2\, dm$$

since $\delta_{kl} = 1$. Using equation (5-4) (Chapter 5), this result becomes

$$-\delta_{ij} \int r^2\, dm$$

The first and third terms are therefore equal and cancel out; hence

$$I'_{X_i X_j} = \sum_k \sum_l \alpha_{ik} \alpha_{jl} I_{X_k X_l} \qquad (10\text{-}13)$$

and

$$I_{X_i X_j} = \sum_k \sum_l \alpha_{ki} \alpha_{lj} I'_{X_k X_l} \qquad (10\text{-}14)$$

These are the tensor transformation equations used to compute the moment and products of inertia with respect to a rotated system of coordinate axes.

10-4. Suggested References

10-1. *Engineering Mechanics, Statics and Dynamics*, Irving H. Shames, Prentice-Hall, Inc.

10-2. *Principles of Mechanics of Solids and Fluids*, Vol. 1, "Particles and Rigid Body Mechanics," Hsuan Yeh and Joel I. Abrams, McGraw-Hill Book Company.

10-3. *Nonlinear Theory of Continuous Media*, A. Cemal Eringen, McGraw-Hill Book Company.

Differentiations
of Vectors and Tensors

11-1. Covariant and Intrinsic or Absolute Derivatives of Contravariant Vectors and Tensors

Many of the fundamental relations in engineering and in the engineering and physical sciences involve rates of change. For orthogonal Cartesian coordinate systems, the rates of change are expressed by simple derivatives. When curvilinear coordinate systems are employed, expressions for the rates of change are no longer simple derivatives of the variables. For example, radial and Coriolis accelerations are not simple derivatives of the velocity. Procedures will now be studied so that the rates of change may be formulated for any arbitrary coordinate system.

Consider a vector **A** which has covariant and contravariant components A_i and A^j, respectively.

The vector **A** may be represented as

$$\mathbf{A} = A^j\mathbf{g}_j = A_i\mathbf{g}^i \qquad (11\text{-}1)$$

Here the base vectors $\mathbf{g}_j$ and $\mathbf{g}^i$ in terms of a curvilinear system may be represented by

$$\mathbf{g}_j = \mathbf{g}_j(z^1, z^2, z^3) \quad \text{and} \quad \mathbf{g}^i = \mathbf{g}^i(z_1, z_2, z_3)$$

Taking the partial derivative of equation (11-1) with respect to z^k gives

$$\frac{\partial \mathbf{A}}{\partial z^k} = \frac{\partial (A^j\mathbf{g}_j)}{\partial z^k} = \frac{\partial A^j}{\partial z^k}\,\mathbf{g}_j + A^j\frac{\partial \mathbf{g}_j}{\partial z^k}$$

Employing equation (9-26) gives

$$\frac{\partial \mathbf{A}}{\partial z^k} = \frac{\partial A^j}{\partial z^k}\, \mathbf{g}_j + A^j \begin{Bmatrix} m \\ j\,k \end{Bmatrix} \mathbf{g}_m$$

Replacing by m the repeated index j in the first term on the right-hand side of the equation yields

$$\frac{\partial \mathbf{A}}{\partial z^k} = \frac{\partial A^m}{\partial z^k}\, \mathbf{g}_m + \begin{Bmatrix} m \\ j\,k \end{Bmatrix} \mathbf{g}_m A^j$$

Rearranging gives

$$\frac{\partial \mathbf{A}}{\partial z^k} = \left[\frac{\partial A^m}{\partial z^k} + \begin{Bmatrix} m \\ j\,k \end{Bmatrix} A^j \right] \mathbf{g}_m$$

The expression within the brackets is the covariant derivative of a contravariant vector; it is designated by the symbol $D_k A^m$. Hence

$$\frac{\partial \mathbf{A}}{\partial z^k} = D_k A^m \mathbf{g}_m \tag{11-2}$$

and

$$D_k A^m = \left[\frac{\partial A^m}{\partial z^k} + \begin{Bmatrix} m \\ j\,k \end{Bmatrix} A^j \right] \tag{11-3}$$

Since equation (11-2) has precisely the same structure as equation (11-1), one might conclude that $D_k A^m$ is a tensor. This concept will be verified.

It will now be demonstrated that the covariant derivative of a contravariant vector A^i is a mixed tensor of the second order. The transformation equation for a contravariant vector A^i is

$$\overset{'}{A}{}^i = \frac{\partial z'^i}{\partial z^\alpha}\, A^\alpha$$

Taking the partial derivative of $\overset{'}{A}{}^i$ with respect to z'^j gives

$$\frac{\partial \overset{'}{A}{}^i}{\partial z'^j} = \frac{\partial z'^i}{\partial z^\alpha}\left(\frac{\partial A^\alpha}{\partial z^\beta} \frac{\partial z^\beta}{\partial z'^j} \right) + A^\alpha \left(\frac{\partial^2 z'^i}{\partial z^\alpha\, \partial z^\beta} \frac{\partial z^\beta}{\partial z'^j} \right) \tag{11-4}$$

E. B. Christoffel in 1869, obtained the following general equation (Problem 11-16).

$$\frac{\partial^2 z'^i}{\partial z^\alpha\, \partial z^\beta} = \begin{Bmatrix} c \\ \alpha\,\beta \end{Bmatrix} \frac{\partial z'^i}{\partial z^c} - \begin{Bmatrix} i \\ a\,b \end{Bmatrix}' \frac{\partial z'^a}{\partial z^\alpha} \frac{\partial z'^b}{\partial z^\beta}$$

Substituting this relation into equation (11-4) gives

$$\frac{\partial \overset{\prime}{A}^i}{\partial z'^j} = \frac{\partial z'^i}{\partial z^\alpha}\left(\frac{\partial A^\alpha}{\partial z^\beta}\frac{\partial z^\beta}{\partial z'^j}\right) + A^\alpha \begin{Bmatrix} c \\ \alpha\ \beta \end{Bmatrix} \frac{\partial z'^i}{\partial z^c}\frac{\partial z^\beta}{\partial z'^j} - A^\alpha \begin{Bmatrix} i \\ a\ b \end{Bmatrix}\frac{\partial z^\beta}{\partial z'^j}\frac{\partial z'^a}{\partial z^\alpha}\frac{\partial z'^b}{\partial z^\beta}$$

or

$$\frac{\partial \overset{\prime}{A}^i}{\partial z'^j} + A^\alpha \begin{Bmatrix} i \\ a\ b \end{Bmatrix}\frac{\partial z^\beta}{\partial z'^j}\frac{\partial z'^a}{\partial z^\alpha}\frac{\partial z'^b}{\partial z^\beta} = \frac{\partial A^\alpha}{\partial z^\beta}\frac{\partial z'^i}{\partial z^\alpha}\frac{\partial z^\beta}{\partial z'^j} + A^\alpha \begin{Bmatrix} c \\ \alpha\ \beta \end{Bmatrix}\frac{\partial z'^i}{\partial z^c}\frac{\partial z^\beta}{\partial z'^j}$$

Changing the repeated index α to c in the first term on the right side of the equality, remembering that $\partial z^b/\partial z'^j = \delta_j{}^b$ in the second term on the left side of the equality, and replacing $A^\alpha(\partial z'^a/\partial z^\alpha)$ by $\overset{\prime}{A}^a$ gives

$$\left[\frac{\partial \overset{\prime}{A}^i}{\partial z'^j} + \begin{Bmatrix} i \\ a\ j \end{Bmatrix}\overset{\prime}{A}^a\right] = \left[\frac{\partial A^c}{\partial z^\beta} + \begin{Bmatrix} c \\ \alpha\ \beta \end{Bmatrix}A^\alpha\right]\frac{\partial z'^i}{\partial z^c}\frac{\partial z^\beta}{\partial z'^j} \qquad (11\text{-}5)$$

This is the transformation equation for a mixed tensor of the second order; covariant derivatives of tensors are therefore tensors.

For rectangular Cartesian coordinate systems the Christoffel symbols are zero; consequently, the covariant derivatives reduce to the usual partial derivatives.

The covariant derivatives express rates of change of physical quantities which are independent of the coordinate systems used; hence they are extremely important in the analysis of physical systems.

Consider the vector **A** to be a function of the coordinates z^i and of time t; thus

$$\mathbf{A} = A^k(z^i, t)\mathbf{g}_k(z^i)$$

If the vector **A** is a physical quantity to be associated with a system which is itself in motion with respect to the coordinate frame, the coordinates z^i, that is, the location of the system, also change with time; hence

$$\mathbf{A} = A^k[z^i(t), t]\ \mathbf{g}_k[z^i(t)]$$

The velocity field in fluid mechanics is an example of such a vector. Taking the derivative of **A** with respect to time gives

$$\frac{d\mathbf{A}}{dt} = \frac{d}{dt}(A^k\mathbf{g}_k) = \frac{dA^k}{dt}\mathbf{g}_k + A^k\frac{\partial \mathbf{g}_k}{\partial z^l}\frac{dz^l}{dt}$$

where

$$\frac{dA^k}{dt} = \frac{\partial A^k}{\partial t} + \frac{\partial A^k}{\partial z^l}\left(\frac{dz^l}{dt}\right)$$

According to equation (9-26) $\partial \mathbf{g}_k/\partial z^l$ may be replaced by $\begin{Bmatrix} m \\ k\,l \end{Bmatrix} \mathbf{g}_m$; hence

$$\frac{d\mathbf{A}}{dt} = \frac{dA^k}{dt}\,\mathbf{g}_k + A^k \begin{Bmatrix} m \\ k\,l \end{Bmatrix} \mathbf{g}_m \frac{dz^l}{dt}$$

Changing the dummy index k to m in the first term on the right and rearranging gives

$$\frac{d\mathbf{A}}{dt} = \left[\frac{dA^m}{dt} + A^k \begin{Bmatrix} m \\ k\,l \end{Bmatrix} \frac{dz^l}{dt} \right]\mathbf{g}_m \tag{11-6}$$

The bracketed quantity is the intrinsic or absolute derivative of the contravariant vector A^m with respect to t; it is denoted by $\delta A^m/\delta t$; that is,

$$\frac{\delta A^m}{\delta t} = \frac{dA^m}{dt} + A^k \begin{Bmatrix} m \\ k\,l \end{Bmatrix} \frac{dz^l}{dt} \tag{11-7}$$

Substituting for dA^m/dt in equation (11-7) gives

$$\frac{\delta A^m}{\delta t} = \frac{\partial A^m}{\partial t} + \frac{\partial A^m}{\partial z^l}\frac{dz^l}{dt} + A^k \begin{Bmatrix} m \\ k\,l \end{Bmatrix} \frac{dz^l}{dt}$$

Rearranging,

$$\frac{\delta A^m}{\delta t} = \frac{\partial A^m}{\partial t} + \left[\frac{\partial A^m}{\partial z^l} + A^k \begin{Bmatrix} m \\ k\,l \end{Bmatrix} \right]\frac{dz^l}{dt} \tag{11-8}$$

The bracketed quantity represents the covariant derivative of the contravariant vector A^m; hence the absolute or intrinsic derivative may be written

$$\frac{\delta A^m}{\delta t} = \frac{\partial A^m}{\partial t} + D_l A^m \frac{dz^l}{dt} \tag{11-9}$$

In summary, we may write for the contravariant vector A^m the expressions

$$\frac{\delta A^m}{\delta t} = \frac{dA^m}{dt} + A^k \begin{Bmatrix} m \\ k\,l \end{Bmatrix} \frac{dz^l}{dt} \tag{11-7}$$

$$\frac{\delta A^m}{\delta t} = \frac{\partial A^m}{\partial t} + \left[\frac{\partial A^m}{\partial z^l} + A^k \begin{Bmatrix} m \\ k\,l \end{Bmatrix} \right]\frac{dz^l}{dt} \tag{11-8}$$

$$\frac{\delta A^m}{\delta t} = \frac{\partial A^m}{\partial t} + D_l A^m \frac{dz^l}{dt} \tag{11-9}$$

$$\left(\frac{\delta A^m}{\delta t}\right)\mathbf{g}_m = \frac{d\mathbf{A}}{dt} = \frac{d(A^m\mathbf{g}_m)}{dt} \tag{11-10}$$

$$(D_l A^m)\mathbf{g}_m = \frac{\partial \mathbf{A}}{\partial z^l} = \frac{\partial(A^m\mathbf{g}_m)}{\partial z^l} \tag{11-11}$$

It may be shown that the covariant derivative of a second-order contravariant tensor A^{ij} is

$$D_k A^{ij} = \frac{\partial A^{ij}}{\partial z^k} + \begin{Bmatrix} i \\ m\ k \end{Bmatrix} A^{mj} + \begin{Bmatrix} j \\ m\ k \end{Bmatrix} A^{im} \qquad (11\text{-}12)$$

The procedure for placing the indices in the proper position when writing the covariant derivative of a contravariant tensor is a simple procedure once the student is familiar with the subject matter. In the beginning stages of learning the technique, the steps which are discussed in the following paragraphs may be of value. In order to illustrate the procedure, let us formulate the covariant derivative of the third-order contravariant tensor A^{ijk}.

STEP 1

Since there are three contravariant indices, there must be three Christoffel symbols following the partial derivative term. In skeleton form the expression becomes

$$D_n A^{ijk} = \frac{\partial A^{ijk}}{\partial z^n} + \begin{Bmatrix} \ \\ \ \end{Bmatrix} A^{\cdots} + \begin{Bmatrix} \ \\ \ \end{Bmatrix} A^{\cdots} + \begin{Bmatrix} \ \\ \ \end{Bmatrix} A^{\cdots}$$

STEP 2

Each of the Christoffel symbols must carry the index denoting the differentiation, in this case n. Thus

$$D_n A^{ijk} = \frac{\partial A^{ijk}}{\partial z^n} + \begin{Bmatrix} \ \\ \ n \end{Bmatrix} A^{\cdots} + \begin{Bmatrix} \ \\ \ n \end{Bmatrix} A^{\cdots} + \begin{Bmatrix} \ \\ \ n \end{Bmatrix} A^{\cdots}$$

STEP 3

The contravariant indices of the tensor A^{ijk} appear in the Christoffel symbols in the same order as they appear in the original tensor.

$$D_n A^{ijk} = \frac{\partial A^{ijk}}{\partial z^n} + \begin{Bmatrix} i \\ \ n \end{Bmatrix} A^{\cdots} + \begin{Bmatrix} j \\ \ n \end{Bmatrix} A^{\cdots} + \begin{Bmatrix} k \\ \ n \end{Bmatrix} A^{\cdots}$$

STEP 4

The dummy indices are next placed in the Christoffel symbols in the lower left-hand position and, in sequence, in the tensors associated with each Christoffel symbol.

$$D_n A^{ijk} = \frac{\partial A^{ijk}}{\partial z^n} + \begin{Bmatrix} i \\ m\ n \end{Bmatrix} A^{m\cdot\cdot} + \begin{Bmatrix} j \\ m\ n \end{Bmatrix} A^{\cdot m\cdot} + \begin{Bmatrix} k \\ m\ n \end{Bmatrix} A^{\cdot\cdot m}$$

STEP 5

The remaining superscripts in the tensors associated with each Christoffel symbol appear in the same position as in the original tensor; however, the dummy index replaces one of the original indices in the original tensor A^{ijk}.

$$D_n A^{ijk} = \frac{\partial A^{ijk}}{\partial z^n} + \begin{Bmatrix} i \\ m\ n \end{Bmatrix} A^{mjk} + \begin{Bmatrix} j \\ m\ n \end{Bmatrix} A^{imk} + \begin{Bmatrix} k \\ m\ n \end{Bmatrix} A^{ijm} \quad (11\text{-}13)$$

11-2. Covariant and Intrinsic or Absolute Derivatives of Covariant Vectors and Tensors

A vector $\mathbf{A}$ may be represented in terms of the covariant components as follows.

$$\mathbf{A} = A_i \mathbf{g}^i \quad (11\text{-}1)$$

Differentiating with respect to z^k results in

$$\frac{\partial \mathbf{A}}{\partial z^k} = \frac{\partial (A_i \mathbf{g}^i)}{\partial z^k} = \frac{\partial A_i}{\partial z^k} \mathbf{g}^i + A_i \frac{\partial \mathbf{g}^i}{\partial z^k}$$

Substituting for $\partial \mathbf{g}^i / \partial z^k$ from equation (9-26a) gives

$$\frac{\partial \mathbf{A}}{\partial z^k} = \frac{\partial A_i}{\partial z^k} \mathbf{g}^i - A_i \begin{Bmatrix} i \\ k\ j \end{Bmatrix} \mathbf{g}^j$$

Replacing the repeated index i in the first term on the right-hand side of the equality by j and rearranging gives

$$\frac{\partial \mathbf{A}}{\partial z^k} = \left[\frac{\partial A_j}{\partial z^k} - A_i \begin{Bmatrix} i \\ k\ j \end{Bmatrix} \right] \mathbf{g}^j \quad (11\text{-}14)$$

The quantity in brackets is known as the covariant derivative of a covariant vector A_j; it is designated by the symbol $D_k A_j$. Hence

$$D_k A_j = \left[\frac{\partial A_j}{\partial z^k} - A_i \begin{Bmatrix} i \\ k\ j \end{Bmatrix} \right] \quad (11\text{-}15)$$

The intrinsic or absolute derivative of a covariant vector, A_j, may be developed in a manner similar to that used for the contravariant vector. Hence

$$\frac{\delta A_j}{\delta t} = \frac{dA_j}{dt} - \begin{Bmatrix} k \\ j\, i \end{Bmatrix} A_k \frac{dz^i}{dt} \tag{11-16}$$

or

$$\frac{\delta A_j}{\delta t} = \frac{\partial A_j}{\partial t} + \left[\frac{\partial A_j}{\partial z^i} - A_k \begin{Bmatrix} k \\ j\, i \end{Bmatrix}\right] \frac{dz^i}{dt}$$

or

$$\frac{\delta A_j}{\delta t} = \frac{\partial A_j}{\partial t} + D_i A_j \frac{dz^i}{dt} \tag{11-17}$$

The covariant derivative of a second-order covariant tensor A_{ij} is expressed as

$$D_n A_{ij} = \frac{\partial A_{ij}}{\partial z^n} - \begin{Bmatrix} m \\ i\, n \end{Bmatrix} A_{mj} - \begin{Bmatrix} m \\ j\, n \end{Bmatrix} A_{im} \tag{11-18}$$

Since

$$\begin{Bmatrix} m \\ j\, n \end{Bmatrix} = \begin{Bmatrix} m \\ n\, j \end{Bmatrix} \quad \text{and} \quad \begin{Bmatrix} m \\ i\, n \end{Bmatrix} = \begin{Bmatrix} m \\ n\, i \end{Bmatrix}$$

equation (11-18) may be written

$$D_n A_{ij} = \frac{\partial A_{ij}}{\partial z^n} - \begin{Bmatrix} m \\ n\, i \end{Bmatrix} A_{mj} - \begin{Bmatrix} m \\ n\, j \end{Bmatrix} A_{im} \tag{11-19}$$

The steps for establishing the proper location of the indices are now presented to aid the student in acquiring skill in this technique. The covariant derivative of the tensor A_{ijk} will be formulated according to the following steps.

STEP 1

Since there are three covariant indices, there must be three Christoffel symbols following the partial derivative term, each preceded by a negative sign. In skeleton form the expression becomes

$$D_n A_{ijk} = \frac{\partial A_{ijk}}{\partial z^n} - \begin{Bmatrix} \ \ \\ \ \ \end{Bmatrix} A_{\ldots} - \begin{Bmatrix} \ \ \\ \ \ \end{Bmatrix} A_{\ldots} - \begin{Bmatrix} \ \ \\ \ \ \end{Bmatrix} A_{\ldots}$$

STEP 2

Each of the Christoffel symbols must carry the index denoting the differentiation, in this case n. Hence

$$D_n A_{ijk} = \frac{\partial A_{ijk}}{\partial z^n} - \left\{ \begin{matrix} \\ n \end{matrix} \right\} A_{...} - \left\{ \begin{matrix} \\ n \end{matrix} \right\} A_{...} - \left\{ \begin{matrix} \\ n \end{matrix} \right\} A_{...}$$

STEP 3

The covariant indices of the tensor A_{ijk} appear in the Christoffel symbols in the same order as they appear in the original tensor.

$$D_n A_{ijk} \frac{\partial A_{ijk}}{\partial z^n} - \left\{ \begin{matrix} \\ i\ n \end{matrix} \right\} A_{...} - \left\{ \begin{matrix} \\ j\ n \end{matrix} \right\} A_{...} - \left\{ \begin{matrix} \\ k\ n \end{matrix} \right\} A_{...}$$

STEP 4

The dummy indices are next placed in the Christoffel symbols at the upper level in sequence and in the tensors associated with each Christoffel symbol.

$$D_n A_{ijk} = \frac{\partial A_{ijk}}{\partial z^n} - \left\{ \begin{matrix} m \\ i\ n \end{matrix} \right\} A_{m..} - \left\{ \begin{matrix} m \\ j\ n \end{matrix} \right\} A_{.m.} - \left\{ \begin{matrix} m \\ k\ n \end{matrix} \right\} A_{..m}$$

STEP 5

The subscripts in the tensors associated with each Christoffel symbol appear in the same position as in the original tensor; however, the dummy index replaces one of the original indices in the tensor A_{ijk}.

$$D_n A_{ijk} = \frac{\partial A_{ijk}}{\partial z^n} - \left\{ \begin{matrix} m \\ i\ n \end{matrix} \right\} A_{mjk} - \left\{ \begin{matrix} m \\ j\ n \end{matrix} \right\} A_{imk} - \left\{ \begin{matrix} m \\ k\ n \end{matrix} \right\} A_{ijm}$$

The absolute or intrinsic derivative of a second-order covariant tensor A_{ij} is expressed as

$$\frac{\delta A_{ij}}{\delta t} = \frac{d A_{ij}}{dt} - \left\{ \begin{matrix} m \\ i\ n \end{matrix} \right\} A_{mj} \frac{dz^n}{dt} - \left\{ \begin{matrix} m \\ j\ n \end{matrix} \right\} A_{im} \frac{dz^n}{dt}$$

$$= \frac{\partial A_{ij}}{\partial t} + D_n A_{ij} \frac{dz^n}{dt} \qquad (11\text{-}20)$$

11-3. Covariant and Intrinsic or Absolute Derivatives of an Invariant

The covariant derivatives of an invariant or scalar A is the same as the partial derivative. That is,

$$D_k A = \frac{\partial A}{\partial z^k} \tag{11-21}$$

The absolute or intrinsic derivative of the invariant A is the same as the total derivative; hence

$$\frac{\delta A}{\delta t} = \frac{dA}{dt} = \frac{\partial A}{\partial t} + D_n A \frac{dz^n}{dt} \tag{11-22}$$

11-4. Covariant and Intrinsic or Absolute Derivatives of Mixed Tensors

The procedures presented for covariant differentiation may be applied to mixed tensors. For example,

$$D_k(A_j^{\ i}) = \frac{\partial A_j^{\ i}}{\partial z^k} - \left\{ \begin{matrix} a \\ j\ k \end{matrix} \right\} A_a^{\ i} + \left\{ \begin{matrix} i \\ a\ k \end{matrix} \right\} A_j^{\ a}$$

$$D_q(A_{kl}^{\ \ j}) = \frac{\partial A_{kl}^{\ \ j}}{\partial z^q} - \left\{ \begin{matrix} s \\ k\ q \end{matrix} \right\} A_{sl}^{\ \ j} - \left\{ \begin{matrix} s \\ l\ q \end{matrix} \right\} A_{ks}^{\ \ j} + \left\{ \begin{matrix} j \\ q\ s \end{matrix} \right\} A_{kl}^{\ \ s}$$

$$D_m A_k^{\ ij} = \frac{\partial A_k^{\ ij}}{\partial z^m} + \left\{ \begin{matrix} i \\ a\ m \end{matrix} \right\} A_k^{\ aj} + \left\{ \begin{matrix} j \\ a\ m \end{matrix} \right\} A_k^{\ ia} - \left\{ \begin{matrix} a \\ k\ m \end{matrix} \right\} A_a^{\ ij}$$

$$D_q(A_{mn}^{\ \ jkl}) = \frac{\partial A_{mn}^{\ \ jkl}}{\partial z^q} - \left\{ \begin{matrix} s \\ m\ q \end{matrix} \right\} A_{sn}^{\ \ jkl} - \left\{ \begin{matrix} s \\ n\ q \end{matrix} \right\} A_{ms}^{\ \ jkl}$$

$$+ \left\{ \begin{matrix} j \\ q\ s \end{matrix} \right\} A_{mn}^{\ \ skl} + \left\{ \begin{matrix} k \\ q\ s \end{matrix} \right\} A_{mn}^{\ \ jsl} + \left\{ \begin{matrix} l \\ q\ s \end{matrix} \right\} A_{mn}^{\ \ jks} \tag{11-23}$$

By a similar procedure the absolute or intrinsic derivative of a mixed tensor may be obtained; for example,

$$\frac{\delta A_{jk}^{\ \ i}}{\delta t} = \frac{dA_{jk}^{\ \ i}}{dt} + \left\{ \begin{matrix} i \\ a\ d \end{matrix} \right\} A_{jk}^{\ \ a} \frac{dz^d}{dt} - \left\{ \begin{matrix} a \\ j\ b \end{matrix} \right\} A_{ak}^{\ \ i} \frac{dz^b}{dt} - \left\{ \begin{matrix} a \\ k\ b \end{matrix} \right\} A_{ja}^{\ \ i} \frac{dz^b}{dt}$$

$$\frac{\delta A_{jk}^{\ \ i}}{\delta t} = \frac{\partial A_{jk}^{\ \ i}}{\partial t} + D_n A_{jk}^{\ \ i} \frac{dz^n}{dt}$$

Also

$$\frac{\delta A_k^{ij}}{\delta t} = \frac{dA_k^{ij}}{dt} + \begin{Bmatrix} i \\ a\ d \end{Bmatrix} A_k^{aj} \frac{dz^d}{dt} + \begin{Bmatrix} j \\ a\ d \end{Bmatrix} A_k^{ia} \frac{dz^d}{dt} - \begin{Bmatrix} a \\ k\ b \end{Bmatrix} A_a^{ij} \frac{dz^b}{dt}$$

$$(11\text{-}24)$$

11-5. The Covariant and Intrinsic or Absolute Derivatives of the Metric and Conjugate Tensors and the Kronecker Delta

According to the rules of covariant differentiation the covariant derivative of the metric tensor g_{ij} is

$$D_k g_{ij} = \frac{\partial g_{ij}}{\partial z^k} - \begin{Bmatrix} l \\ k\ i \end{Bmatrix} g_{lj} - \begin{Bmatrix} l \\ k\ j \end{Bmatrix} g_{il}$$

The last two terms are the Christoffel symbols of the first kind, since by definition

$$[ki, j] = g_{lj} \begin{Bmatrix} l \\ k\ i \end{Bmatrix}$$

Substituting gives

$$D_k g_{ij} = \frac{\partial g_{ij}}{\partial z^k} - [ki, j] - [kj, i]$$

According to equation (9-27),

$$\frac{\partial g_{ij}}{\partial z^k} = [ik, j] + [kj, i]$$

Therefore

$$D_k g_{ij} = 0 \qquad (11\text{-}25)$$

According to the procedures for covariant differentiation, the covariant derivative of the Kronecker delta is

$$D_i(\delta_k{}^j) = \frac{\partial \delta_k{}^j}{\partial z^i} + \begin{Bmatrix} j \\ i\ l \end{Bmatrix} \delta_k{}^l - \begin{Bmatrix} l \\ i\ k \end{Bmatrix} \delta_l{}^j$$

The value of $\partial \delta_k{}^j / \partial z^i$ is zero because $\delta_k{}^j$ is equal to 1 or 0. Hence

$$D_i \delta_k{}^j = \begin{Bmatrix} j \\ i\ l \end{Bmatrix} \delta_k{}^l - \begin{Bmatrix} l \\ i\ k \end{Bmatrix} \delta_l{}^j = \begin{Bmatrix} j \\ i\ k \end{Bmatrix} - \begin{Bmatrix} j \\ i\ k \end{Bmatrix} = 0$$

Therefore

$$D_i(\delta_k{}^j) = 0 \qquad (11\text{-}26)$$

The covariant derivative of the conjugate tensor g^{jk} will be determined.

According to equation (8-4)

$$g_{ij}g^{jk} = \delta_i{}^k$$

Differentiating gives

$$D_l g_{ij}g^{jk} = g_{ij}D_l g^{jk} + g^{jk}\,D_l g_{ij}$$

or

$$D_l\,\delta_i{}^k = g_{ij}\,D_l g^{jk} + g^{jk}\,D_l g_{ij}$$

It has already been shown that $D_l\delta_i{}^k$ and $D_l g_{ij}$ are both zero. Since g_{ij} cannot be zero for all conditions, in order to satisfy the last equation $D_l g^{jk}$ must be zero. Hence

$$D_l g^{jk} = 0 \tag{11-27}$$

The absolute derivative of the metric g_{ij} may be expressed as

$$\frac{\delta g_{ij}}{\delta t} = \frac{dg_{ij}}{dt} - \begin{Bmatrix} m \\ i\ n \end{Bmatrix} g_{mj}\frac{dz^n}{dt} - \begin{Bmatrix} m \\ j\ n \end{Bmatrix} g_{im}\frac{dz^n}{dt}$$

or

$$\frac{\delta g_{ij}}{\delta t} = \frac{\partial g_{ij}}{\partial t} + D_n g_{ij}\frac{dz^n}{dt}$$

but

$$D_n g_{ij} = 0, \qquad \left(\frac{\partial g_{ij}}{\partial t}\right)_{z^k} = 0$$

Therefore

$$\frac{\delta g_{ij}}{\delta t} = 0 \tag{11-28}$$

The absolute derivative of the fundamental tensor is zero.

Also it may be shown that

$$\frac{\delta g^{ij}}{\delta t} = 0 \tag{11-29}$$

and

$$\frac{\delta\,\delta_n{}^m}{\delta t} = 0 \tag{11-30}$$

11-6. Ricci's Theorem

Ricci's theorem states that the covariant derivatives of the fundamental tensors, metric and conjugate tensors, are zero. This means that in covariant differentiation the terms g_{ij}, g^{ij}, and $\delta_j{}^i = g_{jl}g^{li}$ are considered constants. For example,

$$D_m A_{ijk} = D_m(g_{ai}A_{jk}{}^a) = g_{ai}\, D_m(A_{jk}{}^a)$$
$$g_{ij}\, D_k A^j = D_k(g_{ij}A^j) = D_k(A_i)$$

11-7. The Contravariant Derivative

The contravariant derivative D^k is defined by the equation

$$D^k = g^{kj}\, D_j \tag{11-31}$$

We may immediately deduce that

$$D^k g_{ij} = 0 \tag{11-32}$$
$$D^k g^{ij} = 0 \tag{11-33}$$
$$D^k \delta_j{}^i = 0 \tag{11-34}$$

In forming the covariant and contravariant derivatives, g_{ij}, g^{ij}, and $\delta_j{}^i$ are considered constants.

$$D^k A_{\ldots}^{\ldots} = g^{kj}\, D_j A_{\ldots}^{\ldots}$$
$$= D_j(g^{kj}A_{\ldots}^{\ldots})$$

Also

$$D^k A_k = g^{kj}\, D_j A_k = D_j A^j$$

From these developments it is apparent that obtaining the contravariant derivative is equivalent to raising the index on a covariant derivative.

11-8. Covariant and Intrinsic or Absolute Differentiation of Sums and Products of Tensors

The rules for covariant and intrinsic differentiation for sums and products of tensors are the same as for ordinary differentiation.

The covariant derivative of the sum of two of the same types of tensors is

$$D_k(A_j{}^i + B_j{}^i) = D_k A_j{}^i + D_k B_j{}^i \tag{11-35}$$

The covariant derivative of the product of two tensors is analogous to the ordinary derivative of a product; that is,

$$D_m(A_{ij}B^{kl}) = B^{kl}(D_m A_{ij}) + A_{ij}(D_m B^{kl}) \qquad (11\text{-}36)$$

The absolute derivative of a product of two tensors is obtained in a similar manner. Thus

$$\frac{\delta A_s^{\,r} B_u}{\delta t} = B_u \frac{\delta A_s^{\,r}}{\delta t} + A_s^{\,r} \frac{\delta B_u}{\delta t} \qquad (11\text{-}37)$$

11-9. The Second Covariant Derivative of a Covariant Tensor

The steps required to carry out the covariant differentiation of $D_j A_i$ with respect to k are analogous to those required for the differentiation of a second-order tensor A_{ij}. The equation is therefore

$$D_k(D_j A_i) = \frac{\partial(D_j A_i)}{\partial z^k} - \left\{ {l \atop j\,k} \right\} D_l A_i - \left\{ {l \atop i\,k} \right\} D_j A_l$$

$$= \frac{\partial}{\partial z^k}\left(\frac{\partial A_i}{\partial z^j} - \left\{ {l \atop i\,j} \right\} A_l \right) - \left\{ {l \atop j\,k} \right\}\left(\frac{\partial A_i}{\partial z^l} - \left\{ {n \atop i\,l} \right\} A_n \right)$$

$$- \left\{ {l \atop i\,k} \right\}\left(\frac{\partial A_l}{\partial z^j} - \left\{ {m \atop l\,j} \right\} A_m \right)$$

Carrying out the differentiation gives

$$D_k D_j A_i = \frac{\partial^2 A_i}{\partial z^k\,\partial z^j} - A_l \frac{\partial \left\{ {l \atop i\,j} \right\}}{\partial z^k} - \left\{ {l \atop i\,j} \right\} \frac{\partial A_l}{\partial z^k} - \left\{ {l \atop j\,k} \right\} \frac{\partial A_i}{\partial z^l}$$

$$+ \left\{ {l \atop j\,k} \right\}\left\{ {n \atop i\,l} \right\} A_n - \left\{ {l \atop i\,k} \right\} \frac{\partial A_l}{\partial z^j} + \left\{ {l \atop i\,k} \right\}\left\{ {m \atop l\,j} \right\} A_m \qquad (11\text{-}38)$$

It will now be shown that the second covariant derivative is non-commutative; that is, the order of differentiation is important. This derivative may be expressed as

$$D_k(D_j A_i) \neq D_j(D_k A_i) \qquad (11\text{-}39)$$

The proof will consist in showing that the difference between $D_k(D_j A_i)$ and $D_j(D_k A_i)$ is not zero. Hence, by interchanging

j and k in equation (11-38) and subtracting the result from equation (11-38) we obtain

$$D_k\,(D_j A_i) - D_j\,(D_k A_i) = \frac{\partial^2 A_i}{\partial z^k\,\partial z^j} - \frac{\partial^2 A_i}{\partial z^j\,\partial z^k} - A_l\,\frac{\partial \begin{Bmatrix} l \\ i\,j \end{Bmatrix}}{\partial z^k} + A_l\,\frac{\partial \begin{Bmatrix} l \\ i\,k \end{Bmatrix}}{\partial z^j}$$

$$- \begin{Bmatrix} l \\ i\,j \end{Bmatrix}\frac{\partial A_l}{\partial z^k} + \begin{Bmatrix} l \\ i\,k \end{Bmatrix}\frac{\partial A_l}{\partial z^j} - \begin{Bmatrix} l \\ j\,k \end{Bmatrix}\frac{\partial A_i}{\partial z^l} + \begin{Bmatrix} l \\ k\,j \end{Bmatrix}\frac{\partial A_i}{\partial z^l}$$

$$+ \begin{Bmatrix} l \\ j\,k \end{Bmatrix}\begin{Bmatrix} n \\ i\,l \end{Bmatrix} A_n - \begin{Bmatrix} l \\ k\,j \end{Bmatrix}\begin{Bmatrix} n \\ i\,l \end{Bmatrix} A_n - \begin{Bmatrix} l \\ i\,k \end{Bmatrix}\frac{\partial A_l}{\partial z^j} + \begin{Bmatrix} l \\ i\,j \end{Bmatrix}\frac{\partial A_l}{\partial z^k}$$

$$+ \begin{Bmatrix} l \\ i\,k \end{Bmatrix}\begin{Bmatrix} m \\ l\,j \end{Bmatrix} A_m - \begin{Bmatrix} l \\ i\,j \end{Bmatrix}\begin{Bmatrix} m \\ l\,k \end{Bmatrix} A_m$$

Simplifying gives

$$D_k\,(D_j A_i) - D_j\,(D_k A_i)$$

$$= A_l\left[\frac{\partial \begin{Bmatrix} l \\ i\,k \end{Bmatrix}}{\partial z^j} - \frac{\partial \begin{Bmatrix} l \\ i\,j \end{Bmatrix}}{\partial z^k} + \begin{Bmatrix} m \\ i\,k \end{Bmatrix}\begin{Bmatrix} l \\ m\,j \end{Bmatrix} - \begin{Bmatrix} m \\ i\,j \end{Bmatrix}\begin{Bmatrix} l \\ m\,k \end{Bmatrix}\right]$$

The expression in brackets is a mixed tensor of rank four, and it is designated by the symbol R^l_{ijk}; hence

$$\left[\frac{\partial \begin{Bmatrix} l \\ i\,k \end{Bmatrix}}{\partial z^j} - \frac{\partial \begin{Bmatrix} l \\ i\,j \end{Bmatrix}}{\partial z^k} + \begin{Bmatrix} m \\ i\,k \end{Bmatrix}\begin{Bmatrix} l \\ m\,j \end{Bmatrix} - \begin{Bmatrix} m \\ i\,j \end{Bmatrix}\begin{Bmatrix} l \\ m\,k \end{Bmatrix}\right] = R^l_{ijk} \quad (11\text{-}40)$$

If the order of differentiation is to be immaterial, R^l_{ijk} must be zero. In general this is not the case. A necessary condition to ensure that the order of differentiation is immaterial, is that R^l_{ijk} vanish identically.

The fourth-rank tensor R^l_{ijk} is the mixed Riemann-Christoffel tensor, the Riemann-Christoffel tensor of the second kind, or the curvature tensor.

The associated tensor R_{ijkl} is known as the covariant Riemann-Christoffel tensor, the Riemann-Christoffel tensor of the first kind, or the covariant curvature tensor. The relation between the curvature and covariant tensors is

$$R_{ijkl} = g_{i\beta}R^\beta_{jkl} \quad (11\text{-}41)$$

The Riemann-Christoffel tensor of the first kind, R_{ijkl}, may be written in determinant form as follows.

$$R_{ijkl} = \begin{vmatrix} \dfrac{\partial}{\partial z^k} & \dfrac{\partial}{\partial z^l} \\ [jk, i] & [jl, i] \end{vmatrix} + \begin{vmatrix} \begin{Bmatrix} a \\ j\,k \end{Bmatrix} & \begin{Bmatrix} a \\ j\,l \end{Bmatrix} \\ [ik, a] & [il, a] \end{vmatrix}$$

The covariant tensor has n^4 components, but they are not all independent. The following relations may be verified directly.

$$R_{hijk} = -R_{ihjk}$$
$$R_{hijk} = -R_{hikj}$$
$$R_{hijk} = R_{jkhi}$$
$$R_{hijk} + R_{hjki} + R_{hkij} = 0$$

Because of the skew symmetry, $R_{hijk} = 0$, if $h = i$ or $j = k$. As an example, if $n = 2$, the only non-vanishing components are

$$R_{1212}, \quad R_{1221}, \quad R_{2112}, \quad R_{2121}$$

They are related as follows.

$$R_{1221} = -R_{1212} = R_{2112} = -R_{2121}$$

There is then only one independent non-vanishing component.

11-10. The Laplacian Operator, $\nabla^2 = (\nabla \cdot \nabla) = D_k D^k$

The contravariant derivative D^k has been defined by the expression

$$D^k = g^{kj} D_j \tag{11-31}$$

Consider the operator $D^k D_k$. Now

$$D_k D^k A_{\cdots}^{\cdots} = D_k (D^k A_{\cdots}^{\cdots}) = D_k(g^{kj} D_j A_{\cdots}^{\cdots})$$
$$= g^{kj} D_k D_j A_{\cdots}^{\cdots}$$

But

$$g^{kj} D_k = D^j$$

Hence

$$D_k \, D^k A^{\cdots}_{\cdots} = D^j \, D_j A^{\cdots}_{\cdots}$$

Let x^i represent rectangular Cartesian coordinates in three-dimensional space. Then

$$D_k = \frac{\partial}{\partial x^k} \quad \text{and} \quad D^k = \frac{\partial}{\partial x^k}$$

and

$$D_k \, D^k = \frac{\partial^2}{(\partial x^1)^2} + \frac{\partial^2}{(\partial x^2)^2} + \frac{\partial^2}{(\partial x^3)^2} = \nabla^2 \qquad (11\text{-}42)$$

From this we see that $D_k \, D^k$ is the Laplacian operator.

$$\nabla^2 \phi = D_k \left(g^{kj} \frac{\partial \phi}{\partial x^j} \right)$$

$$= \frac{\partial}{\partial x^k} \left(g^{kj} \frac{\partial \phi}{\partial x^j} \right) + \left\{ \begin{matrix} k \\ m \; k \end{matrix} \right\} g^{mj} \frac{\partial \phi}{\partial x^j}$$

But, from equation (9-32),

$$\left\{ \begin{matrix} k \\ k \; m \end{matrix} \right\} = \frac{1}{2} \frac{\partial (\ln g)}{\partial z^m} = \frac{1}{\sqrt{g}} \frac{\partial \sqrt{g}}{\partial z^m}$$

Substitution into the expression for $\nabla^2 \phi$ gives

$$\nabla^2 \phi = D_k \, D^k \phi = \frac{\partial}{\partial x^k} \left(g^{kj} \frac{\partial \phi}{\partial x^j} \right) + \frac{1}{\sqrt{g}} \frac{\partial \sqrt{g}}{\partial x^m} \left(g^{mj} \frac{\partial \phi}{\partial x^j} \right)$$

This represents the derivative of a product, which is

$$D_k \, D^k \phi = \nabla^2 \phi = \sum_k \sum_j \frac{1}{\sqrt{g}} \frac{\partial}{\partial x^k} \left(\sqrt{g} \, g^{kj} \frac{\partial \phi}{\partial x^j} \right) \qquad (11\text{-}43)$$

If the system under consideration is orthogonal,

$$D_i \, D^i \phi = \nabla^2 \phi = \sum_{i=1}^{3} \frac{1}{\sqrt{g}} \frac{\partial}{\partial x^i} \left(\frac{\sqrt{g}}{g_{ii}} \frac{\partial \phi}{\partial x^i} \right) \qquad (11\text{-}44)$$

Example 11-1

If f is an invariant, evaluate $\nabla^2 f$ in terms of spherical polar coordinates r, ϕ, θ as shown in Fig. 11-1.

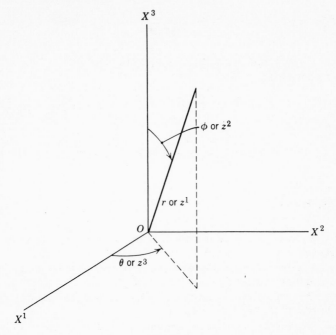

X^3

ϕ or z^2

r or z^1

O

X^2

θ or z^3

X^1

Fig. 11-1.

For spherical coordinates,

$$(ds)^2 = (dr)^2 + (r\,d\phi)^2 + (r\sin\phi\,d\theta)^2$$

$$g_{11} = 1, \quad g_{22} = r^2, \quad g_{33} = r^2\sin^2\phi$$

$$g_{ij} = \begin{pmatrix} 1 & 0 & 0 \\ 0 & r^2 & 0 \\ 0 & 0 & r^2\sin^2\phi \end{pmatrix}$$

$$g = |g_{ij}| = r^4\sin^2\phi, \quad \sqrt{g} = r^2\sin\phi$$

$$g^{ij} = \begin{pmatrix} 1 & 0 & 0 \\ 0 & 1/r^2 & 0 \\ 0 & 0 & \dfrac{1}{r^2\sin^2\phi} \end{pmatrix}$$

$$\nabla^2 f = \frac{1}{\sqrt{g}} \frac{\partial}{\partial x^k}\left(\sqrt{g}\, g^{kj}\, \frac{\partial f}{\partial x^j} \right)$$

$$g^{11} = 1, \quad g^{22} = \frac{1}{r^2}, \quad g^{33} = \frac{1}{r^2 \sin^2 \phi} \qquad \therefore \ k = j, \text{ otherwise } g^{kj} = 0$$

$$\nabla^2 f = \frac{1}{r^2 \sin \phi} \left[\overset{k=j=1}{\frac{\partial}{\partial r}\left(r^2 \sin \phi \ \frac{\partial f}{\partial r} \right)} + \overset{k=j=2}{\frac{\partial}{\partial \phi}\left(r^2 \sin \phi \ \frac{1}{r^2} \frac{\partial f}{\partial \phi} \right)} \right.$$

$$\left. + \overset{k=j=3}{\frac{\partial}{\partial \theta}\left(r^2 \sin \phi \ \frac{1}{r^2 \sin^2 \phi} \frac{\partial f}{\partial \theta} \right)} \right]$$

Hence

$$\nabla^2 f = \frac{1}{r^2} \frac{\partial}{\partial r}\left(r^2 \frac{\partial f}{\partial r} \right) + \frac{1}{r^2} \frac{\partial}{\partial \phi}\left(\sin \phi \ \frac{\partial f}{\partial \phi} \right) + \frac{1}{r^2 \sin^2 \phi} \frac{\partial^2 f}{\partial \theta^2}$$

11-11. Problems

11-1. Express the covariant derivatives of the following contravariant tensors with respect to z^k: (a) A^l; (b) A^{lm}; (c) A^{lmn}.

11-2. Express the intrinsic or absolute derivatives of the contravariant tensors in Problem 11-1.

11-3. Write the covariant derivatives of the following covariant tensors with respect to z^k: (a) A_i; (b) A_{ij}; (c) A_{ijk}.

11-4. Express the intrinsic or absolute derivatives of the covariant tensors in Problem 11-3.

11-5. Verify the following equations.

$$D_k g_{ij} = \frac{\partial g_{ij}}{\partial z^k} - \begin{Bmatrix} m \\ k\ i \end{Bmatrix} g_{mj} - \begin{Bmatrix} m \\ k\ j \end{Bmatrix} g_{im}$$

$$= \frac{\partial g_{ij}}{\partial z^k} - [ki, j] - [kj, i] = 0$$

11-6. If z^r are the coordinates and ϕ is an invariant, determine whether or not $\partial^2 \phi / \partial z^r \ \partial z^s$ is a tensor.

11-7. Write the covariant derivatives of the following mixed tensors with respect to z^i: (a) $A_k{}^j$; (b) $A_{kl}{}^j$; (c) A_{mno}^{jkl}.

11-8. For the mixed tensors of Problem 11-7 write the intrinsic or absolute derivatives.

11-9. Show that

$$D_\alpha A_i{}^\alpha = \frac{1}{\sqrt{g}} \frac{\partial(\sqrt{g}\ A_i{}^\alpha)}{\partial z^\alpha} - A_\beta{}^\alpha \begin{Bmatrix} \beta \\ i\ \alpha \end{Bmatrix}$$

11-10. If $A = A_{rs} z^r z^s$ and A_{rs} are constants, verify the expressions:

(a) $$\frac{\partial A}{\partial z^r} = (A_{rs} + A_{sr}) z^s$$

(b) $$\frac{\partial^2 A}{\partial z^r \ \partial z^s} = A_{rs} + A_{sr}$$

11-11. Verify the expression
$$D_k \delta_j{}^i = 0$$
11-12. Show that

$$R_{ijkl} = \frac{\partial}{\partial z^k}[jl, i] - \frac{\partial}{\partial z^l}[jk, i] + \begin{Bmatrix} a \\ j\,k \end{Bmatrix}[il, a] - \begin{Bmatrix} a \\ j\,l \end{Bmatrix}[ik, a]$$

11-13. Prove that

$$R_{ijkl} = \frac{1}{2}\left[\frac{\partial^2 g_{il}}{\partial z^j\,\partial z^k} + \frac{\partial^2 g_{jk}}{\partial z^i\,\partial z^l} - \frac{\partial^2 g_{ik}}{\partial z^j\,\partial z^l} - \frac{\partial^2 g_{jl}}{\partial z^i\,\partial z^k} \right.$$
$$\left. + g^{ab}([jk, b][il, a] - [jl, b][ik, a]) \right]$$

11-14. If

$$\begin{Bmatrix} s \\ r\,s \end{Bmatrix} = \frac{1}{\sqrt{g}}\frac{\partial}{\partial z^r}\sqrt{g},$$

prove that

$$D_r A^r = \frac{1}{\sqrt{g}}\frac{\partial}{\partial z^r}(\sqrt{g}\,A^r)$$

11-15. If f is an invariant, evaluate $\nabla^2 f$ in terms of cylindrical coordinates.

11-16. Develop the following equation which was obtained by E. B. Christoffel in 1869:

$$\frac{\partial^2 z^m}{\partial z'^i\,\partial z'^j} = \begin{Bmatrix} c \\ i\,j \end{Bmatrix}'\frac{\partial z^m}{\partial z'^c} - \begin{Bmatrix} m \\ a\,b \end{Bmatrix}\frac{\partial z^a}{\partial z'^i}\frac{\partial z^b}{\partial z'^j}$$

11-12. References

11-1. *Vector and Tensor Analysis*, G. E. Hay, Dover Publications, Inc.

11-2. *Theory and Problems of Vector Analysis*, M. R. Spiegel, Schaum Publishing Company.

11-3. *Tensor Analysis: Theory and Applications*, I. S. Sokolnikoff, John Wiley and Sons, Inc.

11-4. *Vector and Tensor Analysis*, H. Lass, McGraw-Hill Book Company.

11-5. *Vector Analysis with an Introduction to Tensor Analysis*, A. P. Wills, Dover Publications, Inc.

11-6. *Vector and Tensor Analysis*, N. Coburn, The Macmillan Company.

11-7. *Concepts from Tensor Analysis and Differential Geometry*, T. Y. Thomas, Vol. 1 of *Mathematics in Science and Engineering*, Academic Press.

11-8. *Nonlinear Theory of Continuous Media*, A. Cemil Eringen, McGraw-Hill Book Company.

Components of Tensors, Relative Tensors, and Cartesian Tensors

12-1. The Covariant, Contravariant, and Physical Components of Vectors and Tensors

Several procedures may be used for determining the covariant, contravariant, and physical components of a vector. The physical components are, by convention, taken to be the projections of the vector onto the tangents to the parametric lines, that is, the parallel projection in the direction of the base vectors $\mathbf{g}_i$ as discussed in Section 1-5 of Chapter 1. Consider a vector $\mathbf{A}$ whose magnitude is designated by the symbol A. This vector will be referred to a primed system $(\acute{X}^1, \acute{X}^2, \acute{X}^3)$ as well as to an unprimed system (X^1, X^2, X^3).

A general expression for vector $\mathbf{A}$ may be written as

$$\mathbf{A} = A^i \mathbf{g}_i = \frac{A^i \mathbf{g}_i}{\sqrt{g_{ii}}} \sqrt{g_{ii}}$$

The term $\mathbf{g}_i/\sqrt{g_{ii}}$ is a unit vector along $\mathbf{g}_i$, and it will be designated by the symbol $\mathbf{e}_i$. Hence

$$\mathbf{A} = \sqrt{g_{ii}} \, A^i \mathbf{e}_i$$

From this we see that the expression in general for the physical components of a vector **A** is

$$A^{(i)} = \sqrt{g_{ii}}\, A^i \qquad \text{(no summation on } i\text{)}$$

The index i in parentheses is used to designate a physical component in order to avoid confusion with the covariant index.

For orthogonal curvilinear coordinates the expression for the physical components may also be written as follows.

$$A^{(i)} = \frac{A^i}{\sqrt{g^{ii}}} \qquad \text{(no summation on } i\text{)}$$

For an orthogonal curvilinear system, g_{11}, g_{22}, g_{33} would have values and all others would be zero. Hence the physical components of the vector denoted by $A^{(1)}$, $A^{(2)}$, and $A^{(3)}$ expressed in orthogonal coordinates are

$$A^{(1)} = \sqrt{g_{11}}\, A^1 = \frac{A^1}{\sqrt{g^{11}}}$$

$$A^{(2)} = \sqrt{g_{22}}\, A^2 = \frac{A^2}{\sqrt{g^{22}}}$$

$$A^{(3)} = \sqrt{g_{33}}\, A^3 = \frac{A^3}{\sqrt{g^{33}}}$$

It should be emphasized that the expressions $\sqrt{g_{ii}}\, A^i$ are general and are not limited to an orthogonal system.

The physical components may also be found from the general expression for the magnitude of a vector. If the coordinates are orthogonal, equation (8-19) becomes

$$A = \sqrt{g_{11}A^1A^1 + g_{22}A^2A^2 + g_{33}A^3A^3}$$

If $A^{(1)}$, $A^{(2)}$, and $A^{(3)}$ represent the magnitude of the projections of the vector on the tangents to the parametric lines,

$$A = \sqrt{(A^{(1)})^2 + (A^{(2)})^2 + (A^{(3)})^2}$$

The physical components obtained by comparing the terms in the last two equations are the same as those previously established.

The physical components are used in vector analysis. It is important to emphasize that the values for the physical components change for each new coordinate system. The physical components are seldom used in tensor analysis.

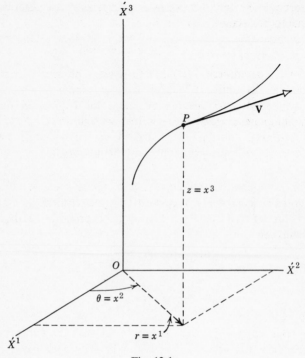

Fig. 12-1.

Example 12-1

Determine the contravariant, covariant, and physical components of the velocity of a particle P moving in space in terms of cylindrical coordinates as shown in Fig. 12-1.

The transformation equations from Cartesian $\overset{'}{x}{}^i$ coordinates to cylindrical x^i coordinates are

$$\overset{'}{x}{}^1 = x^1 \cos x^2 = r \cos \theta$$
$$\overset{'}{x}{}^2 = x^1 \sin x^2 = r \sin \theta$$
$$\overset{'}{x}{}^3 = x^3 \qquad\ \ = z$$

The inverse transformation equations are

$$x^1 = \sqrt{(\overset{'}{x}{}^1)^2 + (\overset{'}{x}{}^2)^2}$$
$$x^2 = \text{arc} \tan \frac{\overset{'}{x}{}^2}{\overset{'}{x}{}^1}$$
$$x^3 = \overset{'}{x}{}^3$$

Consider the vector **V** to represent the velocity of point P as it moves along the general curve shown.

The components of the velocity vector referred to the primed Cartesian coordinates $\dot{x}^i$ are

$$\overset{'}{v}{}^i = \overset{'}{v}_i = \frac{d\overset{'}{x}{}^i}{dt}$$

The contravariant components of the velocity vector **V** referred to the unprimed coordinates x^i (cylindrical coordinates) may be found from the following transformation equation.

$$v^i = \frac{\partial x^i}{\partial \overset{'}{x}{}^j}\, \overset{'}{v}{}^j$$

However,

$$\overset{'}{v}{}^j = \frac{d\overset{'}{x}{}^j}{dt}$$

Therefore

$$v^i = \frac{\partial x^i}{\partial \overset{'}{x}{}^j}\frac{d\overset{'}{x}{}^j}{dt} = \frac{dx^i}{dt}$$

From this relation it may be concluded that the contravariant components of the velocity vector are the time derivatives of the position coordinates of P. That is,

$$\{v^i\} = \left\{\frac{dx^1}{dt},\, \frac{dx^2}{dt},\, \frac{dx^3}{dt}\right\} = \left\{\frac{dr}{dt},\, \frac{d\theta}{dt},\, \frac{dz}{dt}\right\}$$

The covariant velocity components referred to the unprimed components may be found from the following transformation.

$$v_i = \frac{\partial \overset{'}{x}{}^j}{\partial x^i}\, \overset{'}{v}_j$$

Also, we know that

$$v_i = g_{ij} v^j$$

Hence

$$v_i = g_{ij} v^j = \frac{\partial \overset{'}{x}{}^j}{\partial x^i}\, \overset{'}{v}_j$$

In order to determine the covariant components in cylindrical coordinates it is necessary to know the values of the metric tensor g_{ij}.

This tensor was calculated in Chapter 7 for cylindrical coordinates and found to be

$$g_{11} = 1, \quad g_{22} = r^2, \quad g_{33} = 1$$

All others are zero.

The covariant components are therefore

For $i = 1, j = 1, 2, 3,$

$$v_1 = g_{11}v^1 + g_{12}v^2 + g_{13}v^3 = 1v^1 + 0 + 0 = \frac{dx^1}{dt} = \frac{dr}{dt}$$

In a similar manner,

$$v_2 = g_{21}v^1 + g_{22}v^2 + g_{23}v^3 = 0 + (x^1)^2 \frac{dx^2}{dt} + 0 = (x^1)^2 \frac{dx^2}{dt} = r^2 \frac{d\theta}{dt}$$

$$v_3 = g_{31}v^1 + g_{32}v^2 + g_{33}v^3 = 0 + 0 + 1 \frac{dx^3}{dt} = \frac{dx^3}{dt} = \frac{dz}{dt}$$

The covariant components are, therefore,

$$\{v_i\} = \left\{ \frac{dx^1}{dt}, (x^1)^2 \frac{dx^2}{dt}, \frac{dx^3}{dt} \right\} = \left\{ \frac{dr}{dt}, r^2 \frac{d\theta}{dt}, \frac{dz}{dt} \right\}$$

The physical components may be found from the general expression for the magnitude of a vector; namely,

$$v = \sqrt{v^i v_i} = \sqrt{v^1 v_1 + v^2 v_2 + v^3 v_3}$$

Substituting gives

$$v = \sqrt{ \left(\frac{dx^1}{dt} \right)^2 + (x^1)^2 \left(\frac{dx^2}{dt} \right)^2 + \left(\frac{dx^3}{dt} \right)^2 }$$

The physical components are therefore

$$\{v\} = \left\{ \frac{dx^1}{dt}, x^1 \frac{dx^2}{dt}, \frac{dx^3}{dt} \right\} = \left\{ \frac{dr}{dt}, r \frac{d\theta}{dt}, \frac{dz}{dt} \right\}$$

12-2. Relative Tensors

A relative vector of weight one will be defined in such a manner that the transformation equation is expressed as

$$\acute{A}^k = \left| \frac{\partial z^i}{\partial z'^j} \right| A^s \frac{\partial z'^k}{\partial z^s} \tag{12-1}$$

Here the expression $|\partial z^i/\partial z'^j|$ is the Jacobian of the transformation.

If the Jacobian is equal to unity, equation (12-1) is identical with that for the transformation equation for a contravariant vector; that is,

$$\acute{A}^k = A^s \frac{\partial z'^k}{\partial z^s} \tag{6-1}$$

Consider next a number of relative vectors of weight one, each transforming in accordance with equation (12-1).

$$\acute{A}^k = \left| \frac{\partial z^i}{\partial z'^j} \right| A^n \frac{\partial z'^k}{\partial z^n}$$

$$\acute{B}^l = \left| \frac{\partial z^i}{\partial z'^j} \right| B^m \frac{\partial z'^l}{\partial z^m}$$

$$\acute{C}^m = \left| \frac{\partial z^i}{\partial z'^j} \right| C^p \frac{\partial z'^m}{\partial z^p}$$

The product of these relative vectors could be expressed as

$$\acute{A}^k\acute{B}^l\acute{C}^p_{...} = \left[\left| \frac{\partial z^i}{\partial z'^j} \right| \left| \frac{\partial z^i}{\partial z'^j} \right| \cdots \right] [A^nB^mC^p_{...}] \left[\frac{\partial z'^k}{\partial z^n} \frac{\partial z'^l}{\partial z^m} \cdots \right]$$

Let W represent the number of relative vectors. The product may then be expressed as

$$\acute{T}^{kl\cdots} = \left| \frac{\partial z^i}{\partial z'^j} \right|^W T^{nm\cdots} \frac{\partial z'^k}{\partial z^n} \frac{\partial z'^l}{\partial z^m} \cdots \tag{12-2}$$

where $\acute{T}^{kl\cdots}$ represents $\acute{A}^k\acute{B}^l\acute{C}^p_{...}$, and $T^{nm\cdots}$ the term $A^nB^mC^p_{...}$.

This equation is the transformation equation of a relative tensor of weight W, where $|\partial z^i/\partial z'^j| = J$ is the Jacobian or functional determinant of the transformation relating the coordinates z and $\acute{z}$.

It may therefore be stated that a set of quantities $A^{ij\cdots}_{mn\cdots}$ are the components of a relative tensor of weight W, contravariant in the subscripts $ij_{...}$ and covariant in the subscripts $mn_{...}$ if and only if they transform according to the equation

$$\acute{A}^{\alpha\cdots}_{\beta\cdots} = J^W A^{i\cdots}_{m\cdots} \frac{\partial z'^\alpha}{\partial z^i} \cdots \frac{\partial z^m}{\partial z'^\beta} \cdots \tag{12-3}$$

The difference between absolute and relative tensors lies in the term containing the Jacobian raised to the Wth power. The Jacobian, J, is assumed to be neither zero nor infinite. The symbol W is an integer.

It is apparent that, if the weight is zero, the equation reduces to those already developed for absolute tensors. If the weight is unity, the relative tensor is called a tensor density.

Relative tensors of the same type and weight may be added; in this event the sum is a relative tensor of the same type and weight.

The inner and outer products of relative tensors having weights W_1 and W_2 respectively, are relative tensors of weight $W_1 + W_2$.

Consider the following relative tensors of weight W_1 and W_2.

$$A_\beta^{'\alpha} = J^{W_1} \frac{\partial z'^\alpha}{\partial z^q} \frac{\partial z^r}{\partial z'^\beta} A_r^{\,q}$$

$$B_k^{'ij} = J^{W_2} \frac{\partial z'^i}{\partial z^l} \frac{\partial z'^j}{\partial z^m} \frac{\partial z^n}{\partial z'^k} B_n^{\,lm}$$

The outer product is therefore

$$A_\beta^{'\alpha} B_k^{'ij} = J^{(W_1+W_2)} \frac{\partial z'^\alpha}{\partial z^q} \frac{\partial z^r}{\partial z'^\beta} \frac{\partial z'^i}{\partial z^l} \frac{\partial z'^j}{\partial z^m} \frac{\partial z^n}{\partial z'^k} A_r^{\,q} B_n^{\,lm}$$

The inner product, which is a contraction of the outer product; is also a relative tensor of weight $W_1 + W_2$.

A quantity A is a relative invariant of weight W, if it transforms according to the relation

$$A' = \left| \frac{\partial z^i}{\partial z'^j} \right|^W A = J^W A \tag{12-4}$$

An absolute invariant or scalar is a relative invariant having a weight of zero, since in this case

$$A' = A \tag{12-5}$$

Consider the metric tensor whose determinate is g and whose elements are g_{ij}. The elements transform according to the relation

$$g'_{lm} = \frac{\partial z^i}{\partial z'^l} \frac{\partial z^j}{\partial z'^m} g_{ij}$$

Taking the determinant of both sides gives

$$g' = \left| \frac{\partial z^i}{\partial z'^l} \right| \left| \frac{\partial z^j}{\partial z'^m} \right| g = J^2 g$$

Hence

$$\sqrt{g'} = J\sqrt{g}$$

Since W is unity, $\sqrt{g}$ is a tensor of weight one and is an invariant.

Consider an invariant B of weight one and a relative tensor $A_{jk}{}^i$ of weight W. The transformation equation for B is

$$\overset{'}{B} = JB$$

Taking the Wth power gives

$$(\overset{'}{B})^W = J^W B^W$$

According to equation (12-2) the transformation equation for $A_{jk}{}^i$ is

$$\overset{'}{A}_{st}{}^r = J^W A_{jk}{}^i \frac{\partial \overset{'}{z}{}^r}{\partial z^i} \frac{\partial z^j}{\partial \overset{'}{z}{}^s} \frac{\partial z^k}{\partial \overset{'}{z}{}^t}$$

Multiplying both sides by $(B)^{-W}$ and rearranging gives

$$\left[\frac{B^{-W}}{J^W} \overset{'}{A}_{st}{}^r\right] = [B^{-W}A_{jk}{}^i] \frac{\partial \overset{'}{z}{}^r}{\partial z^i} \frac{\partial z^j}{\partial \overset{'}{z}{}^s} \frac{\partial z^k}{\partial \overset{'}{z}{}^t}$$

But

$$\frac{B^{-W}}{J^W} = \overset{'}{B}{}^{-W}$$

Hence

$$[\overset{'}{B}{}^{-W}\overset{'}{A}_{st}{}^r] = [B^{-W}A_{jk}{}^i] \frac{\partial \overset{'}{z}{}^r}{\partial z^i} \frac{\partial z^j}{\partial \overset{'}{z}{}^s} \frac{\partial z^k}{\partial \overset{'}{z}{}^t}$$

This is at once recognized as the transformation equation for an absolute tensor; hence $B^{-W}A_{jk}{}^i$ is an absolute tensor.

Any relative tensor of weight W may be transformed into an absolute tensor by multiplying it by the $(-W)$ power of a relative invariant of weight one. Since $\sqrt{g}$ is a relative invariant of weight one, it is convenient to use it for converting a relative tensor to an absolute one.

Let $A_k{}^{ij}$ be a relative tensor of weight W. In order to transform this into an absolute tensor, it is only necessary to multiply it by $(\sqrt{g})^{-W}$ or $g^{-W/2}$; hence

$$A_k{}^{ij}g^{-W/2} = B_k{}^{ij}$$

which is an absolute tensor.

The covariant derivative of a relative tensor $A_k{}^{ij}$ of weight W can be determined from the covariant derivative of the corresponding absolute tensor $B_k{}^{ij}$. Such a calculation gives

$$D_m A_k{}^{ij} = \frac{\partial A_k{}^{ij}}{\partial z^m} + \left\{ \begin{matrix} i \\ a \; m \end{matrix} \right\} A_k{}^{aj} + \left\{ \begin{matrix} j \\ a \; m \end{matrix} \right\} A_k{}^{ia}$$

$$- \left\{ \begin{matrix} a \\ k \; m \end{matrix} \right\} A_a{}^{ij} - W \left\{ \begin{matrix} a \\ m \; a \end{matrix} \right\} A_k{}^{ij} \quad (12\text{-}6)$$

If $A_k{}^{ij}$ is an absolute tensor ($W = 0$), the last term does not appear in the covariant derivative.

Covariant differentiation of a relative tensor changes the character of the tensor but not the weight.

The absolute or intrinsic derivative of the relative tensor A^i would be

$$\frac{\delta A^i}{\delta t} = \frac{\partial A^i}{\partial t} + [D_m A^i] \frac{dz^m}{dt} \quad (12\text{-}7)$$

12-3. Cartesian Tensors

In many engineering problems the transformation is from one rectangular Cartesian system to another rectangular Cartesian system. Vectors and tensors transformed between two rectangular Cartesian systems are called Cartesian vectors and tensors.

For a Cartesian rectangular coordinate system the metric g_{ij} is unity or zero; hence we may write

$$g_{ij} = \delta_{ij}$$

For a vector A_i we may write

$$A_i = g_{ij}A^j = \delta_{ij}A^j = A^i$$

There is no distinction between a covariant and contravariant index for this system.

In a similar manner, for higher-order Cartesian tensors,

$$A_{ij} = A^{ij}$$

The transformation relations for Cartesian tensors are

$$A_i' = \frac{\partial x_i'}{\partial x_j} A_j \quad (12\text{-}8)$$

$$A_{ij}' = \frac{\partial x_i'}{\partial x^k} \frac{\partial x_j'}{\partial x^l} A_{kl} \quad (12\text{-}9)$$

Absolute differentiation of Cartesian tensors is equivalent to ordinary differentiation; that is,

$$\frac{\delta A_{...}}{\delta t} = \frac{dA_{...}}{dt} \tag{12-10}$$

Covariant differentiation reduces to partial differentiation; that is,

$$D_k A_{...} = \frac{\partial A_{...}}{\partial x_k} \tag{12-11}$$

For rectangular Cartesian coordinates the Christoffel symbols vanish.

12-4. Problems

12-1. Compute, in terms of spherical coordinates, the contravariant, covariant, and physical components of the velocity of a particle moving through space.

12-2. Compute the divergence $D_k A^k$ of a vector $\mathbf{A}$ in terms of (a) cylindrical coordinates, and (b) spherical coordinates.

12-3. If A_i are the covariant components of a vector for an orthogonal curvilinear system Z^i, determine the physical components if the form of the metric is

$$(ds)^2 = (h_1 \, dz^1)^2 + (h_2 \, dz^2)^2 + (h_3 \, dz^3)^2$$

12-4. If A^{ij} is an absolute tensor, show that the determinant $|A^{ij}|$ is a relative invariant of weight -2.

12-5. Show that

$$D_i(g^{1/2} A^i) = g^{1/2} \, D_i A^i$$

12-6. If A^i is a relative tensor of weight one, show that $D_i A^i = \partial A^i / \partial z^i$.

12-7. If $A_{jk}{}^i$ is a relative tensor of weight W, show that $g^{-W/2} A_{jk}{}^i$ is an absolute tensor.

12-8. Show that $\sqrt{g}$ is a relative tensor of weight one.

12-9. Consider the tensor relation

$$(X) B_n{}^{lm} = D_{qn}{}^m$$

In this equation $B_n{}^{lm}$ is an arbitrary tensor of weight W_1, and $D_{qn}{}^m$ is a known relative tensor of weight W_2. Show that (X) is a relative tensor of weight $(W_2 - W_1)$.

12-5. Suggested References

12-1. *Nonlinear Theory of Continuous Media*, A. C. Eringen, McGraw-Hill Book Company.
12-2. *Vector Analysis*, Murray R. Spiegel, Schaum Publishing Company.
12-3. *Concepts from Tensor Analysis and Differential Geometry*, Vol. I of *Mathematics in Science and Engineering*, T. Y. Thomas, Academic Press.
12-4. *Vector and Tensor Analysis*, G. E. Hay, Dover Publications, Inc.
12-5. *Tensor Analysis: Theory and Applications*, I. S. Sokolnikoff, John Wiley and Sons, Inc.
12-6. *Applications of Tensor Analysis*, A. J. McConnell, Dover Publications Inc.
12-7. *Vector and Tensor Analysis*, L. Brand, John Wiley and Sons, Inc.
12-8. *Vector Analysis with an Introduction to Tensor Analysis*, A. P. Wills, Dover Publications, Inc.
12-9. *Cartesian Tensors*, Harold Jeffreys, The University Press, Cambridge, England.
12-10. *Methods of Mathematical Physics*, Harold Jeffreys, The University Press, Cambridge, England.

13

The Permutation Symbols
and the Kronecker Delta

13-1. Introduction

The permutation symbols e^{ijk} and e_{ijk} and the generalized Kronecker delta are important concepts in tensor analysis. Relations between the permutation symbols and the generalized Kronecker delta will now be developed.

By way of introducing the permutation symbols for a two-dimensional system (e^{ij} or e_{ij}), consider the determinant

$$a = |a_j^{\ i}| = \begin{vmatrix} a_1^{\ 1} & a_2^{\ 1} \\ a_1^{\ 2} & a_2^{\ 2} \end{vmatrix} = a_1^{\ 1}a_2^{\ 2} - a_2^{\ 1}a_1^{\ 2}$$

We shall show that this can be written in shorthand form as

$$a = |a_j^{\ i}| = \begin{vmatrix} a_1^{\ 1} & a_2^{\ 1} \\ a_1^{\ 2} & a_2^{\ 2} \end{vmatrix} = e^{ij}a_i^{\ 1}a_j^{\ 2} = e_{ij}a_1^{\ i}a_2^{\ j} \qquad (13\text{-}1)$$

The permutation symbols (e^{ij} or e_{ij}) are defined in such a manner that the following conditions hold.

1. If either the subscripts or the superscripts are composed of the same numbers,

$$e^{ij} \quad \text{or} \quad e_{ij} = 0$$

Examples:

$$e^{11} = 0, \quad e_{22} = 0$$

2. If the subscripts or superscripts are composed of separately distinct numbers which are in the same sequence as the integers 1, 2,

$$e^{ij} \quad \text{or} \quad e_{ij} = 1$$

Examples:

$$e^{12} = 1, \quad e_{12} = 1$$

3. If the subscripts or the superscripts are composed of separately distinct numbers which are not in natural sequence,

$$e^{ij} \quad \text{or} \quad e_{ij} = -1$$

Examples:

$$e^{21} = -1, \quad e_{21} = -1$$

The value for $e^{ij}a_j{}^1a_j{}^2$ will now be expanded and the value compared with the value for the determinant $|a_j{}^i|$.

Expanding gives

$$e^{ij}a_i{}^1a_j{}^2 = e^{11}a_1{}^1a_1{}^2 + e^{12}a_1{}^1a_2{}^2 + e^{21}a_2{}^1a_1{}^2 + e^{22}a_2{}^1a_2{}^2$$
$$e^{ij}a_i{}^1a_j{}^2 = a_1{}^1a_2{}^2 - a_2{}^1a_1{}^2$$

Note that both expressions are identical.

13-2. The Generalized Kronecker Delta

The value of the generalized Kronecker delta $\delta_{\alpha\beta}{}^{ij}$ depends on the indices $ij\alpha\beta$ for which the following restrictions hold.

1. If all the indices in either the subscripts or the superscripts are not distinct, then $\delta_{\alpha\beta}{}^{ij} = 0$. Let $i = j$; then

$$\delta_{\alpha\beta}{}^{ii} = 0$$

The same situation prevails if $\alpha = \beta$; for example,

$$\delta_{\alpha\beta}{}^{11} = 0, \quad \delta_{22}{}^{ij} = 0, \quad \delta_{11}{}^{11} = 0$$

2. If the superscripts are not the same set of numbers as the subscripts, then $\delta_{\alpha\beta}{}^{ij} = 0$; for example,

$$\delta_{12}{}^{73} = 0, \quad \delta_{53}{}^{14} = 0$$

3. If the superscripts are an even permutation of the subscripts, then $\delta_{\alpha\beta}{}^{ij} = 1$, whereas, if the superscripts are an odd permutation of the subscripts, then $\delta_{\alpha\beta}{}^{ij} = -1$.

If an even number of permutations is required to arrange the superscripts in the same sequence as the subscripts, the value of the Kronecker delta is 1, and, if an odd number is required, the result is -1.

Consider $\delta_{12}{}^{21}$. In order to change the numbers in the superscripts into the same sequence as the subscripts it is necessary to interchange 2 and 1. This means that one permutation is required; hence the result is -1. Suppose the Kronecker delta is $\delta_{21}{}^{21}$. Since superscripts and subscripts are in the same sequence,

$$\delta_{21}{}^{21} = \delta_{12}{}^{12} = 1$$

The generalized Kronecker delta may be written as follows.

$$\delta_{\alpha\beta}{}^{ij} = \begin{vmatrix} \delta_\alpha{}^i & \delta_\beta{}^i \\ \delta_\alpha{}^j & \delta_\beta{}^j \end{vmatrix} = \delta_\alpha{}^i\delta_\beta{}^j - \delta_\beta{}^i\delta_\alpha{}^j \tag{13-2}$$

Example 13-1

Show that

$$\delta_{\alpha\beta}{}^{rs}a^{\alpha\beta} = a^{rs} - a^{sr}$$

According to equation (13-2) this relation may be written

$$a^{\alpha\beta}\delta_{\alpha\beta}{}^{rs} = a^{\alpha\beta}\begin{vmatrix} \delta_\alpha{}^r & \delta_\beta{}^r \\ \delta_\alpha{}^s & \delta_\beta{}^s \end{vmatrix} = a^{\alpha\beta}(\delta_\alpha{}^r\delta_\beta{}^s - \delta_\beta{}^r\delta_\alpha{}^s)$$

If $\alpha = r$ and $\beta = s$ in the first expression in the parentheses, and $\beta = r$ and $\alpha = s$ in the second expression, then and only then will these products have values other than zero; hence

$$\delta_{\alpha\beta}{}^{rs}a^{\alpha\beta} = a^{rs}\delta_r{}^r\delta_s{}^s - a^{sr}\delta_r{}^r\delta_s{}^s = a^{rs} - a^{sr} \qquad \text{(no summation on } r \text{ or } s\text{)}$$

13-3. The Relationship between the Permutation Symbols and the Generalized Kronecker Delta

The permutation system may also be defined in terms of the generalized Kronecker delta by the relations

$$e^{i_1i_2} = \delta_{12}^{i_1i_2} \tag{13-3}$$

$$e_{i_1i_2} = \delta_{i_1i_2}^{12} \tag{13-4}$$

194   *Multilinear Analysis*

Numerically $\delta_{12}^{i_1i_2} = \delta_{i_1i_2}^{12}$ because interchanging the rows and columns of a determinant does not change the magnitude. Consequently, as far as numerical values are concerned,

$$e^{ij} = \delta_{12}{}^{ij} = \delta_{ij}{}^{12} = e_{ij} \tag{13-5}$$

The e^{ij} and e_{ij} terms are numerically the same. Thus equation (13-5) is tensorially correct only for Cartesian tensors. Thus, for Cartesian tensors,

$$e_{rs} = \delta_{rs}{}^{12}$$

and

$$e_{rt} = e^{rt}$$

or

$$e_{rt} = e^{rt} = \delta_{12}{}^{rt}$$

We may also directly verify the following equality.

$$e^{\alpha\beta}e_{ij} = \delta_{ij}{}^{\alpha\beta} \tag{13-6}$$

13-4. The Permutation Symbols for a Three-Dimensional System

In the discussion dealing with a two-dimensional system a four-element determinant was introduced; now we shall consider a nine-element determinant.

$$a = |a_j{}^i| = \begin{vmatrix} a_1{}^1 & a_2{}^1 & a_3{}^1 \\ a_1{}^2 & a_2{}^2 & a_3{}^2 \\ a_1{}^3 & a_2{}^3 & a_3{}^3 \end{vmatrix} = a_1{}^1a_2{}^2a_3{}^3 + a_1{}^3a_2{}^1a_3{}^2$$
$$+ a_1{}^2a_2{}^3a_3{}^1 - a_1{}^3a_2{}^2a_3{}^1 - a_3{}^3a_1{}^2a_2{}^1 - a_1{}^1a_3{}^2a_2{}^3$$

An analogous shorthand notation is

$$a = |a_j{}^i| = e^{ijk}a_i{}^1a_j{}^2a_k{}^3 = e_{ijk}a_1{}^ia_2{}^ja_3{}^k$$

The permutation symbol, e^{ijk} or e_{ijk}, is defined in such a manner that the following conditions hold.

1. If any two of the indices are equal,

$$e^{ijk} \quad \text{or} \quad e_{ijk} = 0$$

For example,

$$e^{112} = 0, \quad e_{233} = 0$$

2. If an even number of permutations are required to arrange the indices in the sequence 1, 2, 3,

$$e^{ijk} \quad \text{or} \quad e_{ijk} = 1$$

For example, what is the value of e_{312}? In order to place the indices 312 in sequence it is necessary to interchange first the 1 and 3 and then the 2 and 3. Hence two permutations are required and the value for e_{312} is 1.

3. If an odd number of permutations are required to arrange the indices in the sequence 1, 2, 3,

$$e^{ijk} \quad \text{or} \quad e_{ijk} = -1$$

For example, what is the value of e_{321}? In order to arrange the indices 321 in the order 123 it is only necessary to interchange the 3 and 1. Hence one permutation is required and the value for e_{321} is -1.

The summation $e^{ijk}a_i{}^1a_j{}^2a_k{}^3$ will be expanded and compared with the expression for the determinant $|a_j{}^i|$. The indices i, j, k range over the integers 1, 2, and 3.

Expanding gives

$$
\begin{aligned}
e^{ijk}a_i{}^1a_j{}^2a_k{}^3 &= e^{111}a_1{}^1a_1{}^2a_1{}^3 + e^{112}a_1{}^1a_1{}^2a_2{}^3 + e^{113}a_1{}^1a_1{}^2a_3{}^3 \\
&\quad + e^{121}a_1{}^1a_2{}^2a_1{}^3 + e^{122}a_1{}^1a_2{}^2a_2{}^3 + e^{123}a_1{}^1a_2{}^2a_3{}^3 \\
&\quad + e^{131}a_1{}^1a_3{}^2a_1{}^3 + e^{132}a_1{}^1a_3{}^2a_2{}^3 + e^{133}a_1{}^1a_3{}^2a_3{}^3 \\
&\quad + e^{211}a_2{}^1a_1{}^2a_1{}^3 + e^{212}a_2{}^1a_1{}^2a_2{}^3 + e^{213}a_2{}^1a_1{}^2a_3{}^3 \\
&\quad + e^{221}a_2{}^1a_2{}^2a_1{}^3 + e^{222}a_2{}^1a_2{}^2a_2{}^3 + e^{223}a_2{}^1a_2{}^2a_3{}^3 \\
&\quad + e^{231}a_2{}^1a_3{}^2a_1{}^3 + e^{232}a_2{}^1a_3{}^2a_2{}^3 + e^{233}a_2{}^1a_3{}^2a_3{}^3 \\
&\quad + e^{311}a_3{}^1a_1{}^2a_1{}^3 + e^{312}a_3{}^1a_1{}^2a_2{}^3 + e^{313}a_3{}^1a_1{}^2a_3{}^3 \\
&\quad + e^{321}a_3{}^1a_2{}^2a_1{}^3 + e^{322}a_3{}^1a_2{}^2a_2{}^3 + e^{323}a_3{}^1a_2{}^2a_3{}^3 \\
&\quad + e^{331}a_3{}^1a_3{}^2a_1{}^3 + e^{332}a_3{}^1a_3{}^2a_2{}^3 + e^{333}a_3{}^1a_3{}^2a_3{}^3 \\
&= a_1{}^1a_2{}^2a_3{}^3 + a_1{}^3a_2{}^1a_3{}^2 + a_1{}^2a_2{}^3a_3{}^1 \\
&\quad - a_1{}^3a_2{}^2a_3{}^1 - a_3{}^3a_1{}^2a_2{}^1 - a_1{}^1a_3{}^2a_2{}^3
\end{aligned}
$$

Since this expression is the same as the determinant expansion, the following relation is valid.

$$
a = |a_j{}^i| = \det a_j{}^i = \begin{vmatrix} a_1{}^1 & a_2{}^1 & a_3{}^1 \\ a_1{}^2 & a_2{}^2 & a_3{}^2 \\ a_1{}^3 & a_2{}^3 & a_3{}^3 \end{vmatrix} = \begin{array}{c} e^{ijk}a_i{}^1a_j{}^2a_k{}^3 \\ \text{or} \\ e_{ijk}a_1{}^ia_2{}^ja_3{}^k \end{array} \qquad (13\text{-}7)
$$

Since interchanging the rows and columns of a determinant does not change its value, we also have

$$a = |a_j{}^i| = \det a_j{}^i = \begin{vmatrix} a_1{}^1 & a_1{}^2 & a_1{}^3 \\ a_2{}^1 & a_2{}^2 & a_2{}^3 \\ a_3{}^1 & a_3{}^2 & a_3{}^3 \end{vmatrix} = \begin{matrix} e_{ijk}a_1{}^i a_2{}^j a_3{}^k \\ \text{or} \\ e^{ijk}a_i{}^1 a_j{}^2 a_k{}^3 \end{matrix}$$

Equation (13-7) can also be written

$$a e_{rst} = e_{ijk}a_r{}^i a_s{}^j a_t{}^k, \quad a e^{rst} = e^{ijk}a_i{}^r a_j{}^s a_k{}^t \tag{13-8}$$

This result can be verified by giving value to r, s, t and recalling that interchanging columns in a determinant changes the sign of the determinant.

From equation (13-8) we can establish the tensor character of the permutation symbols. Consider first

$$a e_{rst} = e_{ijk}a_r{}^i a_s{}^j a_t{}^k$$

Let

$$a_j{}^i = \frac{\partial z^i}{\partial z'^j}$$

Then

$$a = \left| \frac{\partial z^i}{\partial z'^j} \right| = J$$

so

$$e_{rst} = J^{-1} \frac{\partial z^i}{\partial z'^r} \frac{\partial z^j}{\partial z'^s} \frac{\partial z^k}{\partial z'^t} e_{ijk}$$

which is a relative tensor transformation.

Now consider

$$a e^{rst} = e^{ijk}a_i{}^r a_j{}^s a_k{}^t$$

Let

$$a_j{}^i = \frac{\partial z'^i}{\partial z^j}$$

Then

$$a = |a_j{}^i| = \frac{1}{J}$$

and

$$e^{rst} = J \frac{\partial z'^r}{\partial z^i} \frac{\partial z'^s}{\partial z^j} \frac{\partial z'^t}{\partial z^k} e^{ijk}$$

which is also a relative tensor transformation.

We may therefore state that the permutation symbols e_{ijk} and e^{ijk} are components of relative tensors of weight -1 and 1, respectively. The corresponding absolute third-order contravariant tensor is $e^{ijk}/\sqrt{g}$, and the corresponding absolute third-order covariant tensor is $\sqrt{g}\, e_{ijk}$.

13-5. Symmetric and Skew-Symmetric Tensors

Consider a system A_{rs} with two subscripts. This system is termed symmetric if each component is unaltered in value when the indices are interchanged. Hence

$$A_{rs} = A_{sr}$$

The same result holds for systems having two superscripts; that is,

$$A^{ij} = A^{ji}$$

A system having more than two subscripts is symmetric in two of the subscripts if the components are unaltered when the two indices are interchanged. If the system is completely symmetric, the interchange of any two subscripts will not change the value of the components. For example, the system A_{ijk} is completely symmetric if

$$A_{ijk} = A_{ikj} = A_{jik} = A_{jki} = A_{kij} = A_{kji}$$

The same result holds true for the system A^{ijk}.

The system A_{rs} is skew-symmetric if the interchange of indices alters the sign, but not the numerical value of the component; hence

$$A_{rs} = -A_{sr}$$

A system may be skew-symmetric with respect to two subscripts, or it may be completely skew-symmetric. An example of a completely skew-symmetric system of the third order is

$$A_{ijk} = -A_{ikj} = -A_{jik} = A_{jki} = A_{kij} = -A_{kji}$$

The same result applies to the system A^{ijk}.

The permutation symbol e_{ijk} represents a skew-symmetric system whose components have the values $0, +1, -1$. If A_{rst} is any skew-symmetric system of the third order, then

$$A_{rst} = A_{123} e_{rst}$$

The inner product of a skew-symmetric tensor and a symmetric tensor will now be considered. Let the inner product be represented by I_k:

$$I_k = e_{ijk}A^iA^j$$

Change the dummy indices i to j and j to i to obtain

$$I_k = e_{jik}A^jA^i$$

Interchange i and j in e_{jik}; then

$$I_k = -e_{ijk}A^jA^i = -I_k$$

or

$$2I_k = 0$$

Therefore

$$I_k = 0$$

From this we may conclude that the inner product of a skew-symmetric tensor and a symmetric tensor is zero. This is an important result which is often used in tensor analysis.

13-6. The Covariant Derivative of $e^{ijk}/\sqrt{g}$ and $e_{ijk}\sqrt{g}$

The covariant derivative of the absolute tensor $e^{jkl}/\sqrt{g}$ may be found as follows.

$$D_i\left(\frac{e^{jkl}}{\sqrt{g}}\right) = \frac{\partial(e^{jkl}/\sqrt{g})}{\partial x^i} + \begin{Bmatrix} j \\ i\ p \end{Bmatrix}\frac{e^{pkl}}{\sqrt{g}} + \begin{Bmatrix} k \\ i\ p \end{Bmatrix}\frac{e^{jpl}}{\sqrt{g}} + \begin{Bmatrix} l \\ i\ p \end{Bmatrix}\frac{e^{jkp}}{\sqrt{g}}$$

Consider the first term on the right side.

$$\frac{\partial(e^{jkl}/\sqrt{g})}{\partial x^i} = \frac{1}{\sqrt{g}}\frac{\partial e^{jkl}}{\partial x^i} + e^{jkl}\frac{\partial(1/\sqrt{g})}{\partial x^i}$$

$$= e^{jkl}\frac{\partial(1/\sqrt{g})}{x^i} = -\frac{e^{jkl}}{2g^{3/2}}\frac{\partial g}{\partial x^i}$$

However, it has been shown that

$$\frac{\partial g}{\partial x^i} = 2g\begin{Bmatrix} p \\ p\ i \end{Bmatrix}$$

Hence

$$\frac{\partial(e^{jkl}/\sqrt{g})}{\partial x^i} = -\frac{e^{jkl}}{2g^{3/2}}2g\begin{Bmatrix} p \\ p\ i \end{Bmatrix} = -\frac{e_{jkl}}{\sqrt{g}}\begin{Bmatrix} p \\ p\ i \end{Bmatrix}$$

Substituting in the original equation gives

$$D_i\left(\frac{e^{jkl}}{\sqrt{g}}\right) = -\frac{e^{jkl}}{\sqrt{g}}\begin{Bmatrix} p \\ p\ i \end{Bmatrix} + \begin{Bmatrix} j \\ i\ p \end{Bmatrix}\frac{e^{pkl}}{\sqrt{g}} + \begin{Bmatrix} k \\ i\ p \end{Bmatrix}\frac{e^{jpl}}{\sqrt{g}} + \begin{Bmatrix} l \\ i\ p \end{Bmatrix}\frac{e^{jkp}}{\sqrt{g}}$$

We shall now show that the right-hand side of the preceding relation is zero.

Let $j = 1$, $k = 2$, and $l = 3$.

$$D_i\left(\frac{e^{jkl}}{\sqrt{g}}\right) = -\frac{e^{123}}{\sqrt{g}}\begin{Bmatrix} p \\ p\ i \end{Bmatrix} + \begin{Bmatrix} 1 \\ i\ p \end{Bmatrix}\frac{e^{p23}}{\sqrt{g}} + \begin{Bmatrix} 2 \\ i\ p \end{Bmatrix}\frac{e^{1p3}}{\sqrt{g}} + \begin{Bmatrix} 3 \\ i\ p \end{Bmatrix}\frac{e^{12p}}{\sqrt{g}}$$

Summing over p gives

$$\begin{aligned}
D_i\left(\frac{e^{jkl}}{\sqrt{g}}\right) =& -\frac{e^{123}}{\sqrt{g}}\left[\begin{Bmatrix} 1 \\ 1\ i \end{Bmatrix} + \begin{Bmatrix} 2 \\ 2\ i \end{Bmatrix} + \begin{Bmatrix} 3 \\ 3\ i \end{Bmatrix}\right] \\
&+ \begin{Bmatrix} 1 \\ i\ 1 \end{Bmatrix}\frac{e^{123}}{\sqrt{g}} + \begin{Bmatrix} 1 \\ i\ 2 \end{Bmatrix}\frac{e^{223}}{\sqrt{g}} \\
&+ \begin{Bmatrix} 1 \\ i\ 3 \end{Bmatrix}\frac{e^{323}}{\sqrt{g}} + \begin{Bmatrix} 2 \\ i\ 1 \end{Bmatrix}\frac{e^{113}}{\sqrt{g}} + \begin{Bmatrix} 2 \\ i\ 2 \end{Bmatrix}\frac{e^{123}}{\sqrt{g}} \\
&+ \begin{Bmatrix} 2 \\ i\ 3 \end{Bmatrix}\frac{e^{133}}{\sqrt{g}} + \begin{Bmatrix} 3 \\ i\ 1 \end{Bmatrix}\frac{e^{121}}{\sqrt{g}} + \begin{Bmatrix} 3 \\ i\ 2 \end{Bmatrix}\frac{e^{122}}{\sqrt{g}} \\
&+ \begin{Bmatrix} 3 \\ i\ 3 \end{Bmatrix}\frac{e^{123}}{\sqrt{g}} \\
=& -\frac{1}{\sqrt{g}}\begin{Bmatrix} 1 \\ 1\ i \end{Bmatrix} - \frac{1}{\sqrt{g}}\begin{Bmatrix} 2 \\ 2\ i \end{Bmatrix} - \frac{1}{\sqrt{g}}\begin{Bmatrix} 3 \\ 3\ i \end{Bmatrix} \\
&+ \begin{Bmatrix} 1 \\ i\ 1 \end{Bmatrix}\frac{1}{\sqrt{g}} + \begin{Bmatrix} 2 \\ i\ 2 \end{Bmatrix}\frac{1}{\sqrt{g}} + \begin{Bmatrix} 3 \\ i\ 3 \end{Bmatrix}\frac{1}{\sqrt{g}}
\end{aligned}$$

But

$$\begin{Bmatrix} 1 \\ 1\ i \end{Bmatrix} = \begin{Bmatrix} 1 \\ i\ 1 \end{Bmatrix}, \quad \begin{Bmatrix} 2 \\ 2\ i \end{Bmatrix} = \begin{Bmatrix} 2 \\ i\ 2 \end{Bmatrix}, \quad \text{and} \quad \begin{Bmatrix} 3 \\ 3\ i \end{Bmatrix} = \begin{Bmatrix} 3 \\ i\ 3 \end{Bmatrix}$$

Substituting gives

$$D_i\left(\frac{e^{jkl}}{\sqrt{g}}\right) = 0 \tag{13-9}$$

Since $D_i(e^{jkl}/\sqrt{g})$ is a skew-symmetric tensor in $(j,\ k,\ l)$, any component is simply a scalar multiple of the component for $j = 1$, $k = 2$, $l = 3$. Consequently, equation (13-9) is generally valid.

Consider next the value for $D_l(\sqrt{g}\,e_{ijk})$.

$$D_l(\sqrt{g}\,e_{ijk}) = \frac{\partial \sqrt{g}\,e_{ijk}}{\partial x^l} - \begin{Bmatrix} p \\ i\ l \end{Bmatrix} \sqrt{g}\,e_{pjk} - \begin{Bmatrix} p \\ j\ l \end{Bmatrix} \sqrt{g}\,e_{ipk} - \begin{Bmatrix} p \\ k\ l \end{Bmatrix} \sqrt{g}\,e_{ijp}$$

Consider the first term on the right side of the relation.

$$\frac{\partial(\sqrt{g}\,e_{ijk})}{\partial x^l} = \sqrt{g}\,\frac{\partial e_{ijk}}{\partial x^l} + e_{ijk}\frac{\partial \sqrt{g}}{\partial x^l} = e_{ijk}\frac{\partial \sqrt{g}}{\partial x^l}$$

However, it has been shown that

$$\frac{\partial \sqrt{g}}{\partial x^l} = \sqrt{g}\begin{Bmatrix} p \\ p\ l \end{Bmatrix}$$

Hence

$$\frac{\partial \sqrt{g}\,e_{ijk}}{\partial x^l} = e_{ijk}\sqrt{g}\begin{Bmatrix} p \\ p\ l \end{Bmatrix}$$

Substituting in the original equation gives

$$D_l(\sqrt{g}\,e_{ijk}) = e_{ijk}\sqrt{g}\begin{Bmatrix} p \\ p\ l \end{Bmatrix} - \begin{Bmatrix} p \\ i\ l \end{Bmatrix}\sqrt{g}\,e_{pjk}$$
$$- \begin{Bmatrix} p \\ j\ l \end{Bmatrix}\sqrt{g}\,e_{ipk} - \begin{Bmatrix} p \\ k\ l \end{Bmatrix}\sqrt{g}\,e_{ijp}$$

Let $i = 1$, $j = 2$, $k = 3$.

$$D_l(\sqrt{g}\,e_{ijk}) = e_{123}\sqrt{g}\begin{Bmatrix} p \\ p\ l \end{Bmatrix} - \begin{Bmatrix} p \\ 1\ l \end{Bmatrix}\sqrt{g}\,e_{p23}$$
$$- \begin{Bmatrix} p \\ 2\ l \end{Bmatrix}\sqrt{g}\,e_{1p3} - \begin{Bmatrix} p \\ 3\ l \end{Bmatrix}\sqrt{g}\,e_{12p}$$

Summing over p gives

$$D_l(\sqrt{g}\,e_{ijk}) = e_{123}\sqrt{g}\begin{Bmatrix} 1 \\ 1\ l \end{Bmatrix} + e_{123}\sqrt{g}\begin{Bmatrix} 2 \\ 2\ l \end{Bmatrix} + e_{123}\sqrt{g}\begin{Bmatrix} 3 \\ 3\ l \end{Bmatrix}$$
$$- \begin{Bmatrix} 1 \\ 1\ l \end{Bmatrix}\sqrt{g}\,e_{123} - \begin{Bmatrix} 2 \\ 1\ l \end{Bmatrix}\sqrt{g}\,e_{223} - \begin{Bmatrix} 3 \\ 1\ l \end{Bmatrix}\sqrt{g}\,e_{323}$$
$$- \begin{Bmatrix} 1 \\ 2\ l \end{Bmatrix}\sqrt{g}\,e_{113} - \begin{Bmatrix} 2 \\ 2\ l \end{Bmatrix}\sqrt{g}\,e_{123} - \begin{Bmatrix} 3 \\ 2\ l \end{Bmatrix}\sqrt{g}\,e_{133}$$
$$- \begin{Bmatrix} 1 \\ 3\ l \end{Bmatrix}\sqrt{g}\,e_{121} - \begin{Bmatrix} 2 \\ 3\ l \end{Bmatrix}\sqrt{g}\,e_{122} - \begin{Bmatrix} 3 \\ 3\ l \end{Bmatrix}\sqrt{g}\,e_{123}$$

$$D_l(\sqrt{g}\,e_{ijk}) = \sqrt{g}\begin{Bmatrix} 1 \\ 1\ l \end{Bmatrix} + \sqrt{g}\begin{Bmatrix} 2 \\ 2\ l \end{Bmatrix} + \sqrt{g}\begin{Bmatrix} 3 \\ 3\ l \end{Bmatrix}$$
$$- \begin{Bmatrix} 1 \\ 1\ l \end{Bmatrix}\sqrt{g} - \begin{Bmatrix} 2 \\ 2\ l \end{Bmatrix}\sqrt{g} - \begin{Bmatrix} 3 \\ 3\ l \end{Bmatrix}\sqrt{g} = 0$$
$$D_l(\sqrt{g}\,e_{ijk}) = 0 \qquad (13\text{-}10)$$

By the reasoning used in connection with equation (13-9), we may conclude that equation (13-10) is also true in general. Consider the value of the following.

$$D_i\left(\frac{e^{ijk}}{\sqrt{g}}\, D_j A_k\right)$$

This may be expressed as

$$\frac{e^{ijk}}{\sqrt{g}}\, D_i\,(D_j A_k) + D_j A_k\, D_i\left(\frac{e^{ijk}}{\sqrt{g}}\right)$$

However,

$$D_i\left(\frac{e^{ijk}}{\sqrt{g}}\right) = 0$$

and hence

$$D_i\left(\frac{e^{ijk}}{\sqrt{g}}\, D_j A_k\right) = \frac{e^{ijk}}{\sqrt{g}}\, D_i\,(D_j A_k)$$

From this we may conclude that the term $e^{ijk}/\sqrt{g}$ may be treated as a constant under covariant differentiation.

13-7. The Generalized Kronecker Delta for a Three-Dimensional System

The Kronecker delta for a three-dimensional system may be represented as follows.

$$\delta^{ijk}_{\alpha\beta\gamma} = \begin{vmatrix} \delta_\alpha{}^i & \delta_\beta{}^i & \delta_\gamma{}^i \\ \delta_\alpha{}^j & \delta_\beta{}^j & \delta_\gamma{}^j \\ \delta_\alpha{}^k & \delta_\beta{}^k & \delta_\gamma{}^k \end{vmatrix} \tag{13-11}$$

In a manner similar to that described for a two-dimensional system the following conditions define $\delta^{ijk}_{\alpha\beta\gamma}$.

1. If two subscripts or two superscripts have the same value, or if the subscripts are not the same set of numbers as the superscripts, then $\delta^{ijk}_{\alpha\beta\gamma} = 0$. For example,

$$\delta^{312}_{323} = 0, \quad \delta^{122}_{123} = 0, \quad \delta^{322}_{133} = 0$$

2. If the subscripts and superscripts are separately distinct and in the same sequence, $\delta^{ijk}_{\alpha\beta\gamma} = 1$. If an even number of permutations

are required to rearrange the subscripts or superscripts in the same sequence, then $\delta_{\alpha\beta\gamma}^{ijk} = 1$. For example,

$$\delta_{123}^{123} = 1, \quad \delta_{231}^{123} = 1, \quad \delta_{321}^{321} = 1$$

3. If the subscripts and superscripts are separately distinct and an odd number of permutations is required to arrange them in the same sequence, $\delta_{\alpha\beta\gamma}^{ijk} = -1$. For example,

$$\delta_{213}^{123} = -1, \quad \delta_{4321}^{1243} = -1$$

Example 13-2

Show that $\delta_{ijk}^{ijk} = 3!$ if $i, j, k = 1, 2, 3$.

$$
\begin{aligned}
\delta_{ijk}^{ijk} &= \delta_{111}^{111} + \delta_{112}^{112} + \delta_{113}^{113} + \delta_{121}^{121} + \delta_{122}^{122} + \delta_{123}^{123} + \delta_{131}^{131} \\
&+ \delta_{132}^{132} + \delta_{133}^{133} + \delta_{211}^{211} + \delta_{212}^{212} + \delta_{213}^{213} + \delta_{221}^{221} + \delta_{222}^{222} \\
&+ \delta_{223}^{223} + \delta_{231}^{231} + \delta_{232}^{232} + \delta_{233}^{233} + \delta_{311}^{311} + \delta_{312}^{312} + \delta_{313}^{313} \\
&+ \delta_{321}^{321} + \delta_{322}^{322} + \delta_{323}^{323} + \delta_{331}^{331} + \delta_{332}^{332} + \delta_{333}^{333} \\
&= 6 = 1 \cdot 2 \cdot 3 = 3!
\end{aligned}
$$

Interesting relations may be obtained by contracting the Kronecker delta. Let us, for example, contract $\delta_{\alpha\beta\gamma}^{ijk}$ on k and γ for a range of 3 ($n = 3$).

Evaluating the determinant gives

$$
\delta_{\alpha\beta k}^{ijk} = \begin{vmatrix} \delta_\alpha{}^i & \delta_\beta{}^i & \delta_k{}^i \\ \delta_\alpha{}^j & \delta_\beta{}^j & \delta_k{}^j \\ \delta_\alpha{}^k & \delta_\beta{}^k & \delta_k{}^k \end{vmatrix} = 3\delta_\alpha{}^i\delta_\beta{}^j - \delta_\alpha{}^i\delta_\beta{}^j - 3\delta_\alpha{}^j\delta_\beta{}^i + \delta_\beta{}^i\delta_\alpha{}^j
$$

$$
+ \delta_\alpha{}^j\delta_\beta{}^i - \delta_\beta{}^j\delta_\alpha{}^i = \delta_\alpha{}^i\delta_\beta{}^j - \delta_\alpha{}^j\delta_\beta{}^i = \delta_{\alpha\beta}{}^{ij}
$$

or

$$\delta_{\alpha\beta k}^{ijk} = \delta_{\alpha\beta}{}^{ij} \tag{13-12}$$

Suppose we contract $\delta_{\alpha\beta}{}^{ij}$ on j and β for a range of 3; then

$$
\delta_{\alpha j}{}^{ij} = \begin{vmatrix} \delta_\alpha{}^i & \delta_j{}^i \\ \delta_\alpha{}^j & \delta_j{}^j \end{vmatrix} = \delta_\alpha{}^i\delta_j{}^j - \delta_j{}^i\delta_\alpha{}^j = 3\delta_\alpha{}^i - \delta_\alpha{}^i = 2\delta_\alpha{}^i
$$

We therefore have the following relation.

$$\delta_\alpha{}^i = \tfrac{1}{2}\delta_{\alpha j}{}^{ij} \tag{13-13}$$

From the proof of equation (13-13) we may generalize to the n-dimensional case.

$$\delta_\alpha{}^i = \frac{1}{n-1}\,\delta_{\alpha j}{}^{ij} \qquad (13\text{-}14)$$

The numerical values of $\delta_{\alpha\beta\gamma}^{123}$ and $\delta_{123}^{\alpha\beta\gamma}$ are the same; however, as tensors they are different. The numerical equality is due to the fact that interchanging rows and columns of a determinate does not change the numerical value.

In general form the Kronecker delta may be written

$$\delta_{j_1 j_2 j_3 \ldots j_m}^{i_1 i_2 i_3 \ldots i_m}$$

The analysis used for obtaining the relations between the permutation symbols and the Kronecker delta for a two-dimensional system, when applied to a three-dimensional system, yields the following basic relations.

$$e^{ijk} = \delta_{123}^{ijk} \qquad (13\text{-}15)$$

and

$$e_{ijk} = \delta_{ijk}^{123} \qquad (13\text{-}16)$$

For an n-dimensional system the equations are

$$e^{i_1 i_2 i_3 \ldots i_n} = \delta_{123\ldots n}^{i_1 i_2 i_3 \ldots i_n}$$

and

$$e_{i_1 i_2 i_3 \ldots i_n} = \delta_{i_1 i_2 i_3 \ldots i_n}^{123\ldots n}$$

Consider the product of e_{mn} and e^{st}. By equations (13-15) and (13-16),

$$e_{mn} = \delta_{mn}{}^{12} \quad \text{and} \quad e^{st} = \delta_{12}{}^{st}$$

Hence

$$e_{mn}e^{st} = \delta_{mn}{}^{st}$$

$$e_{lmn}e^{rst} = \delta_{lmn}^{rst}$$

But $\delta_{mn}{}^{st}$ represents the following determinant.

$$\delta_{mn}{}^{st} = \begin{vmatrix} \delta_m{}^s & \delta_n{}^s \\ \delta_m{}^t & \delta_n{}^t \end{vmatrix} = \delta_m{}^s \delta_n{}^t - \delta_n{}^s \delta_m{}^t$$

Therefore

$$e_{rmn}e^{rst} = \delta_m{}^s \delta_n{}^t - \delta_m{}^t \delta_n{}^s \qquad (13\text{-}17)$$

Example 13-3

By use of the preceding equation show that $e^{ijk}e_{ijk} = 6$.

$$e^{ijk}e_{ilm} = \delta_l{}^j \delta_m{}^k - \delta_m{}^j \delta_l{}^k$$

This represents 81 terms.

If $l = j$,
$$e^{ijk}e_{ijm} = \delta_j{}^j\delta_m{}^k - \delta_m{}^j\delta_j{}^k = 3\delta_m{}^k - \delta_m{}^k = 2\delta_m{}^k$$
since
$$\delta_j{}^j = \delta_1{}^1 + \delta_2{}^2 + \delta_3{}^3 = 3$$
If $m = k$,
$$e^{ijk}e_{ijk} = 2\delta_k{}^k = 2(\delta_1{}^1 + \delta_2{}^2 + \delta_3{}^3) = 2(3) = 6$$
Therefore
$$e^{ijk}e_{ijk} = 6$$

The general relations between the Kronecker delta and the permutation symbol may be represented as follows.

$$\delta^{ijk}_{abc} = e_{abc}e^{ijk} \tag{13-18}$$

and

$$\delta_{ab}{}^{ij} = e_{abr}e^{ijr} = \delta^{ijr}_{abr} \tag{13-19}$$

Since e has a weight of 1 and -1, δ^{ijk}_{abc} is an absolute tensor of order 6. On the other hand, $\delta_{ab}{}^{ij}$ formed by contracting δ^{ijk}_{abc} is an absolute tensor of order 4.

It may, therefore, be concluded that there are n types of Kronecker deltas in n-space, ranging from $\delta_a{}^i$ to $\delta^{ijk\ldots n}_{abc\ldots f}$.

If $n = 4$,

$$\delta^{ijkh}_{abcd} = e_{abcd}e^{ijkh}$$

$$\delta^{ijk}_{abc} = \frac{1}{1!}e_{abcd}e^{ijkd} = \frac{1}{1!}\delta^{ijkd}_{abcd}$$

$$\delta_{ab}{}^{ij} = \frac{1}{2!}e_{abcd}e^{ijcd} = \frac{1}{2!}\delta^{ijcd}_{abcd}$$

$$\delta_a{}^i = \frac{1}{3!}e_{abcd}e^{ibcd} = \frac{1}{3!}\delta^{ibcd}_{abcd}$$

Consider the last equation.

$$\delta_a{}^i = \frac{1}{3!}\delta^{ibcd}_{abcd}$$

For an n-dimensional space the right-hand side can be generalized to read

$$\delta^{i_1\ldots i_r i_{r+1}\ldots i_n}_{j_1\ldots j_r j_{r+1}\ldots j_n}$$

The first term will likewise be expressed in equation form as

$$\delta^{i_1\ldots i_r}_{j_1\ldots j_r}$$

The r-dimensional Kronecker delta may now be expressed as

$$(n-r)!\,\delta^{i_1\ldots i_r}_{j_1\ldots j_r} = e^{i_1\ldots i_r i_{r+1}\ldots i_n}e_{j_1\ldots j_r i_{r+1}\ldots i_n} = \delta^{i_1\ldots i_r i_{r+1}\ldots i_n}_{j_1\ldots j_r i_{r+1}\ldots i_n}$$

This indicates a contraction on j's past j_r.

13-8. Problems

13-1. Expand the following expressions for the two-dimensional case: (a) $e^{ij}a_i^2 a_j^1$; (b) $e^{\alpha\beta}a_\alpha{}^i a_\beta{}^j = e^{ij}|a|$.

13-2. Show that $\delta_{ij}{}^{ij} = 2!$ if $i, j = 1, 2$.

13-3. Show that $\delta_{rs}{}^{12}\delta_{12}{}^{rt} = \delta_s{}^t$ if $r, s, t = 1, 2$.

13-4. For a three-dimensional system expand (a) $\delta_{ij}{}^{\alpha\beta}x^i y^j$ and (b) $\delta_{ij}{}^{ij}$.

13-5. Show that

$$\delta_{ij}{}^{\alpha\beta}\frac{\partial\phi_\alpha}{\partial x^\beta} = \frac{\partial\phi_i}{\partial x^j} - \frac{\partial\phi_j}{\partial x^i}$$

13-6. Show that for a range of 4,

$$\delta_\alpha{}^i = \tfrac{1}{3}\delta_{\alpha j}{}^{ij}$$

13-7. Show that

$$e^{ijk}a_i{}^1 a_j{}^2 a_k{}^3 = e_{ijk}a_1{}^i a_2{}^j a_3{}^k$$

13-8. Show that

$$e_{ijk}A_l - e_{ijl}A_k + e_{lkj}A_i - e_{lki}A_j = 0$$

for three-dimensional space.

13-9. Show that $(1/\sqrt{g})e^{ijk}a_{ij}$ is a null vector if a_{ij} is symmetric.

13-10. Determine the value of the expression $e_{ijk}\,D^j\,D^k A^{pq}$.

13-11. Show that

$$\delta_{1\ldots n}^{i_1\ldots i_n}\,\delta_{j_1\ldots j_n}^{1\ldots n} = \delta_{j_1\ldots j_n}^{i_1\ldots i_n}$$

13-12. Show that $\delta_{ijkl}^{ijkl} = 4!$ if $i, j, k, l = 1, 2, 3, 4$.

13-13. Prove by expanding and evaluating the terms for a range of 3 that $e_{rst}e^{rst} = 6$.

13-14. Show that, for Cartesian tensors, $e_{rmn}e_{rst} = \delta_{ms}\delta_{nt} - \delta_{mt}\delta_{ns}$.

13-15. Show that $e^{ijk}e_{ijl} = 2\delta_l{}^k$.

13-16. Evaluate the following expressions in cylindrical coordinates:

$$(a)\ (e^{ijk}/\sqrt{g})\,D_j A_k, \quad (b)\ D_i\,D^i\phi, \quad (c)\ D_i\,D^i A_j.$$

13-17. Solve Problem 13-16 using spherical coordinates.

13-9. Suggested References

13-1. *Vector and Tensor Analysis*, H. Lass, McGraw-Hill Book Company.

13-2. *Vector and Tensor Analysis*, L. Brand, John Wiley and Sons, Inc.

13-3. *Applications of Tensor Analyses*, A. J. McConnell, Dover Publications, Inc.

13-4. *Tensor Analysis: Theory and Applications*, I. S. Sokolnikoff, John Wiley and Sons, Inc.

13-5. *Vector and Tensor Analysis*, G. E. Hay, Dover Publications, Inc.

13-6. *Vector and Tensor Analysis*, N. Coburn, The Macmillan Company.

Vector Quantities
in Tensor Form

14-1. Introduction

Tensor procedures when applied to vector equations result in important simplification. Vector operations must be determined for each different coordinate system. On the other hand, the tensor operations are valid for all coordinate systems. The generalization of vector relations by use of tensors will be illustrated in the following paragraphs.

In tensor notation vectors **A** and **B** are represented by the following components:

$$A^i \text{ or } A_i \quad \text{and} \quad B^j \text{ or } B_j$$

In Cartesian tensor form the expressions are

$$A_i \quad \text{and} \quad B_j$$

The symbols A^i and A_j represent the contravariant and covariant components of the vector **A**.

14-2. Scalar Product of Two Vectors **A** *and* **B**

The scalar or dot product of the two vectors **A** and **B** according to equation (1-5) is

$$\mathbf{A} \cdot \mathbf{B} = |\mathbf{A}|\,|\mathbf{B}|\cos\theta = |\mathbf{A}|\,|\mathbf{B}|\cos(\mathbf{A}, \mathbf{B}) \qquad (1\text{-}5)$$

The scalar product in tensor form is represented by

$$A^i B_i = A_i B^i = g_{ij} A^i B^j = g^{ij} A_i B_j \qquad (14\text{-}1)$$

The Cartesian tensor form of the scalar product is

$$A_i B_i \qquad (14\text{-}2)$$

In these expressions A^i and A_i again represent the contravariant and covariant components of vector **A**.

14-3. The Vector or Cross Product of Two Vectors **A** and **B**

The vector or cross product of two vectors **A** and **B** according to equation (1-8) is

$$\mathbf{C} = \mathbf{A} \times \mathbf{B} = \mathbf{i} A B \sin \alpha \qquad (1\text{-}8)$$

The vector **i** is a unit vector having the same line of direction as **C**.

In Cartesian coordinates **A** × **B** may also be represented by the determinant

$$\mathbf{A} \times \mathbf{B} = \begin{vmatrix} \mathbf{i}_1 & \mathbf{i}_2 & \mathbf{i}_3 \\ A_1 & A_2 & A_3 \\ B_1 & B_2 & B_3 \end{vmatrix} \qquad (1\text{-}11)$$

The components of the vector product of two absolute or relative vectors **A** and **B** defined on a three-dimensional Riemann space in tensor form are

$$\frac{1}{\sqrt{g}} e^{ijk} A_j B_k \qquad (i = 1, 2, 3)$$

or $\qquad\qquad\qquad\qquad\qquad\qquad\qquad\qquad (14\text{-}3)$

$$\sqrt{g}\, e_{ijk} A^j B^k \qquad (i = 1, 2, 3)$$

The validity of one of these relations will be established. Let the vectors **A** and **B** be represented as follows.

$$\mathbf{A} = A_i \mathbf{e}^i \quad \text{and} \quad \mathbf{B} = B_j \mathbf{e}^j$$

Taking the cross product gives

$$\mathbf{A} \times \mathbf{B} = (A_i \mathbf{e}^i) \times (B_j \mathbf{e}^j) = \frac{1}{\sqrt{g}} e^{ijk} A_i B_j \mathbf{e}_k$$

The term $(1/\sqrt{g}) A_i B_j e^{ijk}$ represents the kth component of $\mathbf{A} \times \mathbf{B}$; hence it is the tensor expression for the cross product.

For Cartesian tensors the components of the cross product are

$$e_{ijk} A_j B_k \qquad\qquad (14\text{-}4)$$

14-4. The Vector Product $\mathbf{A} \times (\mathbf{B} \times \mathbf{C})$

Consider transformation of the vector relation $\mathbf{A} \times (\mathbf{B} \times \mathbf{C})$ into tensor form.

Let $(\mathbf{B} \times \mathbf{C}) = \mathbf{F}$; then according to equation (14-3) the nth component of F is

$$F^n = \frac{1}{\sqrt{g}} e^{njk} B_j C_k$$

Now $\mathbf{A} \times (\mathbf{B} \times \mathbf{C}) = \mathbf{A} \times \mathbf{F}$; hence the lth component of $(\mathbf{A} \times \mathbf{F})$ may be written as

$$(\mathbf{A} \times \mathbf{F})_l = \sqrt{g}\, e_{lmn} A^m F^n$$

Replacing the component F^n gives

$$(\mathbf{A} \times \mathbf{F})_l = \sqrt{g}\, e_{lmn} A^m \left(\frac{1}{\sqrt{g}} e^{njk} B_j C_k \right) = e_{lmn} e^{njk} A^m B_j C_k$$

Now

$$e^{njk} = e^{jkn}$$

so

$$e_{lmn} e^{jkn} = \delta_{lm}{}^{jk} = \delta_l{}^j \delta_m{}^k - \delta_l{}^k \delta_m{}^j$$

Substituting gives

$$[\mathbf{A} \times (\mathbf{B} \times \mathbf{C})]_l = A^m B_j C_k \delta_l{}^j \delta_m{}^k - A^m B_j C_k \delta_l{}^k \delta_m{}^j$$

Summing on j and k gives

$$[\mathbf{A} \times (\mathbf{B} \times \mathbf{C})]_l = B_l A^m C_m - C_l A^m B_m \qquad\qquad (14\text{-}5)$$

or

$$\mathbf{A} \times (\mathbf{B} \times \mathbf{C}) = (\mathbf{A} \cdot \mathbf{C})\mathbf{B} - (\mathbf{A} \cdot \mathbf{B})\mathbf{C}$$

14-5. The Scalar Triple Product $\mathbf{A} \cdot (\mathbf{B} \times \mathbf{C})$

The tensor form of the scalar triple product is

$$\sqrt{g}\, e_{ijk} A^i B^j C^k \quad \text{or} \quad \frac{e^{ijk}}{\sqrt{g}}\, A_i B_j C_k \tag{14-6}$$

The Cartesian tensor form is

$$e_{ijk} A_i B_j C_k \tag{14-7}$$

14-6. The Vector Operator ∇

The vector operator ∇ is

$$\nabla = \mathbf{i}_1 \frac{\partial}{\partial x_1} + \mathbf{i}_2 \frac{\partial}{\partial x_2} + \mathbf{i}_3 \frac{\partial}{\partial x_3} = \sum_{r=1}^{3} \mathbf{i}_r \frac{\partial}{\partial x_r} = \mathbf{i}_r \frac{\partial}{\partial x_r} \tag{14-8}$$

14-7. The Divergence of a Vector $\mathbf{A}$, $\nabla \cdot \mathbf{A}$

In general tensor form the divergence is given by

$$D^i A_i \quad \text{or} \quad D_i A^i \quad \text{or} \quad g_{ij} D^i A^j \quad \text{or} \quad g^{ij} D_i A_j \tag{14-9}$$

In Cartesian tensor form it becomes

$$\frac{\partial A_i}{\partial x_i} \tag{14-10}$$

14-8. The Curl or Rotation of a Vector $\mathbf{A}$, $\nabla \times \mathbf{A}$

In tensor form the ith component of the curl is given by

$$\sqrt{g}\, e_{ijk} D^j A^k \quad \text{or} \quad \frac{1}{\sqrt{g}}\, e^{ijk} D_j A_k \tag{14-11}$$

The form in Cartesian tensors is

$$e_{ijk} \frac{\partial A_k}{\partial x_j} \tag{14-12}$$

	Term or Operation	*Vector Terms and Operations in General* Vector Operation
1	Vector	$\mathbf{a}$
2	Scalar or dot product	$\mathbf{a} \cdot \mathbf{b}$
3	Vector or cross product	$\mathbf{a} \times \mathbf{b}$
4	Scalar triple product	$\mathbf{a} \cdot (\mathbf{b} \times \mathbf{c})$
5	Vector triple product	$\mathbf{a} \times (\mathbf{b} \times \mathbf{c}) = \mathbf{b}(\mathbf{a} \cdot \mathbf{c}) - \mathbf{c}(\mathbf{a} \cdot \mathbf{b})$
6	Divergence of $\mathbf{a}$	$\nabla \cdot \mathbf{a}$
7	Divergence of $u\mathbf{a}$	$\nabla u \cdot \mathbf{a} + u \nabla \cdot \mathbf{a}$
8	Divergence of $\mathbf{a} + \mathbf{b}$	$\nabla \cdot \mathbf{a} + \nabla \cdot \mathbf{b}$
9	Divergence of $\mathbf{a} \times \mathbf{b}$	$\mathbf{b} \cdot (\nabla \times \mathbf{a}) - \mathbf{a} \cdot (\nabla \times \mathbf{b})$
10	Curl or rotation of $\mathbf{a}$	$\nabla \times \mathbf{a}$
11	Curl or rotation of $u\mathbf{a}$	$\nabla u \times \mathbf{a} + u \nabla \times \mathbf{a}$
12	Curl or rotation of $\mathbf{a} + \mathbf{b}$	$\nabla \times \mathbf{a} + \nabla \times \mathbf{b}$
13	Curl or rotation of $\mathbf{a} \times \mathbf{b}$	$\mathbf{a}(\nabla \cdot \mathbf{b}) - \mathbf{b}(\nabla \cdot \mathbf{a}) + (\mathbf{b} \cdot \nabla)\mathbf{a} - (\mathbf{a} \cdot \nabla)\mathbf{b}$
14	$\mathbf{a} \times (\nabla \times \mathbf{b})$	$\mathbf{a} \times (\nabla \times \mathbf{b})$
15	$\nabla^2 u$	$\nabla^2 u = \nabla \cdot (\nabla u)$
16	$\nabla^2 \mathbf{a}$	$\nabla^2 \mathbf{a} = (\nabla \cdot \nabla)\mathbf{a}$
17	$\nabla \times (\nabla \times \mathbf{a})$	$\nabla(\nabla \cdot \mathbf{a}) - (\nabla \cdot \nabla)\mathbf{a}$
18	$(\mathbf{a} \cdot \nabla)\mathbf{b}$	$(\mathbf{a} \cdot \nabla)\mathbf{b}$
19	$\mathbf{a}(\nabla \cdot \mathbf{b})$	$\mathbf{a}(\nabla \cdot \mathbf{b})$

* $\sqrt{g} = 1$; all derivatives are ordinary; all notations are subscripts.

14-1

Tensor and Cartesian Tensor Notation

General Tensor Notation	Cartesian Tensor Notation*
A^i or A_i	A_i
$A^i B_i = A_i B^i = g_{ij} A^i B^j = g^{ij} A_i B_j$	$A_i B_i$
$\sqrt{g}\, e_{ijk} A^j B^k$ or $\dfrac{1}{\sqrt{g}} e^{ijk} A_j B_k$	$e_{ijk} A_j B_k$
$\sqrt{g}\, e_{ijk} A^i B^j C^k$ or $\dfrac{e^{ijk}}{\sqrt{g}} A_i B_j C_k$	$e_{ijk} A_i B_j C_k$
$\dfrac{1}{\sqrt{g}} e^{ijk} A_j (\sqrt{g}\, e_{klm} B^l C^m) = e^{ijk} e_{klm} A_j B^l C^m = \delta_{lm}{}^{ij} A_j B^l C^m$	$e_{ijk} A_j\, e_{klm} B_l C_m$
$D^i A_i = D_i A^i = g_{ij} D^i A^j = g^{ij}\, D_i A_j$	$\dfrac{\partial A_i}{\partial x_i}$
$u\, D_i A^i + A^i D_i u$	$u\,\dfrac{\partial A_i}{\partial x_i} + A_i\,\dfrac{\partial u}{\partial x_i}$
$\dfrac{1}{\sqrt{g}}\dfrac{\partial}{\partial x^j}(\sqrt{g}\, A^j) + \dfrac{1}{\sqrt{g}}\dfrac{\partial}{\partial x^i}(\sqrt{g}\, B^i)$ or $D_i A^i + D_i B^i$	$\dfrac{\partial A_j}{\partial x_j} + \dfrac{\partial B_j}{\partial x_j}$
$\dfrac{e^{ijk}}{\sqrt{g}} D_i A_j B_k$	$\dfrac{\partial}{\partial x_i}(e_{ijk} A_j B_k)$
$\sqrt{g}\, e_{ijk} D^j A^k$ or $\dfrac{1}{\sqrt{g}} e^{ijk} D_j A_k$	$e_{ijk}\dfrac{\partial A_k}{\partial x_j}$
$A_k\dfrac{e^{ijk}}{\sqrt{g}} D_j u + u\dfrac{e^{ijk}}{\sqrt{g}} D_j A_k$ or $\sqrt{g}\, e_{ijk} D^j(uA^k)$	$e_{ijk}u\dfrac{\partial A_k}{\partial x_j} + e_{ijk}A_k\dfrac{\partial u}{\partial x_j}$
$\dfrac{1}{\sqrt{g}} e^{ijk} D_j A_k + \dfrac{1}{\sqrt{g}} e^{ijk} D_j B_k$	$e_{ijk}\dfrac{\partial A_k}{\partial x_j} + e_{ijk}\dfrac{\partial B_k}{\partial x_j}$
$\sqrt{g}\, e_{ijk} D^j\left(\dfrac{e^{klm}}{\sqrt{g}} A_l B_m\right)$ or $\delta_{lm}{}^{ij} D_j(A^l B^m)$	$\dfrac{\partial}{\partial x_j}(e_{ijk} e_{klm} A_l B_m)$
$A_j D_i B^j - A^j D_j B_i$ or $\sqrt{g}\, e_{ijk} A^j\dfrac{e^{klm}}{\sqrt{g}} D_l B_m$	$A_j\dfrac{\partial B_j}{\partial x_i} - A_j\dfrac{\partial B_i}{\partial x_j}$
$D_i D^i u$	$\dfrac{\partial}{\partial x_i}\dfrac{\partial}{\partial x_i}u$
$D_j D^j A^i$ or $D_j D^j A_i$	$\dfrac{\partial}{\partial x_i}\dfrac{\partial}{\partial x_i}A_j$
$\sqrt{g}\, e_{ijk} D^j\left(e^{klm}\dfrac{1}{\sqrt{g}} D_l A_m\right) = e_{ijk}e^{klm}D^j D_l A_m = \delta_{ij}{}^{lm}D^j D_l A_m$	$\dfrac{\partial}{\partial x_j}\dfrac{\partial}{\partial x_i}A_j - \dfrac{\partial}{\partial x_j}\dfrac{\partial}{\partial x_i}A_i$
$A_i D^i B_j$ or $A^i D_i B_j$	$A_j\dfrac{\partial B_i}{\partial x_j}$
$A_i D_j B^j$ or $A^i D_j B^j$	$A_i\dfrac{\partial B_j}{\partial x_j}$

14-9. $\nabla \times (\mathbf{A} \times \mathbf{B})$

The relation $\nabla \times (\mathbf{A} \times \mathbf{B})$ will now be transformed into tensor form.

Let $\mathbf{A} \times \mathbf{B} = \mathbf{F}$; then the nth component of $\mathbf{F}$ may be represented as

$$F^n = \frac{e^{nrs}}{\sqrt{g}} A_r B_s$$

and

$$\nabla \times (\mathbf{A} \times \mathbf{B}) = \nabla \times \mathbf{F}$$

Hence, according to equation (14-11),

$$(\nabla \times \mathbf{F})_i = \sqrt{g}\, e_{imn} D^m F^n = e_{imn} e^{nrs} D^m (A_r B_s) \qquad (14\text{-}13)$$

or

$$(\nabla \times \mathbf{F})_i = \delta_{im}{}^{rs} D^m (A_r B_s) = D^m (A_i B_m) - D^m (A_m B_i) \qquad (14\text{-}14)$$

14-10. $\mathbf{A} \times (\nabla \times \mathbf{B})$

The tensor form of $\mathbf{A} \times (\nabla \times \mathbf{B})$ will be considered next.

Let $\mathbf{F}$ represent $(\nabla \times \mathbf{B})$; then the kth component of $(\nabla \times \mathbf{B})$ is

$$(\nabla \times \mathbf{B})^k = (\mathbf{F})^k = \frac{1}{\sqrt{g}} e^{kmn} D_m B_n$$

Now $\mathbf{A} \times (\nabla \times \mathbf{B}) = \mathbf{A} \times \mathbf{F}$; consequently the ith component of $\mathbf{A} \times \mathbf{F}$ is

$$(\mathbf{A} \times \mathbf{F})_i = \sqrt{g}\, e_{ijk} A^j F^k = \sqrt{g}\, \frac{1}{\sqrt{g}} e_{ijk} e^{kmn} A^j D_m B_n$$

Therefore the ith component of $\mathbf{A} \times (\nabla \times \mathbf{B})$ follows:

$$\begin{aligned}
[\mathbf{A} \times (\nabla \times \mathbf{B})]_i &= e_{ijk} e^{mnk} A^j D_m B_n = \delta_{ij}{}^{mn} A^j D_m B_n \\
&= \delta_i{}^m \delta_j{}^n A^j D_m B_n - \delta_i{}^n \delta_j{}^m A^j D_m B_n \\
&= A^j D_i B_j - A^j D_j B_i \qquad (14\text{-}15)
\end{aligned}$$

The components of other vector relations are shown in Table 14-1.

14-11. Problems

14-1. Using Cartesian tensor notation, verify the following vector identities.

(a) $\nabla \cdot (\mathbf{A} \times \mathbf{B}) = \mathbf{B} \cdot (\nabla \times \mathbf{A}) - \mathbf{A} \cdot (\nabla \times \mathbf{B})$

(b) $\nabla \times (\mathbf{A} \times \mathbf{B}) = \mathbf{A}(\nabla \cdot \mathbf{B}) + (\mathbf{B} \cdot \nabla)\mathbf{A} - (\mathbf{A} \cdot \nabla)\mathbf{B} - \mathbf{B}(\nabla \cdot \mathbf{A})$

14-2. Express the following vector equation in Cartesian tensor form.

$$\mathbf{A} \times (\mathbf{B} \times \mathbf{C}) = \mathbf{B}(\mathbf{A} \cdot \mathbf{C}) - \mathbf{C}(\mathbf{A} \cdot \mathbf{B})$$

14-3. Express the following equations in Cartesian tensor form.

(a) $\qquad \nabla \cdot (f\mathbf{A}) = f(\nabla \cdot \mathbf{A}) + (\nabla f) \cdot \mathbf{A}$

(b) $\qquad \nabla \times (f\mathbf{A}) = f(\nabla \times \mathbf{A}) + (\nabla f) \times \mathbf{A}$

14-4. Express the following equation in Cartesian tensor form.

$$\nabla(\mathbf{A} \cdot \mathbf{B}) = (\mathbf{A} \cdot \nabla)\mathbf{B} + (\mathbf{B} \cdot \nabla)\mathbf{A} + \mathbf{A} \times (\nabla \times \mathbf{B}) + \mathbf{B} \times (\nabla \times \mathbf{A})$$

14-5. Express the following in Cartesian tensor form.

(a) $\qquad \nabla \times (\nabla f) = 0$

(b) $\qquad \nabla \cdot (\nabla \times \mathbf{A}) = 0$

(c) $\qquad \nabla \times (\nabla \times \mathbf{A}) = \nabla(\nabla \cdot \mathbf{A}) - (\nabla \cdot \nabla)\mathbf{A}$

14-6. If $\mathbf{X}$ is the position vector, express the following relations in Cartesian tensor form.

(a) $\qquad \nabla \cdot \mathbf{X} = 3$

(b) $\qquad \nabla \times \mathbf{X} = 0$

(c) $\qquad (\mathbf{A} \cdot \nabla)\mathbf{X} = \mathbf{A}$

14-7. One finds in the literature the following Maxwell equations for free space:

$$\nabla \times \mathbf{H} = k \frac{\partial \mathbf{E}}{\partial t}, \quad \nabla \times \mathbf{E} = -\mu \frac{\partial \mathbf{H}}{\partial t}, \quad \nabla \cdot \mathbf{H} = 0, \quad \nabla \cdot \mathbf{E} = 0$$

Express these relations in terms of general curvilinear coordinates, Z^i.

14-8. Evaluate the expressions for the skewed coordinates shown in the figure

(a) $\qquad A_i B^i$

(b) $\qquad \dfrac{e^{ijk}}{\sqrt{g}} A_j B_k$

(c) $\qquad D_i A^i$

X'^i is a set of orthogonal Cartesian axes and X^i is a set of skewed axes obtained by rotating the X'^1 and X'^2 axes through the angle α and β as shown. The axes X^3 and X'^3 coincide. For this system of coordinates the

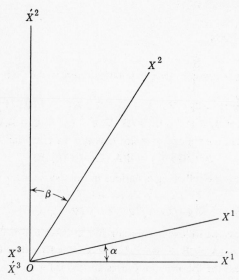

Problem 14-8.

values for g_{ij} are

$$g_{11} = 1$$
$$g_{12} = \sin(\alpha + \beta)$$
$$g_{21} = \sin(\alpha + \beta)$$
$$g_{22} = 1$$

and

$$g_{33} = 1$$

All the Christoffel symbols are zero.

14-12. Suggested References

14-1. *Vector and Tensor Analysis*, G. E. Hay, Dover Publications, Inc.

14-2. *Mathematical Handbook*, G. A. Korn and T. M. Korn, McGraw-Hill Book Company.

14-3. *Tensor Analysis: Theory and Applications*, I. S. Sokolnikoff, John Wiley and Sons, Inc.

14-4. *Cartesian Tensors*, Harold Jeffreys, The University Press, Cambridge, England.

14-5. *Vector Analysis with an Introduction to Tensor Analysis*, A. P. Wills, Dover Publications, Inc.

14-6. *Applications of Tensor Analysis*, A. J. McConnell, Dover Publications, Inc.

14-7. *Theory and Problems of Vector Analysis and an Introduction to Tensor Analysis*, Murray R. Spiegel, Schaum Publishing Company.

Index